D0169193

Jacques Lacan

Twayne's World Authors Series

French Literature

David O'Connell, Editor
Georgia State University

TWAS 817

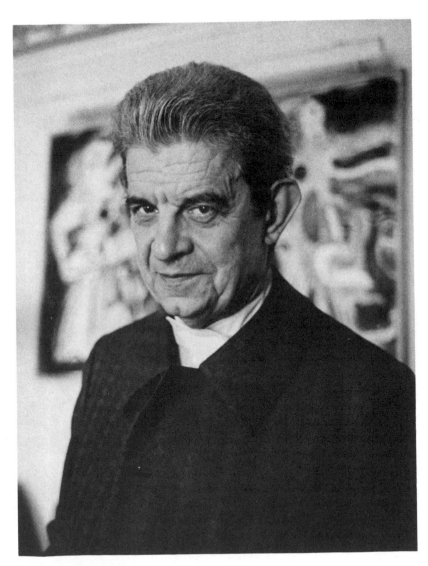

JACQUES LACAN
Photograph courtesy of Jerry Bauer

Jacques Lacan

By Jonathan Scott Lee

Knox College

Twayne Publishers
A Division of G. K. Hall & Co. • *Boston*

Jacques Lacan
Jonathan Scott Lee

Copyright 1990 by G. K. Hall & Co.
All rights reserved.
Published by Twayne Publishers
A Division of G. K. Hall & Co.
70 Lincoln Street
Boston, Massachusetts 02111

Copyediting supervised by Barbara Sutton
Book production by Gabrielle B. McDonald
Book design by Barbara Anderson

Typeset in 11 pt. Garamond
by Huron Valley Graphic, Inc., Ann Arbor, Michigan

Printed on permanent/durable acid-free paper
and bound in the United States of America

First printing 1990
10 9 8 7 6 5 4 3 2 1

Library of Congress Cataloging-in-Publication Data

Lee, Jonathan Scott.
    Jacques Lacan / Jonathan Scott Lee.
        p.   cm. — (Twayne's world authors series ; TWAS 817. French
    Literature)
    Includes bibliographical references.
    ISBN 0-8057-8256-7
    1. Lacan, Jacques, 1901–   —Contributions in criticism.
2. Psychoanalysis and literature. 3. Criticism—History—20th
century.   I. Title.   II. Series: Twayne's world authors series ;
TWAS 817.   III. Series: Twayne's world authors series. French
literature.
PN98.P75L38   1990
801'.95'092—dc20   89-48094
                                                                    CIP

For Maryann, with all my love.

Contents

About the Author

Jonathan Scott Lee is associate professor of philosophy at Knox College in Galesburg, Illinois. His doctoral dissertation (1978) was on the metaphysics of the Greek neoplatonist philosopher Plotinus. His more recent work on contemporary French philosophy can be found in essays on Lacan and Derrida in *PsychCritique*. At the same time, his interests in experimental literature and music have led to essays on Antonin Artaud, Stéphane Mallarmé, and John Cage for such journals as *boundary 2* and the *Revue d'esthétique*. He is married to the painter Maryann Golden Lee.

Preface

The work of the French psychoanalyst Jacques Lacan poses special problems of interpretation. In part, these problems stem from his baroque style, a high form of *préciosité* that has left its indelible mark on a generation of French thinkers. In one of his most influential essays Lacan characterizes his own preferred approach to writing: "Writing is distinguished by a prevalence of the *text* in the sense that this factor of discourse will assume in this essay a factor that makes possible the kind of tightening up that I like in order to leave the reader no other way out than the way in, which I prefer to be difficult."[1] To his taste for difficulty must be added the special bibliographic fact that virtually all of Lacan's texts originated as at least partially extemporaneous oral presentations. Those published during his lifetime tend to reflect a rather large amount of revision meant to increase the "prevalence of the *text*," while those published since his death—primarily the ongoing series of volumes edited by Jacques-Alain Miller and devoted to his weekly or biweekly seminar conducted between 1953 and 1980—raise different problems because of the unique complexities of transcribing Lacan's polyvalent speech.

Another major source of difficulty lies in Lacan's extensive use of sources from a wide variety of intellectual disciplines. While the texts of Freud provide the fundamental context for his work, Lacan does not hesitate to address issues and allude to texts flung far from the boundaries of psychoanalytic theory. The interpreter of Lacan must not only deal with Lacan's own challenging texts but sort out thematic references to the work of such notoriously obscure thinkers as Kant, Hegel, and Heidegger, and be prepared as well for the occasional excursion into the textual details of such literary giants as Sophocles, Racine, and Shakespeare.

This study aims to provide general readers with an introduction to the work of Lacan, an introduction that will both allow readers to formulate an initial assessment of Lacan's significance (particularly in areas outside the confines of psychoanalysis itself) and encourage them to read Lacan's texts for themselves.

After a brief biographical account in chapter 1, chapter 2 provides a review of Lacan's early writings, exploring his gradual theoretical move toward psychoanalysis. The chapter concludes with a close look at the writings on the "mirror stage," which provide an important introduction to the mature theory of the 1950s.

The heart of the book is found in chapters 3 and 4, which review in some detail the major claims of Lacan's mature theory, using as a primary guide his landmark text of 1953, "The Function and Field of Speech and Language in Psychoanalysis." I offer a close review of that text's central arguments, using extensive quotations from Lacan himself to help the reader come to some familiarity with Lacan's notorious style. Chapter 3 pursues the role of structuralism as it helps to shape Lacan's fundamental theories, and quite a bit of space is devoted to unfolding the unique and influential theory of language he developed. The next chapter turns from these highly theoretical issues to concentrate more attention on the details of psychoanalytic practice as understood and outlined in Lacan's teaching. Here I explore the fundamental issue of the relation between psychoanalytic treatment and the concept of "cure" (*la guérison*). I cannot pretend to explore all the ramifications of this daunting text in the space available, nor can I promise to tackle all the points where Lacan's lapidary style joins forces with a complex web of philosophical and literary allusion to make comprehension almost impossible. What I intend is that my review enable readers to turn to Lacan's text with the confidence that they can make it through with a sufficient grasp of the key points.

Subsequent chapters of this study turn to other writings of the 1950s, as well as texts of the 1960s and 1970s, showing how Lacan returned again and again to themes and concepts articulated in 1953, often primarily to elaborate earlier points, sometimes to revise or otherwise transform his early formulations of key concepts. Chapter 5 considers Lacan's influential forays into literary criticism and provides the framework for appreciating his treatments of Poe, Shakespeare, and Sophocles. Chapter 6 pursues various aspects of Lacan's new emphasis on the category of the *real* during the 1960s. The final chapter attempts to sketch and to show the connection between Lacan's two primary interests of the 1970s: the psychoanalytic problem of feminine sexuality and the essentially philosophical problem of evaluating the claims of psychoanalysis to be a science.

Permission to quote from the works of Jacques Lacan has been granted by M. Jacques-Alain Miller and Éditions du Seuil.

Quotations from *Écrits: A Selection* by Jacques Lacan, translated from the French by Alan Sheridan, are used with the permission of W. W. Norton & Co. Inc. © 1977 by Tavistock Publications Ltd.

I would like to thank all those who have helped me bring this study to completion. Special thanks must go to my friend Dr. Donald Moss, who has shown exceptional willingness to read manuscripts and to guide me away from ill-considered descriptions of psychoanalytic practice and theory. My friends and colleagues at Knox College have done much to help me clarify my ideas: particular thanks must go to Bruce Davis, Brenda Fineberg, Nancy Eberhardt, David Amor, Carol Chase, Steven Cohn, and Stephen Fineberg. I owe a special debt to William J. Richardson for his kindly allowing me to quote from his unpublished translation of Lacan's "Kant avec Sade." I am grateful as well for the encouragement of Robert Con Davis and for the assistance of Julie Lindstrom. Knox College and Dean John Strassburger were very generous in their support of a sabbatical during which the bulk of this study was written. I also would like to thank M. Jacques-Alain Miller for his kind and gracious assistance.

My most important debt is to Maryann Golden Lee, who has suffered through my struggles with Lacan with remarkable patience and love.

Jonathan Scott Lee

Knox College

Guide to Abbreviations

References to the works of Jacques Lacan are generally cited in the body of the text using the following abbreviations.

CF *Les complexes familiaux dans la formation de l'individu*
E   *Écrits*
S   Seminars; numerals refer to the chronological list in the Selected Bibliography.
D   *Le désir et son interprétation* (S 6)—the sessions on *Hamlet*
T   *Télévision*

Full references for these texts will be found in the bibliography. Where a source is available in an English translation, that translation has been quoted, and its page reference is given after the French page reference (the two numbers being separated by a slash). I have supplied my own translations for texts not yet available in English.

All references to the works of Freud are always to *The Standard Edition of the Complete Psychological Works of Sigmund Freud*, translated from the German under the general editorship of James Strachey, in collaboration with Anna Freud, 24 volumes (London: Hogarth Press and the Institute of Psycho-Analysis; New York: W.W. Norton, 1953–73). Cited in the notes as *SE*.

List of Figures

Chronology

1901 Jacques-Marie Émile Lacan, the eldest of three children, born to Alfred Lacan and Émilie Baudry Lacan on 13 April in Paris.

1916 While attending the Jesuit Collège Stanislas, begins the serious study of philosophy and embraces atheism.

1919 Begins medical training in the Faculté de médecine de Paris.

1927 Appointed *interne des asiles.*

1930 Studies with Carl Jung in August and September at the Burghölzi clinic in Zurich.

1931 Receives Diplôme de médecine légiste, after three years of work in forensic medicine.

1932 Receives Doctorat d'état in psychiatry, after defending thesis on 7 September. *De la psychose paranoïaque dans ses rapports avec la personnalité.* Appointed *chef de clinique* at the Hôpital Saint-Anne in Paris.

1933 Publishes articles on paranoia in first issues of the surrealist journal *Le minotaure.* Begins attending regularly (with Raymond Queneau, Georges Bataille, Maurice Merleau-Ponty, and André Breton, among others) the lectures on Hegel given by Alexandre Kojève at the École pratique des hautes études (until 1939).

1934 Marries Marie-Louise Blondin in January. After beginning a training psychoanalysis with Rudolf Loewenstein in either 1932 or 1933, Lacan joins the Société psychanalytique de Paris (SPP), officially recognized by the International Psychoanalytic Association (IPA).

1936 Presents paper on the "mirror stage" at the fourteenth congress of the IPA in Marienbad.

1938 "Le complexe, facteur concret de la psychologie familiale" and "Les complexes familiaux en pathologie" appear in the *Encyclopédie française.*

1939   Begins relationship with the actress Sylvia Bataille (née Maklès).

1940   Mobilized to the hospital of Val-de-Grâce.

1941   Marie-Louise divorces Lacan. Judith Bataille (later Lacan) born to Sylvia Bataille and Jacques Lacan.

1945   Publishes articles on mathematical game theory in *Cahiers d'art*.

1946   Emerges as principal theorist in the revitalized SPP.

1949   As member of the SPP's committee on training, Lacan writes new statutes, opening psychoanalytic training to nonmedical candidates.

1951   Initiates a private teaching seminar on Freud's case studies.

1953   Lacan's election to president of SPP on 20 January marks a split within the SPP between medical and nonmedical factions. In June Lacan and others resign under pressure from SPP and form a new professional association, the Société française de psychanalyse (SFP). Presents the text of "Fonction et champ de la parole et du langage en psychanalyse" in Rome on 26 September, with an oral commentary inaugurating the new SFP. Opens his teaching seminar at the Hôpital Saint-Anne to the public for the first time in November. Marries Sylvia Bataille.

1956   Inaugural issue of *La psychanalyse,* the journal of the SFP, is devoted to Lacan.

1959   SFP petitions the IPA for formal affiliation in July.

1961   IPA committee recommends in August that the SFP become a supervised study group of the IPA and, in a series of twenty recommendations, effectively demands the exclusion of Lacan and his closest followers from SFP training programs.

1963   On 13 October, under pressure from the IPA, the SFP's committee on training refuses Lacan permission to continue in the SFP's training program, a decision that is supported by the SFP as a whole on 19 November. On

20 November Lacan announces the end of his seminar at the Hôpital Saint-Anne.

1964 At the invitation of Fernand Braudel, Lacan resumes his seminar under the auspices of the École pratique des hautes études and, with the help of Louis Althusser, reconvenes his public teaching on 15 January at the École normale supérieure. On 21 June Lacan formally founds a new psychoanalytic school and society, the École française de psychanalyse, later renamed the École freudienne de Paris (EFP).

1966 Travels to the United States in October, where he participates in the symposium "The Languages of Criticism and the Sciences of Man" held at Johns Hopkins University. *Écrits,* a large volume of essays, is published in November and quickly becomes a Parisian bestseller. Lacan's daughter Judith marries Jacques-Alain Miller, a young philosopher working closely with Lacan.

1969 In January a Lacanian department of psychoanalysis is founded at the new and controversial Université de Paris-Vincennes. Believed to be in some way responsible for the student-worker revolution of May 1968, Lacan is asked to leave the École normale supérieure. His seminar resumes in the fall in a large amphitheatre at the Faculté de droit, near the Pantheon.

1973 *Les quatre concepts fondamentaux de la psychanalyse,* the seminar of 1964, is published as the first volume in a series of the seminars to be edited by Jacques-Alain Miller, Lacan's son-in-law. Lacan is the subject of a two-part French television interview.

1974 *Télévision.* During the summer and fall Lacan takes charge of the department of psychoanalysis at Vincennes, naming Jacques-Alain Miller as its chair and presiding over a radical transformation of its curriculum.

1975 *Les écrits techniques de Freud,* the seminar of 1953–54, and *Encore,* the seminar of 1972–73, are published.

Travels to the United States in November and December, where he speaks at Yale University, Columbia University, and the Massachusetts Institute of Technology.

1977   *Écrits: A Selection* and *The Four Fundamental Concepts of Psychoanalysis* appear in English translations.

1978   *Le moi dans la théorie de Freud et dans la technique de la psychanalyse,* the seminar of 1954–55, is published.

1979   Lacan and his daughter Judith Miller found the Fondation du champ freudien in February. In September Jacques-Alain Miller is elected to the board of directors of the EFP, precipitating widespread protest within the organization.

1980   Unilaterally dissolves the EFP on 5 January. Lacan's final seminar, *Dissolution!,* takes the form of a series of open letters and messages published in various Parisian media. Travels to Venezuela in July to open the first international congress of the Champ freudien in Caracas. After months of litigation and legal maneuvering, the EFP ratifies its own dissolution on 27 September. Lacan founds the École de la cause freudienne in October, effectively authorizing Jacques-Alain Miller to serve as his successor.

1981   Dies on 9 September after a long struggle with abdominal cancer.

Chapter One
Jacques Lacan: Psychoanalyst and Teacher

Jacques-Marie Émile Lacan was born into an upper-middle-class Parisian household on 13 April 1901.[1] The first child of Alfred and Émilie Baudry Lacan, Jacques-Marie soon shared the family quarters with a sister, Madeleine, and a brother, Marc-François, both of whom enjoyed Christmas as their birthday (in 1903 and 1908, respectively). His parents sent their eldest child to the distinguished Jesuit Collège Stanislas, where he might both prepare himself for a profession and undergo a rigorous religious education. Although similar training led his younger brother to devote himself to the life of a Benedictine monk, the Collège Stanislas seems to have brought the adolescent Jacques-Marie to a crisis in his own faith. By the age of fifteen he had ventured deeply into the study of philosophy—Spinoza emerging as a decisive influence—and this led him to give up Catholicism and embrace atheism. Elisabeth Roudinesco suggests that the loss of a clear sense of authority in his life may have been responsible for the young Lacan's brief interest in the monarchist (and anti-Semitic) Action française movement around this time.[2]

If Émilie Lacan was displeased with her eldest son's religious views, Alfred Lacan was surely satisfied when Jacques (no longer Jacques-Marie) decided upon a career in medicine and enrolled in the Faculté de médecine de Paris. Although he apparently continued to enjoy a rather wild private life, Lacan proceeded through a long, difficult, and classical French psychiatric education. His primary medical residency was at the Hôpital Saint-Anne in Paris, where, as *interne des asiles,* he worked directly under the direction of Gaëtan Gatian de Clérambault. Clérambault's work in psychiatry was focused on the syndrome of "mental automatism," by which he understood features of psychotic delirium that appeared to force themselves upon the patient from the outside, that had no direct connection to other ideas or personality traits of the patient, and that could be assigned some organic cause. Clérambault seems to have influenced Lacan to take special interest in the criminally insane, and Lacan received a Diplôme de médecine légiste in 1931, after three years of work in forensic medicine in Paris and Toulouse. During the summer of 1930 he studied briefly at the clinic of Burghölzi in Zurich, where he apparently worked with Carl Jung and certainly was exposed to the "existential" psychoanalytic theory of Ludwig Binswanger.[3] After defending his thesis on 7 September 1932, Lacan received his Doctorat d'état in psychiatry. The thesis, which stands as Lacan's only published case study, was published the same year as *De la psychose paranoïaque dans ses rapports avec la personnalité* (On paranoid psychosis in its relations with personality).[4] In the thesis Lacan pays homage to his teacher Clérambault by working directly with a criminally psychotic subject exhibiting many of the features of "mental automatism,"[5] but he also directly argues against both Clérambault's emphasis on organic explanation and his fundamental claim that psychotic deliria are essentially unconnected with the patient's other ideas or features of the patient's personality. Indeed, the thesis—although it remains essentially psychiatric in its orientation and style—was clearly paving the way toward Lacan's own acceptance of the integral relation between symptoms and personality found in psychoanalytic theory.

Newly appointed *chef de clinique* at the Hôpital Saint-Anne, Lacan continued his distinguished work in psychiatry. However, during the early 1930s his intellectual and professional interests were taking several different turns. Beginning in 1932 or 1933 he undertook a training psychoanalysis with Rudolph Loewenstein. Although the analysis itself lasted until the late 1930s, Lacan joined the Société psychanalytique de Paris (SPP) in 1934, thereby becoming a practicing psychoanalyst, and with this step emerged into the professional world as a member of the International Psychoanalytic Association (IPA). During this same period Lacan was moving in social circles with such people as André Breton and Salvador Dali, and his friendship with the surrealists led him to publish articles and even a poem in surrealist journals. His friends were no doubt attracted to the young Lacan's interest in the criminally insane—one of the articles he contributed to the review *Le minotaure* was devoted to the notoriously brutal murder that became the basis for Jean Genet's play *Les bonnes* some years later[6]—and he was clearly attracted to the surrealists' experiments in automatic writing.[7] From 1933 to 1939 Lacan followed the influential series of lectures on Hegel given by Alexandre Kojève, a Russian émigré, at the École pratique des hautes études. These lectures, which quite simply transformed twentieth-century French thought, were also attended by Lacan's friends, the writers Georges Bataille and Raymond Queneau, and the philosopher Maurice Merleau-Ponty, as well as the ever-present André Breton.[8] In 1934 Lacan married Marie-Louise Blondin, with whom he was to have three children: Caroline, Thibaut, and Sibylle.

It was during the later 1930s that Lacan became a presence in the international psychoanalytic community. In 1936 he attended the fourteenth congress of the IPA in Marienbad, where he delivered a paper on the "mirror stage," only to be interrupted after ten minutes by Ernest Jones. Despite this unfortunate introduction to the psychoanalytic world, two years later Lacan was commissioned by Henri Wallon to write two long articles on the family for the eighth volume of the distinguished *Encyclopédie française*, a volume devoted to "the mental life" and featuring the work of the most important French psychologists and psychiatrists.[9] Lacan's contributions reveal him to have made a total conversion from the psychiatric position of his thesis to an overtly Freudian and psychoanalytic orientation. Despite his new passion for the theories of Freud, Lacan was notably absent from the reception in Paris for Freud held by Marie Bonaparte in 1939 during Freud's flight from Vienna to England.

Lacan apparently played no public role during the years of World War II, apart from his brief mobilization in 1940 to the hospital of Val-de-Grâce. He continued his private psychoanalytic practice and his work at Saint-Anne, where he briefly treated Antonin Artaud and reportedly claimed that Artaud was incurable.[10] However, Lacan seems to have turned most of his own attention inward during the Nazi occupation. In 1939 he fell in love with Sylvia Bataille (née Maklès), an actress who had come to prominence in the films of Jean Renoir after having separated from Georges Bataille in 1933. When Sylvia became pregnant in 1940, Lacan's wife filed for divorce, which was granted at about the time that Judith Bataille (later Lacan) was born in 1941. It would be another twelve years before Lacan and Sylvia would marry in the eventful year of 1953.

The occupation kept Lacan apart from his new family much of the time. Because the Maklès family was of Jewish extraction, they were under constant threat from the Nazis, and Sylvia spent much of the war living in the free zone in the south of France. Even this relatively safe haven posed dangers, and Elisabeth Roudinesco tells how Lacan himself managed to steal the papers of the Maklès family from the authorities, thereby protecting them from further persecution.[11] Although Lacan visited Sylvia in the south every two weeks, his practice dictated that he spend most of his time in Paris. He seems to have devoted himself to the study of Chinese after moving to an apartment at 5, rue de Lille, across the street from the École des langues orientales.

The years of the occupation were not a time when psychoanalysis flourished in France. The SPP had been forced to close its training institute in 1940, and most of Lacan's work during this time was strictly private. With the end of the war, however, there came a dramatic increase of interest in psychoanalysis in France, and Lacan found himself publishing articles (on mathematical game theory) in *Cahiers d'art*.[12] When the SPP started up again in 1946, Lacan emerged as one of its three central figures, along with Sacha Nacht and Daniel Lagache. Recognized as the most important psychoanalytic theorist in France, Lacan was appointed to the SPP's committee on training in 1948, and he played a decisive role in the drafting of the society's new statutes on training in 1949. Lacan (with the support of Lagache) was the leader of a group within the SPP committed to opening full psychoanalytic training to nonmedical candidates, but in this he came up against the rigorously medical orientation of Nacht. This legitimate difference in philosophical attitude seems to have escalated rather quickly into serious intrainstitutional conflict when Nacht was appointed director of the new SPP training institute in 1952.[13] Enlisting the aid of Marie Bonaparte, the woman who had effectively brought psychoanalysis to France in the first place and who provided most of the funding for the SPP, Lacan managed to force Nacht's resignation, ultimately becoming himself the organization's president on 20 January 1953. It should be added that since 1951 Lacan had conducted, outside the society's auspices, a private teaching seminar devoted to Freud's case studies.

The conflict between Nacht and Lacan was, however, much more than a conflict over the training of nonmedical candidates. Nacht was, perhaps primarily, working against Lacan's own practice of using variable-length sessions in both his therapeutic and his training analyses. Lacan's unwillingness to conform to the standard psychoanalytic practice of the forty-five- or fifty-minute analytic hour became the central issue in a largely personal struggle that split the SPP apart. In June 1953, after only six months as president, Lacan resigned from the organization and, with Lagache and a number of analysts who had been trained by Lacan, formed a new professional association, the Société française de psychanalyse (SFP). As it happened, this apparent resolution of the French conflict became the first battle in an international psychoanalytic war when the newly formed SFP applied to the IPA for official recognition. Nacht, with the support of Marie Bonaparte and Anna Freud, managed to persuade the larger organization to exclude the SFP on a preliminary basis and to form a committee to resolve the question of the new society's possible eventual affiliation with the IPA, a committee that would not actually reach a final decision for more than ten years.

Having been thus cast out of an institution in which he had become the leading figure, Lacan turned to a wider audience. In late September 1953 he went to Rome to attend the Congrès des psychanalystes de langue française, a congress to which he had originally been invited to speak as the president of the SPP. Appearing now as the leader of a new and apparently radical movement, Lacan launched a ferocious attack on the current state of psychoanalytic theory and practice in a text entitled "Fonction et champ de la parole et du langage en psychanalyse" ("The Function and Field of Speech and Language in Psychoanalysis"). In this so-called "Discours de Rome" Lacan argued that psychoanalysis could not ignore the advances in structuralist linguistics and social sciences, and he called for a "return to Freud" that would build bridges between psychoanalysis, Martin Heidegger's version of existentialism, literature, and the other human sciences. In attacking the current state of psychoanalytic thought, Lacan was in effect criticizing the "ego psychology" developed in significant part by his own training analyst, Rudolph Loewenstein, who had moved on to New York after the fall of France. At the same time Lacan was making a case for an approach to psychoanalysis that was in almost every way different from that which had been developed in England and the United States, largely under the influence of Anna Freud.

Lacan's appearance in Rome was followed by the opening of his teaching seminar at Saint-Anne to the public for the first time in November 1953. For the rest of his life the seminar would provide Lacan with a forum in which he could explore his own reformulations of Freudian theory while having a direct and immediate effect on the intellectual life of Paris. By inviting his distinguished friends to the seminar—friends including the anthropologist Claude Lévi-Strauss, the linguist Roman Jakobson (who stayed with Sylvia on his visits to Paris), and the philosophers Maurice Merleau-Ponty and Jean Hyppolite— Lacan was able over the years to turn his lecture hall into something of a laboratory of avant-garde theory. The result of his teaching can be seen most visibly in the astonishing influence of psychoanalytic theory on postwar French thought and in the dramatic rise of public interest in psychoanalysis in France.

Crucial to understanding Lacan's influence during the 1950s and 1960s is the fact that very little of his work was actually available in print. As had been the case with Kojève's celebrated lectures on Hegel during the 1930s, Lacan's seminar worked its way into Parisian intellectual life through its influence on the work of other thinkers. Virtually every major French thinker of the great structuralist and poststructuralist era owes Lacan's work a great debt. The critics Roland Barthes and Julia Kristeva, the philosophers Michel Foucault, Louis Althusser, and Jacques Derrida, and the novelist-critic Philippe Sollers, to name but a few, all either attended Lacan's seminar for some period of time or were caught up in the general debate raised by Lacan's oral teachings. Lacan's own writings during the 1950s were few, were typically published in relatively obscure technical journals, and were themselves mostly dense rewritings of his earlier oral presentations. In 1956 the SFP published the first issue of its own journal, La psychanalyse, devoted to Lacan and featuring the text of "Function and Field," as well as Lacan's own, "authorized" translation of an important essay on Heraclitus by the German existentialist Martin Heidegger.[14] Despite such notable appearances in print, it was not until the publication of Écrits in 1966 that Lacan's work was readily available in any form other than that of his oral seminar. One curious effect of the oral character of most of Lacan's work was the ever-increasing proliferation of unauthorized, "pirate" transcriptions of his seminars. By the early 1980s it was possible to purchase for a relatively modest price virtually every Lacan seminar in a pirate edition from a variety of larger academic bookstores in France.

While Lacan was emerging as the most important psychoanalytic thinker in France, his organization was struggling for international recognition by the IPA. Having been denied membership in 1955 by a committee dominated by Anna Freud and the American ego psychologist Heinz Hartmann, the SFP again petitioned for membership in July 1959.[15] Two years later another committee recommended that the SFP be allowed to become a supervised study group of the larger organization, on the condition that it reform its activities along the lines of twenty recommendations (the so-called Edinburgh demands). These recommendations effectively demanded the exclusion or marginalization of Lacan and his closest followers from his own training program. By the beginning of 1963 it was apparent to the IPA that the Edinburgh demands had not been implemented and that Lacan was still very much at the center of his group's activities. On 2 August 1963 the IPA formally demanded that Lacan be dropped from the SFP's list of approved training analysts by 31 October, and on 13 October the SFP's committee on training (a committee including Lacan's long-time ally Daniel Lagache) did so. This decision was endorsed by a general vote of the SFP on 19 November. The next day Lacan was due to open his scheduled seminar for 1963–64 on the topic, *Les noms-du-père* (The names of the father), but he announced to the assembled crowd at Saint-Anne that the opening session would be his last.[16] (After Lacan's removal, the members who had sided against Lacan formed the new, anti-Lacanian Association psychanalytique de France. In July 1965 it was unanimously admitted into the IPA.)

What Lacan reasonably enough described as his "excommunication" from both the IPA and his own SFP marked, however, a dramatic new turn in the fate of his teaching.[17] At the invitation of the historian Fernand Braudel he continued his seminar under the aegis of the École pratique des hautes études, thus following in Kojève's footsteps, while the Marxist theoretician Louis Althusser arranged for Lacan to bring his seminar to the distinguished lecture halls of the École normale supérieure. As a result of this change in venue, Lacan's audience increased and diversified: no longer were most of his auditors psychoanalysts in training; more and more the seminar came to be attended by young students of philosophy, of literary criticism, and of the human sciences. Among these students was the young philosopher Jacques-Alain Miller, who was soon to marry Lacan's daughter Judith and who would become by the 1970s perhaps the most important influence on Lacan's theoretical work. With this change in his audience, Lacan began to broaden the content of his seminar, and from 1964 through the 1970s he pursued a profoundly original, if difficult, intellectual path in which close study of Freud's texts was intermingled with provocative theorizing drawn from areas as diverse as avant-garde literature and mathematical topology.

On 21 June 1964 Lacan formally founded a new psychoanalytic school and association, the École française de psychanalyse, which was quickly renamed the École freudienne de Paris (EFP). Lacan's goal, as described in the "Founding Act" of the EFP,[18] was to form a psychoanalytic association that could successfully avoid both the IPA's tendency toward hierarchy and its unwillingness to allow the free pursuit of psychoanalytic research and practice. Thus, the EFP encouraged non-medical candidates to enter into training analyses, while an entire section of the school was meant to pursue the complex relations between psychoanalysis, the sciences, and philosophy—"taking inventory of the Freudian field [*le champ freudien*].

" Finally, and certainly most radically, Lacan envisaged the EFP as an institution in which young analysts-in-training could come to the position of *authorizing themselves* as psychoanalysts, thereby in principle destroying the entire hierarchical basis of the IPA's traditional approach to analytic training. In practice, the EFP never quite realized Lacan's stated goals, and he found himself during the 1970s reformulating in several different ways the organization's basic governing principles in an effort to preserve the antiinstitutional character of his own institution.

In October 1966 Lacan traveled for the first time to the United States, where he participated in a landmark symposium held at Johns Hopkins University in Baltimore, "The Languages of Criticism and the Sciences of Man."[19] Lacan thus came to appear as a central figure in the rise of structuralism and poststructuralism in American academic circles, and this accounts for the rather high degree of interest in Lacan among North American literary critics, an interest that has not yet been matched by North American psychoanalysts or philosophers. Shortly after his return to Paris, a large volume of Lacan's collected writings, *Écrits,*[20] was published. Despite the daunting size of the volume and the by then legendary difficulty of Lacan's prose, the *Écrits* sold so well that his publisher rather quickly made selected essays from the collection available in an inexpensive two-volume reprint.[21]

The late 1960s represented the apogee of Lacan's influence among the Parisian intelligentsia. In 1964 Louis Althusser published an important article arguing that Lacan's work had at last opened the door to a successful rapprochement between Marxism and psychoanalysis.[22] This endorsement had the effect of bringing Lacan's work to the attention of still larger numbers of students. When the student-worker revolution of May 1968 nearly brought France to a standstill, Lacan's was one of the voices heard in support of the students' position. Although the student perception of Lacan was ambivalent, his work—both theoretically and institutionally—provided a radical alternative to all hierarchical philosophical systems and social organizations. It was Lacan's apparent encouragement of the events of 1968 that led Robert Flacelière, the director of the École normale supérieure, to demand in March 1969 that Lacan move his seminar to some other venue. This demand produced a number of demonstrations, including a faculty-student occupation of Flacelière's office, but in the end Lacan moved his seminar to a still grander amphitheatre, this time in the Faculté de droit, near the Pantheon.

Meanwhile, the EFP had been caught up since October 1967 in a controversy of its own, stemming from Lacan's attempt to institutionalize the process of the analyst's self-authorization. What was at stake was the pass (*la passe*), a process meant to distinguish between two different categories of analysts within the EFP. Opposition to the pass was in part rooted in the same antihierarchical sentiments that had led to Lacan's own opposition to the IPA. In larger part, however, Lacan's opponents within the EFP were objecting to what they saw as his increasingly authoritarian domination. The institution of the pass required a candidate analyst to describe his or her training analysis to three fellow analysts in training, who in turn would report on this description to a committee of senior EFP analysts. This committee, which in practice always included Lacan, would then approve or reject the candidate's promotion.[23] Thus it seemed that Lacan himself really held all the cards in determining whether or not a candidate would become a *psychanalyste de l'École*. Lacan's apparent domination of the EFP extended to its initial journal, *Scilicet*, which published only anonymous articles, except for those texts actually written by Lacan himself.[24] When the EFP finally voted in January 1969 to approve Lacan's suggested procedure for the pass, a number of his most loyal disciples resigned from the EFP to form yet another psychoanalytic society, le quatrième Groupe.

The revolution of 1968 left in its wake a new and experimental university, the Université de Paris-Vincennes (now Paris VIII). In January 1969 a Lacanian department of psychoanalysis was founded at Vincennes under the direction of Serge Leclaire, and once again the antiinstitutional ideas of Lacan found themselves caught up in an institutional framework. By the summer of 1974 Lacan felt that the curriculum and programs of the department were in sufficient disarray to justify dramatic action, and he stepped in, without any formal authority to do so, appointing Jacques-Alain Miller to the position of chair of the newly renamed Champ freudien and presiding personally over a radical transformation of the program's curriculum in the direction of the mathematical formalization of psychoanalytic theory. While his direct intervention in the academic arena led to yet more defections from the EFP, Lacan's move strengthened the foothold of Lacanian thought within French educational and social institutions. In 1976 a two-year certificate program in clinical psychoanalysis was established at Vincennes, thereby furthering directly Lacan's influence on mental health care in France.

While Lacan's institutional conflicts seemed to be unending, his prominence on the intellectual scene continued to escalate. At the beginning of 1973 Éditions du Seuil brought out the first volume in a series devoted to transcriptions of the complete seminars. This series, only six volumes of which have appeared as of 1989, was initiated by his son-in-law, Jacques-Alain Miller, who convinced Lacan of the value of publishing "authorized" versions of the seminars by producing on his own an *établissement du texte* of the seminar of 1964.[25] With the publication of *Les quatre concepts fondamentaux de la psychanalyse (The Four Fundamental Concepts of Psychoanalysis)*,[26] Lacan's oral teachings first began to reach the larger audience of the printed word. Later in the same year, the French national broadcasting agency (ORTF) produced a two-part documentary television program, aired in January 1974, in which Jacques-Alain Miller asked Lacan a series of alternately teasing and challenging questions, only to receive hermetic and provocative responses.[27] At the end of 1975 Lacan returned to the United States, where he lectured to largely mystified audiences at Yale, Columbia, and MIT on the relation between psychoanalysis and topological knot theory.[28] At about the same time, the new Champ freudien at the Université de Paris-Vincennes established its own journal, *Ornicar?*, in which preliminary transcriptions by Miller of recent Lacan seminars were regularly featured.[29] Further seminars appeared in due course from Éditions du Seuil, as well as numerous translations of Lacan's work in a variety of languages. Nineteen seventy-seven finally saw the appearance in English of both *The Four Fundamental Concepts of Psychoanalysis* and *Écrits: A Selection*.[30]

Early in 1979 Lacan and his daughter Judith Miller cofounded the Fondation du champ freudien as a Lacanian institution separate from the EFP. At the end of September in the same year Jacques-Alain Miller was elected to the board of directors of the EFP after a controversial revision of its bylaws had been passed at Lacan's insistence. Many members of the EFP protested Miller's election, largely because of what was seen as Lacan's unwarranted domination of the École. Lacan's response to the growing mutiny within the EFP was nothing if not spectacular: on 5 January he unilaterally dissolved the EFP, announcing in a "Lettre de dissolution" sent to the EFP's members (and quickly published in *Le Monde)* that he would give those who wished to follow him yet another chance. The tone of this letter is so extraordinary that a portion of it deserves to be quoted:

> If I persevere [*père-sévère*: severe-father], it is because the experiment completed calls for a compensatory counter experiment.
> I don't need many. And there are many whom I don't need.
> I am abandoning them here so that they may show me what they can do, aside from burden me and turn to water a teaching in which everything has been carefully weighed.
> Will those whom I admit with me do any better? At least they can avail themselves of the fact that I am giving them the chance.[31]

This letter was followed by a number of other open letters and messages published in the winter and spring of 1980, fragmentary texts that together effectively constitute the almost disembodied sessions of Lacan's final seminar (S 27).[32] Here Lacan makes his case against the EFP and inaugurates the Cause freudienne, his last venture into the world of psychoanalytic organizations. These final texts, having the appearance of messages from beyond the grave, saw the light of day in the midst of intense litigation and legal maneuvering on the part of a large number of EFP members.[33]

In seriously failing health and clearly bitter over the controversy surrounding his dissolution of the EFP, Lacan traveled to Caracas, Venezuela, in July 1980 to open the first international congress of the Champ freudien. His brief remarks, published as "Le séminaire de Caracas,"[34] announced the impending foundation of a formal organization devoted to the Cause freudienne. In this connection, Lacan reaffirmed the focus of his entire teaching as a "return to Freud," noting that "it's up to you to be Lacanians, if you want. As for me, I am a Freudian."[35] Returning from South America, Lacan sought and received his final vindication, when the EFP as a whole overwhelmingly ratified its own dissolution on 27 September 1980. The next month Lacan formally founded the École de la cause freudienne (ECF), effectively authorizing Jacques-Alain Miller to serve as his successor.

The fall of 1980 saw the end of Lacan's seminar. No longer able to teach publicly, Lacan withdrew to his private psychoanalytic practice and did what he could to consolidate his son-in-law's position within the ECF, in part by naming Miller his literary executor. On 9 September 1981 Lacan died of kidney failure, after a long struggle with abdominal cancer. His last words, as reported by Roudinesco, were: "Je suis obstiné. . . . Je disparais."[36]

Chapter Two

The Family and the Individual

Jacques Lacan began his career as a medically trained psychiatrist, and it was only after successfully defending his doctoral thesis in September 1932 that he entered into a psychoanalysis with Rudolph Loewenstein and began formal psychoanalytic training. Nevertheless, the central argument of his thesis clearly marks a significant move in the direction of psychoanalytic theory. In *De la psychose paranoïaque dans ses rapports avec la personnalité* (1932) Lacan argues that paranoid psychosis cannot be adequately understood by means of organic explanation, and he uses detailed data from a particular case study—the case of Aimée, a patient who had been hospitalized after violently attacking a well-known actress—to build this argument. In this he is arguing against the dominant tradition of French psychiatry. Moreover, Lacan argues against his teacher Clérambault by insisting that, far from being driven automatically by alien notions (Clérambault's "mental automatism"), Aimée's actions and self-descriptions grow inevitably out of her own lived experience. Indeed, the thesis works out at length numerous detailed connections between features of Aimée's delusions and both events in her previous life and well-established characteristics of her personality.[1] In thus emphasizing the essential connection between a psychotic's paranoia and the specific trajectory of her life history, Lacan is self-consciously working his way toward a fundamentally psychodynamic approach to mental illness. It comes as little surprise, then, to see that the extensive bibliography accompanying the thesis includes many references to Freud.[2] For a psychiatrist working in France in the early 1930s, even such an implicit endorsement of Freudian concepts would have appeared at the least "somewhat subversive,"[3] and it is important to bear in mind that psychoanalysis had come to France in a formal way as recently as 1926, with the founding of the Société psychanalytique de Paris (SPP) by Princess Marie Bonaparte and her associates.

Although his thesis remains in the end essentially psychiatric and prepsychoanalytic, Lacan quickly established himself as a psychoanalyst after beginning his analysis with Loewenstein. In 1934 he joined the SPP and the International Psychoanalytic Association (IPA), and he established a private psychoanalytic practice. Just two years later he presented his first explicitly psychoanalytic paper to the fourteenth congress of the IPA in Marienbad. This paper, listed in the *International Journal of Psychoanalysis* for the following year as "The Looking-glass Phase," was not published at that time, but it seems to have led to Lacan's first important psychoanalytic publication, his two articles on the family for the *Encyclopédie française.*

The Family

Volume 8 of the *Encyclopédie française* (1938) is devoted to "the mental life" and features the work of leading French psychologists, psychoanalysts, and psychiatrists from a variety of theoretical perspectives.[4] The editor, Henri Wallon, brought together such traditional psychiatric thinkers as Pierre Janet and Charles Blondel and combined their work with that of such leading psychoanalytic thinkers as Eugène Minkowski and Édouard Pichon. Wallon commissioned Lacan to write two long articles on the family, and the length of these articles made of the comparatively young and relatively unknown Lacan perhaps the *Encyclopédie*'s most important contributor.

Lacan's articles, republished together in 1984 as *Les complexes familiaux dans la formation de l'individu* (The family complexes in the making of the individual), can be seen as remarkably concise and theoretically sophisticated reviews of Freudian theory. However, they also reveal a profoundly original and critical approach to Freud. In a brief introduction to his contributions, Lacan defines the human family as an "institution" and argues that a merely "psychological study" of the family is unable to describe or to explain the systematic ways in which the family reproduces "the structures of behavior and of representation, the play of which overflows the limits of consciousness" (*CF*, 13–14). His emphasis throughout the articles remains firmly upon the concept of *structure*, and Lacan uses this "prestructuralist" notion of structure to combat naively developmental or causal accounts of the relation between the individual and the family.

The first article, "Le complexe, facteur concret de la psychologie familiale" (The complex as a concrete factor of family psychology), elaborates a fundamental distinction between "complex" and "instinct." An instinct depends upon the support of an organic process and serves essentially to regulate this organic functioning in a fixed way. The complexes that Lacan explores, however, are only intermittently related to organic processes and serve, in contrast with the instincts, to supplement organic functioning with sociocultural regulation (*CF*, 32–33). Indeed, the family complexes are what make "the human order" precisely a "subversion of all instinctive fixity" (*CF*, 23). Each complex in effect "reproduces a certain reality of the environment" in the form of an *imago* or "unconscious representation." This imago then serves to unite in a repetitive fashion a number of bodily and psychological reactions, some of which are clearly instinctual (*CF*, 22–24). What Lacan is describing, then, is the way in which imaginary (and fundamentally unconscious) representations shape our bodily and emotional responses to our environments. Put another way, Lacan aims to show how unconscious representations of relations inherent in family structure permanently shape human behavior.

The article goes on to elaborate this theory of the interaction of perceptual stimulus and imaginary representation by considering the three imagoes that represent (and thus reproduce in human action) the fundamental structures of the family: the maternal imago, the fraternal imago, and the paternal imago. The maternal imago lies at the heart of the "weaning complex" and represents not the satisfaction that the mother's breast brings to the infant but "the congenital deficiency" that the infant faces in regard to its bodily needs (*CF*, 33). In adult life the maternal imago is the operative force beneath every philosophical, religious, or political quest: "If it were necessary to define the most abstract form where it is refound, we might characterize it thus: a perfect assimilation of the totality of being. Under this formulation with a slightly philosophical aspect, we can recognize these nostalgias of humanity: the metaphysical mirage of universal harmony, the mystical abyss of affective fusion, the social utopia of a totalitarian guardianship, and every outburst of the obsession with a paradise lost before birth or of the most obscure aspiration toward death" (*CF*, 35).

The fraternal imago characterizes the "intrusion complex" and lies behind the jealousy that attends the young child's realization that his or her identity is inescapably bound up with the identity of others. Lacan is here building on the topic of his 1936 paper and arguing that jealousy "represents not a vital rivalry but a mental identification" (*CF*, 36). The aggressive behavior characteristic of siblings is in fact a product of their more fundamental identification with each other (*CF*, 39). This allows Lacan to argue that the fraternal imago is thus the unconscious basis of human social behavior, and this means that jealousy emerges as "the archetype of social feelings" (*CF*, 46). The paternal imago, finally, is what underlies the Freudian Oedipus complex. Lacan's extensive discussion of this complex focuses on an ambiguity that he suggests is not sufficiently understood by psychoanalytic theorists. While the standard account emphasizes the role of the father in the repression of sexuality, Lacan stresses the parallel process by which the paternal imago sublimates reality for the child (*CF*, 50–51, 55). With the onset of the latency period, the child develops a "disinterested," desexualized appreciation of the structure of his or her environment (*CF*, 58–59), but this appreciation is inevitably tied to a narcissistic self-interest. The post-oedipal child can approach reality in a desexualized fashion precisely because all of his or her sexual interest is turned within (*CF*, 63–64). Consequently, there is a "subversive" tension inherent in the paternal imago and reproduced by the social institution of the bourgeois family: the paternal authority that represses sexuality at the same time serves as the model of sexual adulthood (the ego ideal) for the narcissistic child. The result of this tension is precisely the anxiety and confusion about sexuality characteristic of the modern human condition (*CF*, 70–71). A significant level of Lacan's argument here involves his repudiation of the biologically grounded and anthropologically suspect Freudian myth of the "primal horde"[5] in favor of his own more structural account of the interaction of imaginary representations and external perceptions (*CF*, 54–55).

What is perhaps most remarkable about Lacan's discussion throughout this article is his unwillingness to tie his argument to particular claims of developmental psychology. While there are obvious connections between Lacan's three complexes (with their underlying imagoes) and Freud's phases of infantile sexual development (oral, anal, phallic, and genital),[6] Lacan is much more interested in how unconscious representations dominate human psychology than he is in the Freudian theory of the instincts. His overriding concern remains the way in which behavior is structured by the imagoes. Moreover, his notion of structuring is much more formal than it is causal. The imagoes are not so much causal determinants of human action as patterns or archetypes describing the range of possible human actions. In these respects this early article already foreshadows Lacan's turn to structuralism some fifteen years later.

The second of Lacan's articles for the *Encyclopédie*, "Les complexes familiaux en pathologie" (The family complexes in pathology), extends his theory of the complexes by arguing that these complexes play somewhat different roles in the etiology of different forms of mental illness. With respect to psychosis, Lacan argues that the family complexes perform an essentially formal function, providing fundamental themes worked out in deliria. With respect to neurosis, however, Lacan argues that the complexes actually do perform a causal function, serving to determine characteristic symptoms (CF, 77).

Lacan's thesis about psychotic delirium depends upon his earlier claim that "the evolution of sexuality" in the child is paralleled by "the constitution of reality" in the child's understanding of his or her environment (see CF, 55). What we see in the objects of psychotic delirium is in effect the "stagnation" of sublimation at preliminary stages of the child's appreciation of the constitution of reality (CF, 79, 83, 85). As an example of this Lacan sketches the way megalomania and its attendant psychotic separation from reality might owe their form to a boy's modeling himself upon his brother, taking his brother as his ego ideal. Lacan suggests that the "primitive homosexuality" involved here would produce an ego ideal "too narcissistic not to debase the structure of sublimation" (CF, 86). In this way the fraternal imago and the intrusion complex can be seen to provide a pattern within which the psychotic's behavior will find a place. It is worthy of note that Lacan here is willing to grant that psychosis may well have an organic cause (CF, 87), this cause then producing behavior that conforms to the form or structure laid down by the family complex.

Neurotic behavior, in contrast, has its causal origins in the family complexes. Any formal similarity between a symptom and an imago is merely "contingent" (CF, 88), but neurotic symptoms grow out of precisely the "subversive" tension that Lacan describes in the first of the Encyclopédie articles as stemming from the Oedipus complex. It is the paternal imago's inability satisfactorily to repress sexuality and to serve as a workable model of sexual adulthood that triggers the variety of symptoms that characterize the different neuroses (CF, 95–96). The remainder of the article works out this claim by showing how animal phobias, hysterias, obsessions, and character neuroses all have their source in the sexual ambiguities of the family situation confronting the narcissistic, post-oedipal child. In the final analysis, Lacan's argument comes down to the claim that neurotic symptoms are the product of almost inevitable conflicts between the unconscious imagoes that structure the family situation and the all-too-visible failures of the actual members of a child's family to live up to these structuring representations.

With his sophisticated and critical psychoanalytic account of the family, Lacan's prewar contributions to psychoanalytic theory came to an end. Clearly on the verge of some sort of "structural" rethinking of Freudian theory, Lacan abandoned writing for the duration of World War II, devoting himself instead to his new family, to his private psychoanalytic practice, and to the study of Chinese.

The *Moi* and the Mirror

In the summer of 1949 Lacan attended the sixteenth international congress of the IPA in Zurich and delivered a revised version of his 1936 paper on "The Looking-glass Phase." This new paper was published in the *Revue française de psychanalyse* as "Le stade du miroir comme formateur de la fonction du Je telle qu'elle nous est révélée dans l'expérience psychanalytique" ("The Mirror Stage as Formative of the Function of the I as Revealed in Psychoanalytic Experience") (*E*, 93–100/1–7). This paper, foreshadowed by "L'agressivité en psychanalyse" ("Aggressivity in Psychoanalysis") (*E*, 101–24/8–29), published the previous year in the same journal, marks Lacan's entry into psychoanalytic theory as a distinctive voice. The two papers offer fresh reflections on the nature and constitution of the *moi* (the ego),[7] reflections derived from empirical evidence of child development and from dominant features of the psychoanalytic experience. Specifically, the papers articulate a theory of the *moi* with radical consequences for the then-dominant version of psychoanalytic theory known as ego psychology. Indeed, it is not going too far to say that the series of confrontations with the international psychoanalytic community that marked Lacan's life from the early 1950s on had its theoretical origins in these two early papers. Both papers concern the role of the image in forming the young child's *moi* and offer provocative claims about the continuing importance of the image and of *l'imaginaire* (the imaginary) throughout human life.

The Mirror Stage   "The Mirror Stage" focuses on that period in children's lives, generally between six and eighteen months, when they recognize the image in a mirror as theirs. In his brief meditation on this stage of development, Lacan manages to sketch the framework of a complex theory of personality (or, to use the more Lacanian term, the human subject) and to provide a schematic characterization of the therapeutic efficacy of psychoanalysis, while at the same time developing a thoroughgoing critique of much of modern, Western philosophical reflection on the self.

Central to Lacan's observations is a fundamentally biological fact: the child's recognition of the mirror image comes at a point where she is still effectively incapable of controlling the movements of her body and is still almost totally dependent upon the care of others.[8] The mirror image presents the child with a visual entity that appears whole and that appears to move in a coherent fashion. This image of totality is, then, quite different from the infant's experience of her own bodily existence. Yet observation clearly reveals that the child takes the image to be hers, and in so doing she identifies with the image. Defining *identification* rather precisely as "the transformation that takes place in the subject when he assumes an image" (*E*, 94/2), Lacan goes on to emphasize just how radical a transformation of the infant is involved in this identification with the mirror image: the infant is basically taking herself to be something other than herself; there is thus a fundamental alienation of infant from self marked by the mirror stage; and this alienation lies at the foundation of the very notion of human identity.

In fact, the discordance between the child's inner experience of the body (an experience of the body as made up of discrete body fragments, as yet unintegrated) and the external mirror image which she assumes as an identity (emphasizing the totality and wholeness of this image) opens a split or gap (*béance*)[9] in the subject upon which is built in the course of her development a whole sequence of illusory attempts to overcome an ineluctably alienating identity.[10] Writing of the "primordial form" of the *je* (I)[11] that is "precipitated" in the mirror stage "before it is objectified in the dialectic of identification with the other, and before language restores to it, in the universal, its function as subject" (*E*, 94/2), Lacan notes: "But the important point is that this form situates the agency of the ego [*moi*], before its social determination, in a fictional direction, which will always remain irreducible for the individual alone, or rather, which will only rejoin the coming-into-being of the subject asymptotically, whatever the success of the dialectical syntheses by which he must resolve as *I* [*je*] his discordance with his own reality" (*E*, 94/2). There is a great deal of Lacanian theory implicit in this passage, and perhaps the best way to elucidate it is to juxtapose it with another paragraph from later in the essay:

This development [of the *moi* but also of the neurophysiological system of the child] is experienced as a temporal dialectic that decisively projects the formation of the individual into history. The *mirror stage* is a drama whose internal thrust is precipitated from insufficiency to anticipation—and which manufactures for the subject, caught up in the lure of spatial identification, the succession of phantasies that extends from a fragmented body-image to a form of its totality that I shall call orthopaedic—and, lastly, to the assumption of the armour of an alienating identity, which will mark with its rigid structure the subject's entire mental development. Thus, to break out of the circle of the *Innenwelt* into the *Umwelt* generates the inexhaustible quadrature of the ego's [*moi*] verifications. (*E*, 97/4)

Taking these two passages together, we can outline a series of five stages in the development of the human subject.

1) From its earliest infancy the neonate is basically an uncoordinated collection of natural capacities, few of which do much at this stage to help it survive in its environment. It is here that Lacan emphasizes the "real *specific prematurity of birth* in man" (*E*, 96/4), a lack of bodily integrity that is manifested in later life in sadomasochistic fantasies and dreams of the *corps morcelé* (fragmented body) (*E*, 97/4).

2) Beginning sometime after the age of six months is the mirror stage, that point at which the infant identifies with a visual image of herself. Because this image comes to the infant as a spatially situated unity, the mirror stage in effect marks the infant's assumption of a spatial identity. Lacan's review of the mirror stage suggests that it is itself made up of two independent substages. In the first of these, the infant's identification with the image is "jubilant" (*E*, 94/2), insofar as the image offers the promise of a "totality that I shall call orthopaedic," that is, a totality that makes the child (*pais*) correct or proper (*orthos*) in its form.

3) This joyous affirmation of bodily unity in the image is quickly followed in the mirror stage, however, by a recognition of the gap between the unity of the image and the continuing fragmentary character of the infant's lived experience of her body. Lacan suggests such a recognition when he refers to "the assumption of the armour of an alienating identity." From jubilation to alienation, the double movement of the mirror stage inaugurates the doubts about identity that haunt the human being throughout life. [12]

4) If the mirror stage "precipitates" a "primordial form" of the *je*, this *je* is more fully constituted in the infant's relations with others. The

first stage of this constitution comes in "the dialectic of identification with the other," whereby the identity of the young child is shaped in profound and enduring ways by her adopting the visual identity offered by other people (in particular, by mother, father, and siblings), thus linking her identity to "socially elaborated situations" (E, 98/5).

5) A later stage of the *je's* "social determination" comes with the acquisition of language, beginning roughly at two years of age. It is at this point that the child's visually constituted, essentially imaginary identity rooted in the mirror stage and developed through the identification with others is situated within the preexisting symbolic system of language. Here the *moi* becomes a *je*: the essentially individual identity constructed through the child's image-constituted relations to others is transcended by a universal identity created by and sustained within that broad range of cultural forces that goes by the name of language. The imaginary product of a particular history of visual identifications becomes a genuine human subject, able to use the first person pronoun and to identify herself as the child of a particular family: "I am Joanna Smith."

Much needs to be added to this account, but at this point it is worth emphasizing that the transition from imaginary individuality to symbolic universality itself marks another level of alienation in the human being, a level of alienation that builds upon the earlier alienation grounded in the *béance* between the infant's lived experience of the "fragmented body" and her assumption of a unified imaginary identity in the mirror stage. It should also be remembered that the developmental language in which Lacan couches his account here has already come in for a serious critique in his 1938 articles on the family complexes. Although the very concept of a "mirror stage" would seem to be inherently developmental, implying a series of other stages in the life of a child, it is important to keep in mind that Lacan is more concerned with these stages as formal patterns meaningful only in the light of adult behavior. As Lacan brings the insights of structuralism to bear on psychoanalytic theory during the 1950s, the stages reviewed here and treated as inherently chronological in nature are transformed into structural indices, in relation to which symptoms and patterns of behavior in the psychoanalytic dialogue can be described. This shift of emphasis away from developmental models is motivated at least in part by Lacan's coming to see American ego psychology, with its own special emphasis on the psychological development of ego functions, as the single greatest threat to the integrity of Freud's discovery of the unconscious.

While "The Mirror Stage" offers in schematic form a complex theory of the human personality or subject—and much of Lacan's later work can be seen as elaborating precisely this schema—it also provides in its conclusion an illuminating sketch of the nature and goal of psychoanalytic treatment. The sequence of structural positions presented in the paper provides the basis for tentative and very general definitions of neurosis and madness (*la folie*). The neurotic manifests "the inertia characteristic of the formations of the *I* [*je*]" (*E*, 99/7) and remains caught up in an identity that experiences but does not recognize the various levels of her subjective alienation. The psychotic subject remains rooted in a "captation . . . by the situation" (*E*, 99/7), essentially unable to frame an identity of any sort distinct from that of the environment that envelops him. Alluding to Freud's characterization of analytic therapy in terms of love,[13] Lacan remarks that "psychoanalysis alone recognizes this knot of imaginary servitude that love must always undo again, or sever" (*E*, 100/7). By means of a kind of love (activated in the relation of transference between analysand and analyst), psychoanalysis aims to liberate the neurotic subject from her servitude to an alienating identity, while it hopes to help the psychotic subject take on an identity by "severing" his total identification with aspects of the surrounding world.

Lacan closes the paper with a brief paragraph suggesting how analysis is to achieve these aims: "In the recourse of subject to subject that we preserve, psychoanalysis may accompany the patient to the ecstatic limit of the '*Thou art that*', in which is revealed to him the cipher of his mortal destiny, but it is not in our mere power as practitioners to bring him to the point where the real journey begins" (*E*, 100/7). The therapeutic efficacy of psychoanalysis lies in the ability of its "subject to subject" dialogue to help the analysand recognize and thus come to know the distinct layers of her identity and the complementary levels of her alienation. The message of the analysand's identity—indeed, the meaning of her life—is hidden by a code which the analyst can help the analysand crack. Once the analysand knows what she is, the course of analysis is concluded, and the "real journey" of life begins.

"The Mirror Stage" goes beyond the intrapsychoanalytic context thus far reviewed, however, to address a number of the largest properly philosophical questions about the nature of the human subject and its relation to reality. Indeed, from the very beginning of the essay Lacan situates his reflections in a broad philosophical field, noting that the mirror stage is "an experience that leads us to oppose any philosophy

directly issuing from the *Cogito" (E,* 93/1). The *cogito* in question is of
course Descartes's "Cogito ergo sum" ("I think; therefore, I am"), but
Lacan's reference here clearly goes well beyond the seventeenth-century
philosopher's attempt to ground all human knowledge in the indubitable certainty that thought is possible only for a thinker that exists.[14]
Lacan's true target is the phenomenological tradition of the twentieth
century, growing out of Edmund Husserl's rethinking of Descartes.[15]
In particular, he is concerned with the existentialism of Jean-Paul
Sartre (whose major work, *L'être et le néant* [1943][16] is alluded to at *E,*
98–99/6), which has clear roots in Husserl's attempt to call into question an unthinking epistemological dualism between the subject that
knows and the object that is known. What Descartes, Husserl, and
Sartre (as well as the majority of Western philosophers) share is a
confidence that the human being is essentially a unified, autonomous
subject, fully present to its own consciousness—indeed, essentially
identical with this consciousness—a belief that all human knowledge
can be grounded in the clear self-knowledge of this unified subject, and
a conviction that the moral assessment of human actions is grounded in
the human being's autonomy as a thinking, knowing subject. Freud's
discovery of the unconscious marks a decisive break with this Cartesian
tradition, and Lacan's critique of Cartesianism in "The Mirror Stage"
must be seen as working within the largely tacit context of the theory of
the unconscious. (Lacan himself turns explicitly to the theory of the
unconscious in the years immediately following "The Mirror Stage.")

"The Mirror Stage" undermines the Cartesian subject in a variety of
ways, all of which are elaborated in Lacan's later work and constitute
perhaps the most decisive "decentering" of the subject in postwar
French thought. Lacan's repeated metaphor of "precipitation" (*E,* 94/2,
97/4), for example, immediately drives home the subject's lack of
autonomy. The *moi* is hurled into a largely alien environment by forces
outside its control: the specific prematurity of birth in the human
species, the infant's capacity to identify with a visual image, and the
preexisting cultural network of language and other symbolic systems.[17]
This precipitated *moi* is situated "in a fictional direction" (*E,* 94/2) and
thus is in an important sense illusory, and the *béance* between this
illusory identity and the infant's lived experience of the body provides
the basis for a more or less permanent alienation of the subject from
herself. Moreover, the Cartesian confidence that knowledge of the external world finds its ultimate justification in the subject's certain knowledge of self is replaced in Lacan's essay by the haunting image of the

moi's alienating identity as an armor that prevents its grasp of anything beyond its inner world: "To break out of the circle of the *Innenwelt* into the *Umwelt* generates the inexhaustible quadrature of the ego's [*moi*] verifications" (*E*, 97/4). Just as the circle cannot be squared (this would be its quadrature),[18] so too the *moi* cannot verify its identity in a way allowing it to clarify and theorize the distinction between it and an external reality.

Lacan's anti-Cartesianism is perhaps even more profoundly reflected in some methodological remarks he makes which in turn lead him to call into question apparently fundamental aspects of Freud's theory of the ego. Worried that his reader might suspect that the ultimate evidence for the account of the mirror stage is a matter of "subjective givens" that would depend upon "the unthinkable of an absolute subject" for their verification (*E*, 98/5), Lacan describes his contribution as a "guiding grid for a *method of symbolic reduction*" (*E*, 98/5). I take this to mean that, rather than assuming the existence and intelligibility of the human subject—on the basis of whose existence empirical data can be introduced into a scientific description of the subject's relation to the rest of the world—Lacan means to offer what might be termed a structural account of the existence and intelligibility of the human subject. Such an account "reduces" the subject not to the data of the empirical scientist (which data, it must be emphasized, presuppose the reliability of the human subject) but to the rather complex schema of visual identifications and symbolic determinations briefly sketched in "The Mirror Stage." Lacan's move here radically transforms the notion of knowledge, inasmuch as the empirical data of science are themselves seen to be dependent upon a subject, whose fragile and largely illusory identity is essentially bound up with the existence of others (*E*, 98/5). In place of an empirical science rooted in data whose certainty rests on the epistemological preeminence of the subject, Lacan offers us a vision of knowledge as caught up in an ever-changing dialectic between the data derived from a subject's experience and that subject's complexly mediated identity that shapes the very nature of the data.

This methodological digression leads Lacan to offer toward the end of "The Mirror Stage" a careful but radical critique of Freud. Lacan writes that "our experience . . . teaches us not to regard the ego [*moi*] as centred on the *perception-consciousness system,* or as organized by the 'reality principle'—a principle that is the expression of a scientific prejudice most hostile to the dialectic of knowledge. Our experience shows that we should start instead from the *function of méconnaissance* that characterizes the ego [*moi*] in all its structures, so markedly articulated by Miss Anna Freud" (*E*, 99/6). In this passage Lacan is again emphasizing the theme of alienation discussed earlier: the *méconnaissance* (misrecognition) involved at the heart of the *moi*'s function is simply its being constituted as an illusory identity in the identificatory drama of the mirror stage.[19] But in thus opposing his notion of the *moi* to an inescapably Cartesian notion of the ego or subject as identifiable with consciousness and with perceptual consciousness in particular, Lacan is coming into at least partial conflict with Freud's fairly regular theorization of the ego as intimately tied to what he in fact calls the "perception-consciousness system."[20] Lacan's dismissal of the reality principle here—his explicit insistence that the *moi* has very little at all to do with reality—is shockingly at odds with numerous Freudian texts, and this radical challenge to Freud certainly lies at the theoretical core of the conflict that erupted between Lacan and the international psychoanalytic establishment in the early 1950s. From the perspective of ego psychology, which is grounded in Anna Freud's classic contribution to psychoanalytic theory, *The Ego and the Mechanisms of Defence* (1936),[21] Lacan's decentering of the *moi* away from reality represents a shocking attack: if the *moi* or ego is not the agency of the psyche responsible for adjusting the subject's relations with reality, then psychoanalytic therapy with the aim of strengthening the ego's defenses against those instinctual impulses at odds with reality becomes almost laughably inappropriate.

Finally, Lacan's focusing of attention on the fundamental structures of *méconnaissance* that constitute the *moi*'s illusory identity allows him to develop a stinging critique of Sartrean existentialism as based on the central "illusion of autonomy" that the *moi* adopts as part of its misrecognized identity (*E*, 99/6). Lacan summarizes his position in a passage of remarkable directness: "Existentialism must be judged by the explanations it gives of the subjective impasses that have indeed resulted from it; a freedom that is never more authentic than when it is within the walls of a prison; a demand for commitment, expressing the impotence of a pure consciousness to master any situation; a voyeuristic-sadistic idealization of the sexual relation; a personality that realizes itself only in suicide; a consciousness of the other that can be satisfied only by Hegelian murder"(*E*, 99/6). It is precisely paradoxes such as these, Lacan asserts, that grow out of the illusion that the human subject possesses an absolute freedom, an illusion which in turn rests on Descartes's subject-centered epistemology. And it is precisely paradoxes such as these—in the form of neurotic and even psychotic symptoms—that Lacanian psychoanalytic practice will aim to dissolve.

Narcissism and the Paranoiac *Moi* The central themes of "The Mirror Stage" had been sketched the year before in "Aggressivity in Psychoanalysis." The earlier essay, however, deepens Lacan's radical account of the *moi* by involving it inextricably with a variety of forms of aggression and, in turn, by showing the roots of this aggression in the narcissistic modes of identification that give the *moi* its very identity.

Methodologically, "Aggressivity in Psychoanalysis" builds its argument on the foundations of a close description of the psychoanalytic experience, attempting to explore the "formative function" of images in the subject (*E,* 104/11) by noting the reappearance of certain images in the transference relation between analysand and analyst. The recurrent images at issue here are "the images of castration, mutilation, dismemberment, dislocation, evisceration, devouring, bursting open of the body, in short, the *imagoes* that I have grouped together under the apparently structural term of *imagoes of the fragmented body*" (*E,* 104/11). These images may be assumed to be memories and imaginary reconstructions of the lived bodily experience of the infant prior to the onset of the mirror stage, given Lacan's claims about the *corps morcelé* in "The Mirror Stage." In a careful description of the psychoanalytic dialogue, Lacan emphasizes the way in which the analyst's essential lack of personality within the analytic dialogue fosters in the analysand "that resistance of *amour-propre*" (*E,* 107/13) which in turn results in an aggressive attitude towards the analyst (the negative transference). Using examples of hysteria, obsession, and phobia, Lacan suggests that the negative transference involves "in the patient the imaginary transference on to our person [i.e., that of the analyst] of one of the more or less archaic *imagoes*" of the fragmented body (*E,* 107–8/14–15). In other words, the aggression displayed by an analysand within the analytic dialogue appears as given shape and content by particular, largely visual, images.

This immediately brings us back to the sphere of the mirror stage and Lacan's insistence that the *moi* is itself constituted by the young child's identification with a variety of visual images. In the course of the analyst's attempt to help the analysand recognize what he is ("*Thou art that*"), these images are bound to be revived, and the unpleasantness, even the horror, of the images of the fragmented body, in particular, may be expected to contribute to the analysand's affective relation to the analyst (in the negative transference, once again). The result will often be the analysand's belligerent rejection of whatever it is that may be surfacing in the course of the analytic dialogue. Elaborating Freud's suggestion in his 1925 essay "Negation" that "the content of a repressed image or idea can make its way into consciousness, on condition that it is *negated*,"[22] Lacan insists that it is precisely in the subject's repeated acts of negating, of denying the *moi*'s actual character as an illusory construct, that we see the distinctive character of the *méconnaissance* that lies at the *moi*'s heart (*E*, 108–9/15). Indeed, Lacan goes so far as to maintain that "the characteristic modes of the agency of the ego [*moi*] in dialogue" are the aggressive reactions of "opposition, negation, ostentation, and lying" (*E*, 108/15), so that "the ego [*moi*] represents the centre of all the *resistances* to the treatment of symptoms" (*E*, 118/23).[23]

Much of "Aggressivity in Psychoanalysis" is devoted to making a case for the important thesis that "*Aggressivity is the correlative tendency of a mode of identification that we call narcissistic, and which determines the formal structure of man's ego (moi) and of the register of entities characteristic of his world*" (*E*, 110/16). The theoretical context for this discussion is the notion of narcissism as elaborated in Freud's important paper of 1914, "On Narcissism."[24] This rich paper brings together a number of issues by relating them all to the central claim that the libido directed toward external love objects can be and, at an earlier point in the development of the subject, was in fact directed toward the ego itself. Freud himself virtually defines the ego as essentially narcissistic and deepens the perhaps crude notion of "self-love" by taking narcissism to involve the relation between the ego and an image of its ideal (the so-called ego ideal). He writes: "The development of the ego consists in a departure from primary narcissism and gives rise to a vigorous attempt to recover that state. This departure is brought about by means of the displacement of libido on to an ego ideal imposed from without; and satisfaction is brought about from fulfilling this ideal."[25] This passage strikingly foreshadows Lacan's controversial claim that human identity is itself mediated by others and mediated in particular by images of others.

How, then, does a narcissistic mode of identification determine the formal structure of the *moi*? Returning to Lacan's conception of the mirror stage, we note that the infant's ambivalent identification with his mirror image—an identification that can now be labeled narcissistic— dominates his mental life from the very moment of self-recognition; in particular, the infant's captivation with the mirror image proves a determining factor in his relations with others. According to Lacan, "it is this captation by the *imago* of the human form . . . which, between the ages of six months and two and half years, dominates the entire dialectic of the child's behaviour in the presence of his similars. During the whole of this period, one will record the emotional reactions and the articulated evidences of a normal transitivism. The child who strikes another says that he has been struck; the child who sees another fall, cries" (*E,* 113/19). These "transitive" behaviors stem from the fact that the narcissistic identification with a visual image that constitutes the young *moi* is inherently alienating. Not only is the mirror reflection other than the child, but, once the child begins the game of identifying with visual images, countless images of others offer themselves for identification. As visual images, there are deep similarities between the reflection of the child in a mirror and the visual encounter with another child of similar age or even with an adult. Thus, the disturbing realization of the gap between the child's lived experience of the still minimally competent and functionally fragmented body and his narcissistic identification with the unity of his visual reflection is displaced into various kinds of aggressive tendencies directed towards others. In other words, the discrepancy between the child's fragmented bodily experience and his unified, imaginary identity (a discrepancy often characterized by Lacan with the botanical term *dehiscence*[26]) gives rise to a kind of primordial paranoia in the young *moi*.

The potential for display of aggressive behavior is increased as the child, in his identifying with others, begins to take upon himself the desires manifested in the others' behavior. In modeling oneself on another, one is also modeling one's desires on those of the other, and the inevitable consequence of this is an aggressive rivalry between the child and the other for the object desired by the other.[27] In this way, aggression directed toward others is found at the very center of the *moi*'s structure, as it comes into being through the dialectic of the child's narcissistic identifications with various visual images. Lacan puts this point rather elegantly:

It is in this erotic relation, in which the human individual fixes upon himself an image that alienates him from himself, that are to be found the energy and the form on which this organization of the passions that he will call his ego [*moi*] is based.
This form will crystallize in the subject's internal conflictual tension, which

determines the awakening of his desire for the object of the other's desire. (*E*, 113/19)

From this it follows that "man's ego [*moi*] can never be reduced to his experienced identity" (*E*, 114/20). The *moi* is better understood as a set of structures putting into relationship the individual in question, others, and objects of desire; indeed, all too often it is precisely the unexperienced levels of the *moi*'s structuring that lie behind the characteristic behavior of certain personalities.[28]

Lacan goes on to use this analysis to clarify the resolution of the Oedipus complex. If the key to this resolution lies, in effect, in a nonaggressive identification with the rival, then it is clear that the mirror-stage child's complete narcissistic confusion of self and other provides a useful step toward a satisfactory resolution of the complex. I will turn later to Lacan's mature theory of the Oedipus complex (which goes well beyond the hints found in the paper of 1948), but it is perhaps worth noting here that successful negotiation of the oedipal stage confirms in a relatively stable way the truth of Rimbaud's statement that "Je est un autre."[29] In a flash of trenchant humor, Lacan writes: " 'I'm a doctor' or 'I'm a citizen of the French Republic' . . . certainly presents fewer logical difficulties than the statement, 'I'm a man', which at most can mean no more than, 'I'm like he whom I recognize to be a man, and so recognize myself as being such.' In the last resort, these various formulas are to be understood only in reference to the truth of 'I is an other', an observation that is less astonishing to the intuition of the poet than obvious to the gaze of the psychoanalyst" (*E*, 118/23).

A crucial consequence of Lacan's theory of the *moi* is his startling claim that human knowledge is inherently paranoiac in its "most general structure" (*E*, 111/17).[30] I have already suggested in passing that the aggressiveness that stems from the *béance* between the child's bodily reality and his imaginary identity might be thought of as paranoiac. Lacan goes beyond this to argue in a highly condensed and difficult passage that the forms of aggression manifested in different kinds of paranoia parallel the series of stages in the dialectic between the young, narcissistic *moi*, other people, and various objects of desire (*E*, 110–11/16–17). What all of these forms of aggression have in common is a "stereotypical" quality, an unrealistic pattern of behavior that gives the appearance of being the result of a denial or a halting of the ongoing dialectic of identification between the *moi*, others, and objects. But, of course, it is precisely the denial of the constant flux of our experience that characterizes at the most general level knowledge itself. From the earliest stages of Greek philosophy—for example, Heraclitus (ca. 500 B.C.E.) and, most spectacularly, Plato and Aristotle—knowledge has been identified with a recognition of that which remains the same through or behind or underneath the constantly changing world of our experience. In this sense, knowledge is (virtually by definition) something that offers itself as a replacement for lived experience. Bearing in mind Lacan's notion of the mirror stage, we can naturally situate knowledge claims on the mirror, imaginary side of the gap between bodily reality and imaginary identity: systems of knowledge—from the most fundamental prescientific descriptions of the world to the most highly refined scientific models—aim to provide us with some sort of ultimate unity to put in the place of the apparent chaos and fragmentation of our lived experience in the body. It is surely this promise of unity that gives such systems their perhaps fatal attraction. All this is summed up in a marvelous paragraph, in which Lacan comes as close as he ever does to defining what he calls "paranoic knowledge." He writes: "Now, this formal stagnation is akin to the most general structure of human knowledge: that which constitutes the ego [*moi*] and its objects with attributes of permanence, identity, and substantiality, in short, with entities or 'things' that are very different from the *Gestalten* that experience enables us to isolate in the shifting field, stretched in accordance with the lines of animal desire" (*E,* 111/17).

Thus, "The Mirror Stage" and "Aggressivity in Psychoanalysis" offer us a theory describing the coming-into-being and the structure of the *moi*, a theory that is in many respects an overt challenge to the ego psychology to which Freud's psychoanalytic theory had given birth in England and the United States. Beyond this, these early essays show Lacan in the midst of a sophisticated encounter with fundamental philosophical issues concerning the nature of the self and the character of knowledge. There can be no doubt that Lacan's remarks about the paranoiac structure of what has passed for knowledge (at least in the West) are meant to be brought together with his critique of the Cartesian subject in "The Mirror Stage." If we are to replace the *cogito* with a structural account of the subject as the "precipitate" of a complex dialectic of identification, then we should also expect Lacan to demand that we replace our paranoiac epistemology with a new conception of knowledge. "Aggressivity in Psychoanalysis" allows us to speculate that a Lacanian epistemology would promote systems of knowledge that describe or explain lived experience in terms of "impermanent" and "insubstantial" structures, systems of knowledge that return to "the lines of animal desire" and give up the paranoiac faith in "entities or 'things'."[31] In fact, it is something very much of this sort that Lacan will offer much later in his career as his contribution to the long-standing debate about the scientific status of psychoanalysis.

Despite their theoretical sophistication, these early papers nevertheless betray Lacan's own inability to escape fully the presumptions of phenomenology. The *béance* described in "The Mirror Stage" between the infant's image as recognized in the mirror and her lived experience of a fragmentary and minimally controlled bodily self is a gap apparently fully present to the infant's consciousness. The fundamental alienation that results from her identification with her mirror image is, thus, something essentially *felt* by the young child, and Lacan would seem at this point to be committed to the claim that some such alienating feeling must be a more or less permanent characteristic of human consciousness. To get beyond this conclusion and beyond the demand for a careful phenomenological description of such feelings of alienation, Lacan would need to elaborate a radically antiphenomenological notion of the unconscious, and it is to precisely this that he turns at the beginning of the 1950s. Similarly, the theses of both early papers rest on empirical, scientific data (about mirror recognition and about the phenomena of transitivism), but Lacan's own critique of the phenomenological *cogito* renders problematic the status of empirical claims in general. The turn toward structuralism made by Lacan around 1950 may be seen, in part at least, as an attempt to resituate psychoanalytic theory as an explicitly "nonempirical" science. Thus, if "The Mirror Stage" and "Aggressivity in Psychoanalysis" offer in germ a number of claims that provide the basis for his later theoretical work, these two papers also suffer from defects the repair of which can be seen as one of Lacan's principal tasks in the 1950s.

Chapter Three

From the Imaginary to the Symbolic

September 1953 found Lacan in Rome, having been invited to deliver the official theoretical report of the Société psychanalytique de Paris (SPP) at the Congrès des psychanalystes de langue française. Between the time of his invitation to deliver this report and late September, Lacan and Daniel Lagache had led a secession from the SPP and had formed a new organization of French analysts, the Société française de Psychanalyse (SFP), which was at this time attempting to gain recognition from the International Psychoanalytic Association. Thus, Lacan could no longer represent the SPP at the Rome meeting; nevertheless, he did speak on 26 September, and he used this occasion to launch his own ongoing challenge to the international psychoanalytic community, a challenge that henceforth took the form of his weekly or biweekly seminar. The seminar, which had begun more informally in 1951, continued from autumn of 1953 to the spring of 1980, and it is not at all unfair to see Lacan's teaching career as a sustained elaboration and rethinking of the fundamental positions articulated in Rome in 1953.

The first volume of *La psychanalyse* (1956), the journal of the new SFP, includes two texts relating to Lacan's appearance in Rome. The more important of the two, "Fonction et champ de la parole et du langage en psychanalyse" ("The Function and Field of Speech and Language in Psychoanalysis") was reprinted in *Écrits* (237–322/30–113) and has since found its way into English in two different versions.[1] This long essay originated as the report handed out in Rome at the time of Lacan's lecture (although a number of changes and additions were made in the thirteen years leading up to *Écrits*). Rather than delivering such a substantial text, Lacan chose to speak more or less extemporaneously on a few of the themes of the report: a résumé of his remarks, "Discours de Jacques Lacan (26 sept. 1953)," appears in the same volume of *La psychanalyse* (202–11), together with a transcription of the interventions made by those present (211–42) and of Lacan's responses (242–

55). Lacan's report "The Function and Field of Speech and Language in Psychoanalysis" has rather misleadingly come to be known as the "Discours de Rome."

This study is not the place to launch a detailed account of competing positions within psychoanalytic theory. It may prove helpful, however, to situate Lacan's argument in the 1950s by sketching the alternative psychoanalytic perspectives against which he pursues his theoretical work. Lacan's most vocal opposition is to the movement known as "ego psychology," developed largely in the United States during the late 1940s and early 1950s. Not insignificantly, Lacan's own training analyst, Rudolph Loewenstein, was one of the central figures in the development of this movement, along with Heinz Hartmann and Ernst Kris. Ego psychology focused its attention, predictably enough, on the role of the ego in analytic theory, attempting to bring to psychoanalysis some of the insights of developmental psychology concerning the way ego functions evolve in response to both external and internal (instinctual) stimuli.[2] Following the lead of Anna Freud, the ego psychologists tended to see one of the primary aims of psychoanalytic therapy to be the strengthening of the ego's mechanisms of defense against these various stimuli. There is thus within the theory a comparative depreciation of the importance of the Freudian unconscious, an insistence on the scientific status of psychoanalytic theory, and a willingness to think of the ego in terms of its adaptation to the environment.[3] Lacan is in fundamental disagreement with the whole of ego psychology. As early as "The Mirror Stage" he was insisting on the almost shocking claim—a claim put with equally shocking simplicity in "Some Reflections on the Ego," published in English the same year the Rome conference was held—that the ego or *moi* is fundamentally an illusory identity, inherently weak, alienating and alienated, and a clear hindrance to the curative aims of psychoanalysis. While "Function and Field" carries this argument to a new level, it also initiates two other strands of argument against the international psychoanalytic establishment.

The first of these strands concerns the precipitating cause of his departure from the SPP and of his institutional conflicts with the IPA: his experimental use of variable-length psychoanalytic sessions (the so-called short sessions).[4] Perhaps the most difficult and important dimension of Lacan's argument in "Function and Field" concerns the concept of time, both in the experience of the human subject and in that subject's experience of the psychoanalytic dialogue. Integrally involved in his discussion of these fundamental issues is Lacan's defense of his own use of variable-length analytic sessions to "punctuate" the temporal rhythms of the analysand's experience. In this way, the relatively abstract discussion of time provides a context for Lacan's very concrete challenge to the rules of analytic practice sanctioned by the IPA, as well as a context for the hostility shown to Lacan's ideas by leading members of the IPA (including, most notably, Anna Freud and Marie Bonaparte). I return to this strand of Lacan's argument at some length in chapter 4.

The other approach to psychoanalytic theory that comes under regular critique by Lacan is that known as "object relations" theory. The object relations school (which flourished particularly in England in the wake of the important theoretical work of Melanie Klein, W. R. D. Fairbairn, and D. W. Winnicott) focuses its attention on the interplay of reality and fantasy in the human subject's choice of sexual objects.[5] Lacan is eager to criticize what he sees as this school's unfortunate tendency to move away from a serious theoretical recognition of the importance of speech and language in the phenomena uncovered by psychoanalytic investigation. In the introduction to his report, Lacan sketches what he takes to be the three basic problem areas of contemporary (1950s) psychoanalytic practice and theory (*E*, 242–43/35–36). 1) Largely as a result of Melanie Klein's pioneering work, analysts had become more and more concerned with exploring the role of fantasies. What Lacan calls "the function of the imaginary" (*E*, 242/35) was found to shape the analysands' experience of analysis as well as structuring the very nature of the objects of their choice. 2) Related to this was the rise of object relations theory, with what Lacan sees as a new emphasis on a normative progress of libidinal object choices serving to guide the course of analysis. 3) Finally, new attention was being paid to the role of the countertransference in analysis and thus to the importance in analytic training of dealing with its typical manifestations.

What worried Lacan in 1953 was that all three of these areas in which important new psychoanalytic research was being done shared "the temptation for the analyst to abandon the foundation of speech, and this precisely in areas where, because they border on the ineffable, its use would seem to require a more than usually close examination" (*E*, 243/36). The analyst focusing on fantasy or on normative series of fantasied object relations is generally dealing with preverbal stages of child development or with their regressive reappearances in adult analysands. Yet—and this is Lacan's fundamental point—what these analysts know about such fantasies comes strictly from what their analysands tell them in the course of the analytic dialogue. The preverbal is known only as verbalized in the course of the analysand's speech, and Lacan insists that it is theoretically naive to ignore the ways in which language is bound to shape the reports of fantasy. Similarly, while the new concern with analytic training did not focus on preverbal experience, what Lacan saw in contemporary theory was an obsession with the lived experience of the countertransference. Lacan himself had not completely escaped a similar preoccupation in "The Mirror Stage," yet this emphasis on the phenomenological dimension of analysis is in sharp contrast to Lacan's new emphasis on the ways in which the countertransference manifests itself in the analyst's contribution to the analytic dialogue and thus in the analysand's own speech as well. Lacan's point here is simply that it is the effects of the countertransference on the analytic dialogue (rather than the quality of the analyst's lived experience of countertransference) that are of central importance to psychoanalytic practice and theory.

With this brief sketch of the context of Lacan's manifesto in mind, we may turn now to his text.

The Turn toward Structuralism

We can begin directly with Lacan's basic thesis in 1953 (and throughout his teaching career): psychoanalytic theory can regain its intellectual respectability and rigor and can serve as the foundation for advances in therapeutic technique only if it returns to the role of speech and language in the psychoanalytic experience. Toward the end of the introduction to "Function and Field," Lacan offers the central claim of his report: "As far as I am concerned, I would assert that the technique cannot be understood, nor therefore correctly applied, if the concepts on which it is based are ignored. It is our task to demonstrate that these concepts take on their full meaning only when orientated in a field of language, only when ordered in relation to the function of speech" (E, 246/39). It is this return to the role of language in psychoanalysis that constitutes Lacan's celebrated "return to Freud" and serves to distinguish the trend of his theoretical work from that of object relations theorists as well as ego psychologists. At the same time, it is precisely this return to the role of language in psychoanalysis that marks Lacan's most important revision of Freudian theory. In the preface added to "Function and Field" for its publication in 1956, Lacan makes it clear that his return to the terminology of Freud's theoretical work is to be

made in an intellectual atmosphere very different from that of Freud's
Vienna: "But it seems to me that these terms can only become clear if
one establishes their equivalence to the language of contemporary anthropology, or even to the latest problems in philosophy, fields in
which psychoanalysis could well regain its health" (*E,* 240/32). The
anthropology Lacan has in mind is essentially that of his friend Claude
Lévi-Strauss. Even more fundamentally, as Lacan's text reveals, the
"latest problems in philosophy" are (along with issues raised by the
French existentialists in their reading of Hegel) issues about the distinction between *parole* (speech) and *langue* or *langage* (language), issues
growing out of the structural approach to linguistics initiated by Ferdinand de Saussure.

In short, Lacan quite explicitly reexamines Freudian theory through
the lens of structuralism. This is hardly the place to attempt a systematic introduction to an intellectual movement as complex as French
structuralism.[6] However, a brief review of its most fundamental principles is important to understanding just what is at stake in Lacan's
celebrated bringing together of psychoanalytic theory and structuralist
social science.

Structuralism has its roots in the linguistic theory developed by the
Swiss linguist Ferdinand de Saussure (1857–1913), in lectures given
between 1906 and 1911 at the University of Geneva. After his death
the contents of these lectures were edited into the *Course in General
Linguistics* (1916) by several of Saussure's students.[7] For our purposes,
Saussure's contribution to linguistics (understood as providing the basis
for the elaboration of structuralism) can be reduced to three basic
principles.

1) The subject matter of linguistics is language (what Saussure generally calls *langue*[8] and is often described as the "code") as opposed to
speech (what he calls *parole* and is often described as the "message"). In
other words, what the linguist studies is the more or less abstract
system of grammatical rules and social conventions that make possible
particular uses of language in acts of speech. The linguist is not so
much interested in the details of actual speech in daily life as in the
background system that makes routine speaking meaningful. Saussure
argues for the priority of language to speech on the grounds that what
linguists are concerned with is the "social bond" essential to communication, rather than the individual and fundamentally accidental acts of
communication facilitated by this social bond.[9] Saussure's claim here
rests on the even more fundamental position (made fairly obvious by

the possibility of interlanguage translation) that linguistic meanings are unavoidably a matter of social convention, that the relation between a word and a concept or a thing (between a *signifier* and a *signified,* in the jargon of structuralism) is in principle utterly arbitrary.[10] This approach to linguistic facts allows the structural linguist to move away from the notion (shared by the phenomenological tradition) that meaning is best understood in terms of the individual intentions of speakers. For Saussure, "language is not a function of the speaker, it is a product that is passively assimilated by the individual. It never requires premeditation . . . . Speaking, on the contrary, is an individual act. It is willful and intellectual."[11] From this formulation, it also follows that language is essentially unconscious, something that will be emphasized by Lacan. Another implication of this antiphenomenological approach to language is Saussure's refocusing of linguistic research away from historical, "diachronic" studies of language evolution and towards "synchronic" studies of the static systems of language that make possible actual utterances at a particular point in time.[12]

   2) To his critique of a quasi-phenomenological theory of meaning, Saussure adds a critique of a substantialist theory of language. Language is not a thing, an object to be studied. It is rather an articulated system of differences: "Everything that has been said up to this point boils down to this: in language there are only differences. Even more important: a difference generally implies positive terms between which the difference is set up; but in language there are only differences *without positive terms.*"[13] The meaning of any element in a language is not only arbitrary but utterly dependent upon its relations to all the other elements in the language. Moreover, linguistic meaning cannot be taken to be a function of a preexisting system of concepts or ideas, since concepts too owe their identity to their differential relations to other concepts. "Instead of pre-existing ideas then, we find . . . *values* emanating from the system. When they are said to correspond to concepts, it is understood that the concepts are purely differential and defined not by their positive content but negatively by their relations with the other terms of the system. Their most precise characteristic is in being what the others are not."[14]

   3) Finally, Saussure's approach to linguistics entails a particular concept of explanation, which may fairly be characterized as "structural." In contrast to the "causal" explanation characteristic of the natural sciences—an inherently diachronic, predictive mode of explanation that explains an event by pointing out its determining causes—the

structural linguist explains a speech act by showing it to be one of the possibilities set up by the background language. In unfolding the synchronic system of differences that constitutes a language, the structuralist in effect simultaneously unfolds an indeterminately large (in principle, infinite) number of possible instantiations of the linguistic system in speech. Typically, the demands of structural explanation are effectively met by means of some sort of display of the relevant portion of the background system of language, often by a table of the combinatorial possibilities of a few fundamental elements.

Claude Lévi-Strauss brought Saussure's structuralist principles to anthropology (and more generally to the human sciences) by arguing that forms of human behavior can be (indeed, must be) studied as analogous to utterances, these behaviors making sense only in relation to a background system of rules, which can be thought of as the language of such behaviors. As he himself points out in his inaugural lecture at the Collège de France,[15] Lévi-Strauss is simply following up Saussure's own call for the development of "semiology" as a *"science that studies the life of signs within society,"* a science of which linguistics forms only a part.[16]

In a landmark article of 1945, "Structural Analysis in Linguistics and in Anthropology,"[17] Lévi-Strauss sketches and briefly illustrates the method that he would go on to pursue throughout his lengthy intellectual career. All three of the principles basic to Saussure's structural linguistics can be found there, although Lévi-Strauss borrows his formulations from the Czech linguist, Nikolai Trubetzkoy: "First, structural linguistics shifts from the study of *conscious* linguistic phenomena to study of their *unconscious* infrastructure; second, it does not treat *terms* as independent entities, taking instead as its basis of analysis the *relations* between terms; third, it introduces the concept of *system*—'Modern phonemics does not merely proclaim that phonemes are always part of a system; it *shows* concrete phonemic systems and elucidates their structure'—; finally, structural linguistics aims at discovering *general laws,* either by induction 'or . . . by logical deduction, which would give them an absolute character.' "[18] What Lévi-Strauss most emphasizes here is a conclusion that will prove quite important for the later work of Lacan: the structural mode of explanation, inasmuch as it aims to discover "general laws" by "logical deduction," promises "a social science . . . able to formulate necessary relationships." The article goes on to illustrate precisely (in part by means of a diagram of combinatorial possibilities) such necessary synchronic relationships by showing how the varying kinship systems of five different nonindustrial societies presuppose "the same fundamental relationship between the four pairs of oppositions required to construct the system."[19] What Lévi-Strauss suggests is that structural explanation in anthropology, while it cannot predict the precise form of kinship system that will be found in a given social group, can construct a model showing (in principle) all possible variant kinship systems as transformations of a small number of basic elements. It was to this, admittedly vast, project that Lévi-Strauss devoted his first major book, *The Elementary Structures of Kinship* (1949),[20] a work of crucial importance for Lacan.

What Lacan refers to as "the symbolic" (*le symbolique*) is (at a first degree of approximation) the background system or "language" that makes possible and meaningful the wide variety of human behaviors and, in particular, those evidenced in the course of the psychoanalytic dialogue. When he calls for psychoanalytic theory to situate Freud's fundamental concepts "in a field of language" and to order them "in relation to the function of speech" (*E, 246/39*), Lacan is thus undisguisedly arguing for a structuralist approach to analytic theorizing. Just what the implications of this are for psychoanalysis will be the main burden of the rest of this chapter.

Empty Speech and Full Speech

The first section of "Function and Field" is entitled "Empty Speech and Full Speech in the Psychoanalytic Realization of the Subject." From the beginning Lacan announces his intention to focus on the role of speech (and thus of language) in the psychoanalytic dialogue, but he also emphasizes in his subtitle that at stake in his account of speech is the very being of the subject, the analysand whose discourse has the effect of making real (realizing) his subjectivity. Throughout the reading of "Function and Field," it is important to bear in mind Lacan's dramatic insistence that the psychoanalytic dialogue is the place where a certain kind of subject comes into being or, perhaps more properly, where the subject comes into being in a certain kind of way (psychoanalytically).

Lacan opens the section with a straightforward statement of the importance of speech in psychoanalysis:

Whether it sees itself as an instrument of healing, of training, or of exploration in depth, psychoanalysis has only a single medium: the patient's speech. That this is self-evident is no excuse for our neglecting it. And all speech calls for a reply.

I shall show that there is no speech without a reply, even if it is met only with silence, provided that it has an auditor: this is the heart of its function in analysis. (*E*, 247/40)

Lacan is here resuming a claim made earlier in "Aggressivity in Psychoanalysis," where he had noted that "psychoanalytic action is developed in and through verbal communication, that is, in a dialectical grasp of meaning" (*E*, 102/9). In 1948 he had concluded from this—among other things—that subjectivity has an inherently "bipolar structure" (*E*, 103/10), and this notion is preserved in his insistence now that all speech implies a reply: there is no speaking subject without an auditor who replies; there is no subject without an other.[21]

The treatment of the analytic dialogue in section 1 falls into two parts, the first concerned with the "here and now" of the analysand's free association (*E*, 248–54/41–46) and the second focused on the *anamnesis* or recollection, which makes possible the symbolic interpretation of the analysand's discourse (*E*, 254–65/46–56).

As the analysand observes "the fundamental rule" of psychoanalysis and says whatever comes into his mind,[22] the analyst silently listens. As the analysis continues, what may have begun as the liberating opportunity to speak becomes more and more difficult, and free association becomes a positively difficult labor. The analysand becomes frustrated with the situation and is likely to exhibit a certain amount of aggression toward the analyst. While it may be thought that this frustration is at least in part a result of the analyst's almost inhuman nonintervention in the analysand's discourse, an unwillingness to offer anything more than the silent reply of the attentive auditor, Lacan argues that this frustration is "inherent in the very discourse of the subject" (*E*, 249/41). What the analysand learns in the course of free association is that his identity is essentially illusory, the product of those imaginary identifications and fundamental misrecognitions (*méconnaissances*) described by Lacan in his earlier work on the mirror stage. "For in this labor which he undertakes to reconstruct *for another*, he rediscovers the fundamental alienation that made him construct it [that is, his *moi* identity] *like another*, and which has always destined it to be taken from him *by another*" (*E*, 249/42). Psychoanalysis thus creates a situation in which the analysand is able to come to recognize his alienation and to experience the frustrating gap separating him from this alienated identity. A consequence of this recognition is the parallel recognition that the object of his desire belongs to this imaginary other: in effect, the analysand comes to recognize his own desire as inherently distant from himself. This allows Lacan to offer a stark challenge to the ego psychologists: "This *ego,* whose strength our theorists now define by its capacity to bear frustration, is frustration in its essence. Not frustration of a desire of the subject, but frustration by an object in which his desire is alienated and which the more it is elaborated, the more profound the alienation from his *jouissance* becomes for the subject" (E, 249–50/42). The analytic labor of free association reveals that even the subject's sexual satisfaction (*jouissance*) belongs to an other, an other whom the subject has misrecognized as himself. From the subject's own perspective, then, his speech has been in an important sense "empty": it has been emptied of the subject by being filled with his alienating *moi* identity.

Since a key part of the goal of psychoanalysis is to allow the analysand to escape the objectifications that have plagued him from the time of the mirror stage, "the art of the analyst must be to suspend the subject's certainties until their last mirages have been consumed" (E, 251/43). This the analyst accomplishes by intervening in the constant flow of the analysand's free associating with "punctuation," breaks— such as a carefully phrased question, an appropriately significant cough, or the end of a session—which have the effect of conferring meaning on the analysand's discourse (E, 252/44). Lacan's point is that the empty speech of free association is largely meaningless until it is punctuated by the analyst's replies to the analysand, in the same way that the meaning of a string of words remains essentially indeterminate until a final mark of punctuation retroactively confers upon it a particular sense.

The analyst's carefully chosen breaks in the associative discourse highlight features of the analysand's imaginary *moi* identity, allowing him to grasp, for example, the gap between subject and predicate inherent in a statement of the form, "I am a loving brother." To cut off the analysand's speech at a point such as this is to force him to confront the true meaning of such a statement and to recognize the inevitable discontinuity between one's imaginary identifications ("loving brother") and what one can say about oneself. This will prove a crucial dimension of the psychoanalytic dialogue on Lacan's account, inasmuch as the discontinuity between the *moi* and the *je* (the "I" in terms of which all discourse about the *moi* proceeds) articulates for Lacan what Freud had designated as repression (*Verdrängung*).[23]

It should be clear that Lacan is here resolutely focused on the psychoanalytic dialogue as a matter of language, as existing essentially in speech. The analyst's contact with the analysand is simply through the latter's speech. Contrary to the implicit claims of ego psychology and object relations theory (contrary even to the implicit argument of "The Mirror Stage," with its largely phenomenological analysis of the *béance* separating the infant's lived experience of his fragmented body from the jubilant identification with the mirror image), the analyst is vouchsafed no other reality of the analysand than that of his speech (and the language behind it). To search for a reality lying behind or beyond the analysand's speech is for the analyst to give in to the temptation of misrecognizing for the analysand's *moi* the analyst's own imaginary projections. Hence, the "only object that is within the analyst's reach is the imaginary relation that links him to the subject *qua* ego [*moi*]" (*E*, 253/45), and "it is for this reason that nothing could be more misleading for the analyst than to seek to guide himself by some supposed 'contact' experienced with the reality of the subject" (*E*, 252/44). The proper terrain for the analyst's exploration is nothing other than that discourse in which the analysand's *je* links itself to imaginary *moi* identities,[24] and the entire art of the analyst, if it fundamentally involves the punctuating of this discourse, must rest in grasping the hidden dynamic and meaning of the analysand's apparently empty and meaningless speech.

In other words, the art of the analyst is to help the analysand arrive at a "symbolic interpretation" of his associative discourse, a derivation of meaning that will transform the "empty speech" of the analysand into the "full speech" of the psychoanalytically realized subject (*E*, 254/46). It is with this process of transformation from empty speech to full speech that the latter half of section 1 of "Function and Field" is concerned.

Contrasting his understanding of the effect of the psychoanalytic dialogue with that of psychologists who might stress the role of memory in effecting the psychoanalytic cure, Lacan writes: "But I would say that he [the analysand] has verbalized it [his past] . . . that he has made it pass into the *verbe*, or, more precisely, into the *epos* by which he brings back into present time the origins of his own person. And he does this in a language that allows his discourse to be understood by his contemporaries, and which furthermore presupposes their present discourse" (E, 225/46–47). In other words what is important is not so much the historical accuracy of the analysand's memory as the intersubjectively intelligible narration of his past in the form of a tale or even an epic (the Greek *epos* will bear both senses) of origins.

The analysand's free association, punctuated by the analyst's replies—that is, the psychoanalytic dialogue taken as a dialectical whole—ultimately yields a coherent narrative that has the double effect of constructing the analysand as a subject and of revealing his truth. Lacan explicates this complex claim with the aid of the German philosopher Martin Heidegger, in particular by borrowing from *Being and Time* (1927) Heidegger's notion of "temporality" and of the subject as *"gewesend*—that is to say, as being the one who thus has been" (E, 225/47).[25] In the psychoanalytic dialogue the analysand tells his story, and the very structure of this narrative assures that the narrated events come to have their true significance only in the light of the story's conclusion. That is, the events narrated in free association come to have an anticipatory character as they find a sequential ordering over the course of the analysis. As an autobiography of sorts the analysand's storytelling comes to cast the analysand himself as a subject who has a history. More particularly, the psychoanalytic dialogue constructs in narrative a subject "who thus has been" in relation to a future which is taken to be the subject's own in the course of the psychoanalysis.[26]

This raises an inevitable question: is the analysand's autobiographical narrative true, does it really capture the facts of his history?[27] Lacan's answer to this question is characteristically obscure, but it will prove to be of the utmost importance in understanding the accounts of truth and the real that pop up throughout Lacan's career. Lacan writes:

The ambiguity of the [analysand's] hysterical revelation of the past is due not so much to the vacillation of its content between the imaginary and the real, for it is situated in both. Nor is it because it is made up of lies. The reason is that it presents us with the birth of truth in speech, and thereby brings us up against the reality of what is neither true nor false. At any rate, that is the most disquieting aspect of the problem.

For it is present speech that bears witness to the truth of this revelation in present reality, and which grounds it in the name of that reality. Yet in that reality, only speech bears witness to that portion of the powers of the past that has been thrust aside at each crossroads where the event has made its choice.

. . . I might as well be categorical: in psychoanalytic anamnesis, it is not a question of reality, but of truth, because the effect of full speech is to reorder past contingencies by conferring on them the sense of necessities to come, such as they are constituted by the little freedom through which the subject makes them present. (*E*, 255–56/47–48)

Lacan is arguing here that truth is a function of speech, that outside of the use of language there is no sense to be made of the notion of truth, and thus that the real (or reality)[28] external to the symbolic resources of language is also external to the categories of true and false. In the reality of the psychoanalytic session the only truth that counts is that constituted by the analysand's narration. This idea that the analysand's truth is essentially shaped by the temporality of his telling of his life story is related to Freud's notion of *Nachträglichkeit* or "deferred action" (in French, *après-coup*), the notion that the meaning and psychical effectiveness of early experiences and memories can be and routinely are revised or even constituted for the first time in the light of later experiences.[29] What this narration offers—once it has been punctuated by the interventions of the analyst—is quite simply the meaning of the analysand's life (and it may not be going too far to suggest that this is the only sort of meaning that any life can have). This meaning comes in the way that his tale takes the brute and largely unconnected facts as remembered ("past contingencies") and strings them together to produce a linguistic creation exhibiting something like the inevitability of plot ("the sense of necessities to come"). Borrowing Heidegger's notion of temporality and linking it implicitly with Sartre's analysis of causality in *Being and Nothingness*,[30] Lacan shows how speech and language make possible the subject's truth; this in turn reveals the very constitution of the subject as shaped by the psychoanalytic experience.

It is in precisely these terms that Lacan defines the fundamentals of the psychoanalytic method: "It is certainly this assumption of his history by the subject, insofar as it is constituted by the speech addressed to the other, that constitutes the ground of the new method that Freud called psychoanalysis" (*E*, 257/48). What the psychoanalytic dialogue allows is the analysand's coming to accept the truth of his life story, thus successfully integrating the various features of that life that had never been completely made part of the story. Such integration is possible, however, thanks only to the necessarily dialectical, intersubjective character of the psychoanalytic experience. It is because

his free-associative discourse is necessarily and immediately bound up
with the existence and reply of another speaker that the analysand is
brought to accept as his own the tale he tells in the psychoanalytic
dialogue.[31]

Indeed, Lacan emphasizes that the domain of psychoanalysis, precisely because it is the "concrete discourse" that lives between two
speakers, involves "the transindividual reality of the subject" (E, 257/
49), and this brings us immediately to his notorious conception of the
unconscious as "the discourse of the other" (E, 265/55). What the
psychoanalytic dialogue creates is "the intersubjective continuity of the
discourse in which the subject's history is constituted" (E, 258/49).
The history the analysand comes to accept as his own fills in the various
gaps found in his free-associative discourse, reconstructing the missing
events, motivations, and consequences so as to link the various bits and
pieces of the subject's narration into an intelligible story. While this
history is produced through the interaction—the dialectic—of the
analysand's speech and the analyst's punctuation, what actually fills in
the gaps in the discourse is a third factor, distinct from both the
analysand and the analyst:

It is therefore in the position of a third term that the Freudian discovery of the
unconscious becomes clear as to its true grounding. This discovery may be
simply formulated in the following terms:
    The unconscious is that part of the concrete discourse, insofar as it is
transindividual, that is not at the disposal of the subject in re-establishing the
continuity of his conscious discourse. (E, 258/49)

Crucial to this Lacanian definition of the unconscious is the fact that the
unconscious as the third term making possible "full speech" between
two speakers is not to be confused with what a nonpsychoanalytic
psychology might regard as the "unconscious tendencies" of an individual (E, 258–59/50): the unconscious is neither genuinely individual
nor a matter of dispositions or tendencies. It is rather "the censored
chapter" of the analysand's history, and as such the unconscious is the
dynamic product of the analysand and his (censoring) environment,
existing positively in a variety of the analysand's essentially symbolic
behaviors. Thus, for example, the language of the unconscious can be
read in the speech of the analysand's bodily symptoms, in his putative
memories of childhood, in his idiosyncratic vocabulary, and in the
fragmentary "heroic legends" and other protonarratives out of which

the analysand's self-history is eventually built up.[32] In other words, Lacan's definition of the unconscious is fundamentally structural in the reasonably precise and recognizably Saussurean sense that it specifies the unconscious as one element of a set of structuring factors that taken together provide a characterization and a structural explanation of the human subject.

Lacan takes great pains to distinguish his concept of the history that the subject comes to accept in the course of psychoanalysis from Freud's developmental sequence of instinctual stages (oral, anal, phallic, genital). Not wanting to dispute the explanatory and therapeutic value of Freud's model, Lacan nevertheless wants to insist upon a distinction between primary and secondary "historizations" (*E*, 260–62/51–53). Even if we grant the primordial status of some model of organic development in the young child—and it is worth emphasizing that Lacan's own theory of the mirror stage commits him to certain basic, organically rooted developmental claims—the fact remains that this organic development is lived by a subject (*E*, 262/52–53), and it is this subjective "organization" or primary historization of development that is reconstructed in the secondary historization of the analysand's autobiography. "What we teach the subject to recognize as his unconscious is his history—that is to say, we help him to perfect the present historization of the facts that have already determined a certain number of the historical 'turning-points' in his existence. But if they have played this role, it is already as facts of history, that is to say, insofar as they have been recognized in one particular sense or censored in a certain order" (*E*, 261/52). It must be emphasized that what the psychoanalytic dialogue reveals is not the lived experience of the subject's progress through the developmental stages—the history to be assumed by the subject is not phenomenological—but a historical reconstruction of the subject's progress that makes room for hidden, "censored," portions of his life as well as for remembered life experiences.

Given Lacan's insistence on the importance of speech and language, it stands to reason that the central subjective factor conditioning the child's passage through the developmental stages is her relation to language. Arguing that Freud himself relegated the theory of instincts to "a secondary and hypothetical place" (*E*, 264/54), Lacan emphasizes the primacy of the symbolic over the biological: "To confine ourselves to a more lucid tradition, perhaps we shall understand the celebrated maxim in which La Rochefoucauld tells us that '*il y a des gens qui n'auraient jamais été amoureux, s'ils n'avaient jamais entendu parler de l'amour {There are people who would never have been in love, if they had never heard talk of love},'* not in the Romantic sense of an entirely imaginary 'realization' of love, which would make of this remark a bitter objection on his part, but as an authentic recognition of what love owes to the symbol and of what speech entails of love" (*E*, 264/54). What love owes to the symbol is, apparently, its very existence, and Lacan is here arguing that even the instinctual stages crucial to so much psychoanalytic theory have existence for the subject only through their representation in the symbolic warp of language.

Indeed, if "the unconscious of the subject is the discourse of the other" (*E*, 265/55), then it will come as no surprise that, as Lacan argues throughout the 1950s, "the unconscious is structured in the most radical way like a language" (*E*, 594/234).[33] And if "what the psychoanalytic experience discovers in the unconscious is the whole structure of language,"[34] then it may not be quite so surprising that Lacan can identify an instinct (or, more properly, a drive [*Trieb*]) with "the advent of a signifier" (*E*, 597/236). The familiar claim that the unconscious is outside the control of the individual is transformed into the notion that it is "transindividual": the unconscious is outside the individual's control simply because "language and its structure exist prior to the moment at which each subject at a certain point in his mental development makes his entry into it" (*E*, 495/148). Just what is involved in this linguistic rethinking of the unconscious will be the burden of much of the rest of this book, but at this point all that must be emphasized is the line of thought that leads Lacan to structuralism. From a straightforward reflection on the role of speech and language in the psychoanalytic dialogue, he returns to Freud's insight that the unconscious essentially plays the role of a discourse censored from consciousness, and this leads him to using structural linguistics as the key to theorizing the nature of the unconscious. Theory develops as an attempt to clarify the dynamic of psychoanalytic practice, and the unconscious in particular emerges essentially as a third term making intelligible the dialogue between analysand and analyst.

At this point in his argument, Lacan ends section 1 by using his distinction between the *je* and the *moi* (already introduced in "The Mirror Stage") to highlight and clarify the distinction between the "subjectivity" at issue in psychoanalysis and the "subjective experience" at the heart of most psychological theories from ego psychology to phenomenology. Writing of "the vicissitudes of subjectivity," "the subjective conflict" in the course of which "the 'I' [*je*] wins and loses against the 'ego' [*moi*]" (*E*, 264/55), Lacan notes that "the subject goes well beyond what is experienced 'subjectively' by the individual, exactly as far as the truth he is able to attain" (*E*, 265/55). As we have seen, the truth the analysand attains is the coherent narrative that the *je* gradually becomes able to tell in the course of the psychoanalytic dialogue. This narrative constructed by the analysand and analyst working together—precisely because it ultimately fills in the gaps left in conscious experience and memory—is itself transindividual and goes well beyond what the analysand has "experienced subjectively." The subject's truth, then—the narrative told by the *je*, which itself is realized in the psychoanalytic dialogue—is not to be confused with the conscious, "subjective" experience of the *moi*. Once again, just as he had in "The Mirror Stage," Lacan is standing up to any view of the human subject based on the Cartesian *cogito*. The difference in "Function and Field" is that Lacan has now enriched the *je/moi* distinction, understanding the *je* in terms of symbolic narrative and the *moi* in terms of imaginary identification. That the human subject is essentially a place of conflict between the *je* and the *moi*, between the symbolic and the imaginary, will remain one of Lacan's central theses throughout his career. The final section of "Function and Field," discussed in chapter 4, goes on to elaborate this thesis, bringing in a third dimension or "register" of conceptual analysis, the real (*le réel*), and requiring that the dyadic relation of the symbolic and the imaginary be mediated by the real.

Language in Psychoanalysis

Freud on Language   After opening the second section of "Function and Field" with a recapitulation of his insistence that psychoanalysis has little to do with introspection or with the "subjective" experience held dear by Cartesian approaches to the human subject, Lacan comes to the heart of his concerns in a very direct statement:

If psychoanalysis can become a science (for it is not yet one) and if it is not to degenerate in its technique (and perhaps that has already happened), we must rediscover the sense of its experience.

To this end, we can do no better than to return to the work of Freud. (*E*, 267/57)

Lacan initiates this return to Freud with a brief review of the three formative texts of psychoanalysis, emphasizing that in Freud's most creative period language and its effects were never far from the center of his theoretical concerns. The Interpretation of Dreams (1900),[35] for example, argues that "the dream has the structure of a sentence or, rather, to stick to the letter of the work, of a rebus" (E, 267/57),[36] and Lacan insists that Freud's approach to unraveling the hidden meaning of dreams is profoundly rhetorical. Indeed, Lacan almost gives us an outline for a textbook of dream rhetoric: "Ellipsis and pleonasm, hyperbaton or syllepsis, regression, repetition, apposition—these are the syntactical displacements; metaphor, catachresis, autonomasis, allegory, metonymy, and synecdoche—these are the semantic condensations in which Freud teaches us to read the intentions—ostentatious or demonstrative, dissimulating or persuasive, retaliatory or seductive—out of which the subject modulates his oneiric discourse" (E 268/58). Lacan takes very seriously his rhetorical elucidation of the basic mechanisms of displacement and condensation that Freud had argued transformed the latent dream thoughts into the manifest content of the dream.[37] His procedure here is a nice illustration of his typical treatment of Freud: the return to Freud is really an elaboration of theory at best implicit in and often enough simply consistent with Freud's own theoretical suggestions. Thus, Freud himself does not develop a dream rhetoric, but his analogy of the dream to a rebus or to a sentence is enough to make possible the development of a rhetorical approach to dreams.

From dreams Lacan turns to The Psychopathology of Everyday Life (1901),[38] stressing that the "Freudian slip," unsuccessful as an act, is in fact "a successful, not to say 'well turned', discourse" (E, 268/58) and is thus best understood in terms of the linguistic content that it unconsciously bears. Even more importantly, Lacan points out that Freud's account of overdetermination[39] here is essentially tied to the multiplicity of meaning inherent in the analysand's free associations. It follows that "it is already quite clear that the symptom resolves itself entirely in an analysis of language, because the symptom is itself structured like a language, because it is from language that speech must be delivered" (E, 269/59). The behavior of the neurotic is to be understood, in effect, by looking for the background "language" that makes possible the "speech" of a certain act, and this is how easily Lacan finds an inherently structuralist approach to the human subject in Freud himself.

It is in Jokes and their Relation to the Unconscious (1905),[40] however, that Lacan finds Freud's interest in language at its height. He describes Freud's book as "a work in which the effect of the unconscious is demonstrated to us to its most subtle confines; and the face it reveals to us is that of the spirit in the ambiguity conferred on it by language" (*E*, 270/60). It is the ambiguity of the unconscious that makes it possible for a joke to convey the (unconscious) meaning that makes it a joke and, as such, something unexpected and revelatory. "It is truth in fact that throws off the mask" in the words of a wit, Lacan writes (*E*, 270/60). Given his Heideggerian meditation on truth in section 1 of "Function and Field," it is not at all surprising to find Lacan here returning to his distinction between the *je* or subject who speaks the truth and the *moi* (here called the "individual"), which not only remains unconscious of this truth but maintains its existence only by means of this unconsciousness. He writes, "Nowhere is the intention of the individual more evidently surpassed by what the subject finds—nowhere does the distinction that I make between the individual and the subject make itself better understood—since not only must there have been something foreign to me in what I found for me to take pleasure in it, but it must also remain this way for this find to hit its mark. This takes its place from the necessity, so clearly marked by Freud, of the third listener, always presupposed" (*E*, 271/60). The "third listener" (third, after the subject and the individual, the *je* and the *moi*) is that other who laughs at the subject's joke, often enough allowing the subject to recognize what she has said. What we see in this listener is, of course, the punctuating role of the analyst in the psychoanalytic dialogue: both occupy "the locus of the Other" (*E*, 271/61), which makes it possible (as we shall see) for the truth to emerge from a discourse, whether that discourse is a joke or the life history of an analysand.[41]

Language and the Symbol If language lies at the heart of Freud's own theorizing, then, Lacan nevertheless believes that it is crucial for psychoanalysts to be more systematic and, indeed, more philosophical in their reflections on language than was Freud. Lacan's own contribution in this direction begins with an unmistakably structuralist definition of the relationship between a language and its elements: "What defines any element whatever of a language [*langue*] as belonging to language [*langage*], is that, for all the users of this language [*langue*], this element is distinguished as such in the ensemble supposedly constituted of homologous elements" (*E*, 274/63). In other words, language comes to its speakers more or less as a whole, its elements defined differentially in relation to one another, and what makes something an element of a language is the specific set of relations it bears to the other elements.[42] Consequently, the meaning of a linguistic element is constituted by its relations with other elements of language and not—and this is in radical opposition to any phenomenological approach to language—by the use to which a particular speaker puts it: "The result is that the particular effects of this element of language [*langage*] are bound up with the existence of this ensemble, anterior to any possible link with any particular experience of the subject. And to consider this last link independently of any reference to the first is simply to deny in this element the function proper to language [*langage*]" (*E*, 274/63–64). In short, the "experience" of human subjects, as speakers of a language, is essentially shaped by the language they speak. Language marks a radical otherness at the core of the subject.

The next step in Lacan's argument is to identify this language-grounded otherness within the human subject with the Freudian unconscious, building upon his previous commentary on Freud's use of language in psychoanalytic theorizing. Lacan writes: "For Freud's discovery was that of the field of the effects in the nature of man of his relations to the symbolic order and the tracing of their meaning right back to the most radical agencies of symbolization in being. To ignore this symbolic order is to condemn the discovery to oblivion, and the experience to ruin" (*E*, 275/64). As we have already seen, Lacan defines the unconscious in essentially linguistic terms as "that part of the concrete discourse, insofar as it is transindividual, that is not at the disposal of the subject in re-establishing the continuity of his conscious discourse" (*E*, 258/49). What is clear now is that any understanding of the unconscious is fundamentally an understanding of language, and this means that psychoanalysis is itself a particular way of coming to know a language (that of the analysand) and is thus one of the sciences of the symbolic.

This raises the perhaps inevitable question, what is language? Lacan's approach to this question here involves his trying to distinguish between human language and what might legitimately be described as symbol use in general (for example, by other animals). Lacan begins by granting that the objects exchanged in symbolic activity primordially constitute the existence of some kind of pact among those engaged in the activity (*E*, 272/61).[43] He goes on, however, to insist that "something else" is needed to transform such a symbolic object into an element of language:

> This something completes the symbol, thus making language of it. In order for the symbolic object freed from its usage to become the word freed from the *hic et nunc*, the difference resides not in its material quality as sound, but in its evanescent being in which the symbol finds the permanence of the concept.
>
> Through the word—already a presence made of absence—absence itself gives itself a name in that moment of origin whose perpetual recreation Freud's genius detected in the play of the child. And from this pair of sounds modulated on presence and absence . . . there is born the world of meaning of a particular language in which the world of things will come to be arranged. (*E*, 276/65)

What we find in this passage is a uniquely Lacanian fusion of Freud and Hegel. At the heart of this text is an allusion to the second chapter of *Beyond the Pleasure Principle*,[44] where Freud discusses his eighteen-month-old grandson's attempt to come to grips with his weaning. The little boy quite regularly would take toys and other objects and throw them away from himself, crying "o-o-o-o" as he did so. Freud eventually realized that the child was playing a game and that his barely articulate cry was in fact an infantile representation of the German word *fort*, meaning "gone." Freud describes the significance of this curious game in the following passage, a passage of the very greatest importance to Lacan:

> The child had a wooden reel with a piece of string tied round it. It never occurred to him to pull it along the floor behind him, for instance, and play at its being a carriage. What he did was to hold the reel by the string and very skillfully throw it over the edge of his curtained cot, so that it disappeared into it, at the same time uttering his expressive 'o-o-o-o'. He then pulled the reel out of the cot again by the string and hailed its reappearance with a joyful '*da*' ['there']. This, then, was the complete game—disappearance and return. As a rule one only witnessed its first act, which was repeated untiringly as a game in itself, though there is no doubt that the greater pleasure was attached to the second act.
>
> The interpretation of the game then became obvious. It was related to the child's great cultural achievement—the instinctual renunciation (that is, the renunciation of instinctual satisfaction) which he had made in allowing his mother to go away without protesting. He compensated himself for this, as it

were, by himself staging the disappearance and return of the objects within his reach.[45]

What Lacan particularly emphasizes in this passage is the fact that a rudimentary use of language—"Fort! Da!"—is implicated in the boy's game. What Freud describes as "instinctual renunciation" is accomplished by substituting an inherently linguistic game over which the child has full control for an interpersonal situation within which the child is largely powerless.[46]

Thus, it is Freud who allows us to see the play of presence and absence at the heart of language, although it turns out to be Hegel who will allow us to understand the special importance of absence in language. Following the structuralist understanding of language as a system, what distinguishes mere symbols from words is that, while both are material objects, each of my words is an absence as well as a material presence. More specifically, each of my words is what it is—namely, a word and as such an element of my language—because of its preexistent relations with all the other possible words of my language. My word "mouse" is what it is because of the particular ways in which it resembles and yet differs from "house" or "moose," both phonologically and semantically, and because of the particular syntactic contexts within which it can be used. Nevertheless, these linguistic relations are not present in my words, although my words are what they are because of these absent but effective relations.

Now, what Lacan finds in Hegel (and, in particular, in the Hegel of the *Phenomenology of Spirit* [1807], as interpreted by Alexandre Kojève in his Paris lectures of the 1930s) is essentially the claim that the absences that transform symbols into elements of language constitute what are ordinarily thought of as *concepts*. Kojève relates these absences provocatively (from a Lacanian point of view) to the continual annihilation of the past by time, and as discussed in the next chapter, Lacan uses this notion to link Freud's reflections on the death instinct with Heidegger's notion of the temporalized human being as a being-toward-death. A passage from Kojève may help clarify Lacan's less sweeping use of his reading of Hegel here. "To be sure," Kojève argues,

the Real *endures* in Time as *real*. But by the fact of enduring in *Time*, it is its own *remembrance*: at each instant it realizes its Essence or Meaning, and this is to say that it realizes in the Present what is left of it after its annihilation in the

Past; and this something that is left and that it re-realizes is its *concept*. At the moment when the present Real sinks into the Past, its Meaning (Essence) *detaches itself* from its reality (Existence); and it is here that appears the possibility of retaining this Meaning *outside* of the reality by causing it to pass into the Word. And this Word reveals the Meaning of the Real which *realizes* in the Present its own Past—that is, this same Past that is "eternally" preserved in the Word-Concept.[47]

Where Kojève's Hegel clearly takes the concept or word to "realize" or preserve the vanished empirical past of the thing and thus sees the "word-concept" as constituted by the absence of this past, Lacan grafts on to this reading his essentially structuralist, differential view of language. What results, then, is a rather complex theory of language, according to which the word is constituted by a double absence: that of the thing's past (Hegel-Kojève) and that of the system of language (Saussure). Going somewhat beyond Kojève's claim that the thing's past "is 'eternally' preserved in the Word-Concept," Lacan asserts the fundamental priority of the language or conceptual system—the symbolic—to the "world of things": "Through that which becomes embodied only by being the trace of a nothingness and whose support cannot thereafter be impaired, the concept, saving the duration of what passes by, engenders the thing" (*E*, 276/65). It is the permanence—the eternal preservation—marked by the linguistic-conceptual system that stabilizes "the things originally confused in the *hic et nunc* of the all in the process of coming-into-being," thereby transforming experienced confusion into a more or less systematically arranged world of things: "It is the world of words that creates the world of things" (*E*, 276/65). The most important consequence of this apparently idealistic theory of language is that, among the things created by the world of words, the most important (at least for the psychoanalyst) is the human being himself. "Man speaks, then, but it is because the symbol has made him man" (*E*, 276/65).

Language: Its Structure and Its Laws   Although "Function and Field" repeatedly emphasizes the importance of speech and language in both the theory and the practice of psychoanalysis, it does not actually elaborate Lacan's own account of language. This task was carried out in a relatively unsystematic way in a series of lectures, seminars, and articles that appeared over a five-year period in the

1950s.[48] Because his approach to language is clearly at the heart of Lacan's theoretical enterprise, we must turn our attention away from "Function and Field" to sketch the key elements of this approach.

The fundamental structure of language is reflected in the distinction between the signifier and the signified, which Lacan takes from Saussure and transforms into the "algorithm" S/s, "which is read as: the signifier over the signified, 'over' corresponding to the bar separating the two stages" (E, 497/149) The bar turns out to play an important role in Lacan's reflections, because it marks the *béance* between signifier and signified that is at the heart of the human being's alienation from self. With respect to language in general, however, the bar marks the fact that the signifier/signified distinction carves out "two non-overlapping networks of relations" (E, 414/126).

Lacan's description of the network of the signifier is well within the domain of ordinary structuralism. He characterizes this network as "the synchronic structure of the language material insofar as in that structure each element assumes its precise function by being different from the others" (E, 414/126). With respect to the signified, however, Lacan departs rather radically from the structuralist camp. Where Saussure, for example, understands the signified of a signifier as the concept denoted by that signifier,[49] Lacan defines the signified in terms of the diachronic dimension of language. What is signified is "the diachronic set of the concretely pronounced discourses" (E, 414/126). Thus the relation between signifier and signified is operative within language and does not mark the relation between language and some extralinguistic, conceptual reality. Language is always about language; it is inescapably self-referential; and for Lacan signification "proves never to be resolved into a pure indication of the real, but always refers back to another signification" (E, 414/126). Thus, Lacan brings to his account of language the anticipatory dimension of Heideggerian temporality and the retroactive dimension of Freudian deferred action (*après-coup*). The unfolding chain of signifiers always anticipates a yet-to-be-completed unit of discourse that will give the chain a fixed signification retroactively, and it is the dialectic between individual signifiers and their completed chain that is represented by the algorithm, S/s. From this account, it follows that every language is perfectly capable of covering "the whole field of the signified," since the conception of the signified here precludes there being anything outside of any language that can in fact be signified (E, 498/150).

In "The Agency of the Letter" Lacan illustrates this radical claim that "no signification can be sustained other than by reference to another signification" (*E*, 498/150) with the example of two doors identical in every respect, except that one has written on it "LADIES," while the other bears the legend "GENTLEMEN" (*E*, 499–501/150–52). The one door is what it is only in relation to the other, and the complex material signifier "door-with-'LADIES,' " is meaningful only in relation to the wide variety of actually existent discourses (including human behaviors of all sorts) in which such doors appear. Among other things, Lacan uses this example to stress the fact that the signifier not only can be found in the signified but is responsible for the signified's being what it is.

Crucial to the network of the signifier is that it is "articulated": it is made up of fundamental "differential elements," which are combined "according to the laws of a closed order." Thus signifiers exist only as parts of a "signifying chain" (*E*, 501–2/152–53),[50] and in his later, more algebraic formulations Lacan will designate this signifying chain by "$S_1{\rightarrow}S_2$." This special emphasis on the chain of signifiers derives—as does most Lacanian theory—from reflection on the character of the analytic dialogue. The distinctive feature of the analysand's free-associative discourse is that it is precisely a chain of signifiers; the putative connection between this signifying chain and any reality external to the dialogue is (as we have seen) of questionable importance to the successful proceeding of the dialogue.[51]

The fundamental structure of language, then, is marked by the distinction between the signifier and the signified, and the essential character of the network of the signifier is that it is constituted as a signifying chain. Now, Lacan argues that there are two basic laws that govern the flow of the signifying chain and that thus set in motion the "signifying function" of language. Influenced by Roman Jakobson's study of aphasia,[52] Lacan maintains that the laws of language can be reduced to the processes involved in two figures of speech, *metonymy* and *metaphor*. Metonymy—the classic example of which is the use of "thirty sails" to designate as many ships—involves a combination of signifiers that is grounded solely in "the *word-to-word* connection." As Lacan notes, it is highly unlikely that each ship hoists a single sail, and thus the sail-ship connection is actually found "nowhere but in the signifier" (*E*, 505–6/156). Metonymy combines signifiers without constraints from anything beyond the material of the signifiers themselves. Metaphor, in contrast, involves the substitution of "*one word for another*," where one signifier pushes another out of the signifying chain. Its "poetic" power derives from the fact that metaphor's "occulted signifier," while not actually present in the chain, is nevertheless present in its absence, thanks to "its (metonymic) connection with the rest of the chain" (E, 506–7/156–57). Metaphor's ability to make present something that is absent is the basis for language's ability to represent (in some sense) a reality that is external to and thus absent from language. This metaphoric power remains ultimately dependent upon metonymy, however, reinforcing the centrality of the chain of signifiers for Lacan.

Lacan's account of the structure and laws of language can now be applied to that particular language which is "the discourse of the Other," namely, the unconscious. Elaborating Freud's account of the role of the unconscious in fabricating dreams, Lacan suggests that the basic processes of the "dream-work" can be reconceptualized in terms of language's basic laws.[53] Thus, the inescapable fact that the latent dream thoughts are heavily distorted in the manifest content of the dream can be taken as analogous to the fact that the signified is always beneath the signifier in language, what Lacan often describes as "the sliding [*glissement*] of the signified under the signifier" (E, 511/160). The Freudian mechanism of condensation, by which numerous dream thoughts are consolidated into and distorted by a single new item of the manifest dream, is analogous to the process of metaphor, particularly as both functions serve to substitute one thing for another and thus repress certain features of the unconscious discourse. Similarly, the mechanism of displacement, by which certain characteristics of the latent dream thoughts are associated with radically different elements of the manifest dream, is analogous to the functioning of metonymy, precisely because this mechanism privileges the element-to-element, signifier-to-signifier, relation (see E, 511–12/160–62 and compare E, 621–23/258–59).

In this way Lacan reveals that the Freudian account of dreams is essentially an account of their "linguistic structure" (E, 623/259). It turns out that precisely the same thing can be said about neurotic symptoms and about desire in general. Because a symptom needs to be deciphered in a way analogous to a dream, Lacan argues that a symptom is "a metaphor in which flesh or function is taken as a signifying element" (E, 518/166–67), and he emphasizes that this claim is not itself a metaphor (E, 528/175). An instance of neurotic behavior is itself a signifier substituting for some other signifier that—because it is absent from the manifest behavior of the individual—remains in effect repressed in the unconscious. This repressed signifier must be reconstructed in the course of the psychoanalytic dialogue from the metonymic relations holding between other elements of the analysand's behavior, understanding the whole of this behavior as a signifying chain.

With respect to desire, the situation is a bit more complicated. In "The Direction of the Treatment" Lacan, after stressing that metonymy is "the effect made possible by the fact that there is no signification that does not refer to another signification," maintains that "desire is the metonymy of the want-to-be [*le désir est la métonymie du manque à être*]" (*E, 622–23/259*).[54] Later in the same essay he takes this position one step further by claiming that "if desire is the metonymy of the want-to-be, the ego [*moi*] is the metonymy of desire" (*E, 640/274*). In order to begin to understand these hermetic formulations, we must turn to Lacan's subtle account of the relation between language and desire.

Language and Desire   In the second section of "Function and Field" Lacan introduces a brief categorization of mental disorders with a stunning summary of what we might think of as his structuralist emphasis on the role of the symbolic in the life of the human being. What is most striking about this summary, however, is the clear suggestion that the symbolic register alone cannot fully capture what it is to be a human subject. Lacan writes:

Symbols in fact envelop the life of man in a network so total that they join together, before he comes into the world, those who are going to engender him "by flesh and blood"; so total that they bring to his birth, along with the gifts of the stars, if not with the gifts of the fairies, the shape of his destiny; so total that they give the words that will make him faithful or renegade, the law of the acts that will follow him right to the very place where he *is* not yet and even beyond his death; and so total that through them his end finds its meaning in the last judgement, where the Word absolves his being or condemns it—unless he attain the subjective bringing to realization of being-for-death. (*E, 279/68*)

It is this *unless* that is crucial for the psychoanalyst, since it is precisely the attaining of "the subjective bringing to realization of being-for-death" that is the goal of the analytic dialogue (this Heideggerian dimension of Lacan's account is a major topic of chapter 4). But the possibility for a partial escape from the network of the symbol, for a redemption of the human subject, lies in desire: "Servitude and gran-

deur in which the living being would be annihilated, if desire did not
preserve its part in the interferences and pulsations that the cycles of
language cause to converge on him" (E, 279/68). That desire has the
effect of intervening in the symbolic network and, through that intervention, preserving the human being from symbolic annihilation neces-
sitates a glance at the dynamics of desire.

In the years immediately following "Function and Field," Lacan
developed a theory of desire as the unarticulated remainder left behind
when essentially biological need is articulated in symbolic form as
linguistic demand. A difficult passage from "The Direction of the
Treatment" provides a relatively concise review of this theory:

> Desire is that which is manifested in the interval that demand hollows within
> itself, inasmuch as the subject, in articulating the signifying chain, brings to
> light the want-to-be, together with the appeal to receive the complement from
> the Other, if the Other, the locus of speech, is also the locus of this want.
>   That which is thus given to the Other to fill, and which is strictly that
> which it does not have, since it, too, lacks being, is what is called love, but it
> is also hate and ignorance.
>   It is also what is evoked by any demand beyond the need that is articulated
> in it, and it is certainly that of which the subject remains all the more deprived
> to the extent that the need articulated in the demand is satisfied. (E, 627/263)

We may begin to unpack this dense text by remembering the situation
of the young child as she first begins to acquire language. At this point
she is a congeries of biologically grounded needs and of more or less
fleeting and illusory mirror images of identity. Her recognition of the
béance separating her bodily self from her imaginary *moi* identity in
effect reinforces the sense that not only is this identity alienating—
literally belonging to another—but it is a cover for a fundamental lack
of identity, what Lacan generally refers to as a *manque à être*, a "want-to-
be" or "want-of-being." In beginning to speak, the child is in fact
beginning to deal actively with her essential *béance*.

What the child would appear to ask for, in her first attempts at
speech, is the satisfaction of her bodily *needs*. But what Lacan emphasizes is that the linguistic translation of these needs—what he calls
demand—is inherently interpersonal: demand is always addressed to
another person, at first a parent or caretaker. Indeed, the child is not
simply asking for food when she demands this of her parent; rather, she
is using the demand for food to provoke the parent, the other, into

recognizing her real existence as a force to be contended with. In such recognition is held the promise of something to fill the *béance* between body and *moi*, and it is this which is at the heart of what the child will regard as parental love. In short, the child's demand for food actually masks a deeper longing for recognition by the other, recognition that will in some way make up for the child's fundamental want-of-being. It is this profound but always only implicit longing for recognition— itself essentially a product of the mirror stage—that Lacan designates by the term *desire*.[55]

That desire is metonymy (see *E*, 622–23/259) is a feature of the fact that desire itself can never quite be articulated. No matter what the child or adult demands, it is always merely an object that might satisfy need. Were he to demand recognition explicitly, this demand would require an explicit realization of the subject's essential want-of-being, something that simply cannot be put into words at all.[56] In the desperate and vain attempt to articulate desire, the desiring subject continually moves from one demand to another, from one signifier to another. Each of these signifiers is linked metonymically to the want-of-being, which the desirer hopes will be filled by the other's reply to his demand. Similarly, the *moi* can be seen as the metonymy of desire (see *E*, 640/274), inasmuch as its fleeting images of identity are connected metonymically to the chain of signifiers by means of which the subject tries unsuccessfully to articulate his desire. (Chapter 4 examines Lacan's claim that it is precisely through learning to speak of this essential *béance* that the psychoanalytic cure is effected.)

It is with this account in mind that Lacan remarks in his review of Freud's *Interpretation of Dreams* earlier in "Function and Field": "Man's desire finds its meaning in the desire of the other [*le désir de l'autre*], not so much because the other holds the key to the object desired, as because the first object of desire is to be recognized by the other" (*E*, 268/58). The interpersonal dimension of Lacan's theory as it appears here is quickly transformed, however, as he begins to reflect on the structural features of interpersonal relationships in general. In the long passage from "The Direction of the Treatment" just quoted, Lacan notes that the other to whom desire is directed is radically unable to satisfy this desire, because—as an individual human being just like the child—this other is itself also essentially a want-of-being. However, in this slightly later formulation, Lacan has taken to capitalizing *Autre* (Other), thus emphasizing that the other to whom desire is directed is best understood structurally as playing a particular role in the constitution of this desire. The child's demand is aimed not at the parent as parent, but at the parent as Other capable of recognizing the child's desire. Because the child can be recognized only through speech, it is the language making speech possible that serves as the structural precondition for this recognition. In effect, then, the Other to whom desire is addressed (disguised in the form of demand addressed to the parent) is language itself or, at least, the place of Otherness from which language comes to the struggling subject. This point is put perhaps most perspicaciously in the seminar of 13 June 1956, where Lacan notes that "*the Other is thus the place where is constituted the 'je' which speaks with the one who listens*" (S 3, 309).[57] The Other is thus not "a fellow man" (*E*, 615/253), but the condition structurally necessary for there to be a speaker of language, and this condition is itself utterly distinct—utterly Other—from any individual other (*E*, 430/140). From this, it follows that, "produced as it is by an animal at the mercy of language, man's desire is the desire of the Other" (*E*, 628/264).[58]

Having brought the Other and language into such close proximity, Lacan further relates the Other to the Freudian unconscious. The Otherness of the Other is the place of the unconscious, precisely because speech as it is introduced to the human animal by the Other belongs to no human subject. "*It* speaks [*Ça parle*] in the Other, I say, designating by the Other the very locus evoked by the recourse to speech in any relation in which the Other intervenes" (*E*, 689/285).[59] The human subject is in fact constituted as such by her relation to the Other—by the fact that she speaks—and this essential relation to the Other is present in the subject as the unconscious. Lacan identifies "primal repression" as the result of the inability of the Other's language to articulate desire, this inability leading to desire's being "alienated in needs" (*E*, 690/285–86), just as the child's desire for recognition is masked by and thus alienated in her demand for an object such as the breast. One sign of this alienation internal to the subject is the paradox that "it is first of all for the subject that his speech is a message" (*E*, 634/269). The words that the desiring subject speaks—for example, "I love you"—are meant to evoke from the Other a reply destined for the subject—in this case, "I love you"—but this reply is simply an inverted version of the subject's original speech ("Function and Field," *E*, 298/85).

The Phallus   If the structure of language is essentially captured in the notion of a signifying chain distinguished from the network of the signified, and if the laws of language and thus of the unconscious are reflected in the processes of metonymy and metaphor, it nevertheless remains the case for Lacan that there is a connection between the network of the signifier and that of the signified, the connection of *sens* or "meaning." The metonymical chain of signifiers that constitutes a subject's discourse spreads itself out temporally and thus in a linear fashion, but it is a crucial fact of this signifying chain that it is tied down at various points by the operation of metaphor. Using a favorite analogy, Lacan writes:

> But one has only to listen to poetry, which Saussure was no doubt in the habit of doing, for a polyphony to be heard, for it to become clear that all discourse is aligned along the several staves of a score.
>
> There is in effect no signifying chain that does not have, as if attached to the punctuation of each of its units, a whole articulation of relevant contexts suspended "vertically", as it were, from that point. (*E,* 503/154)

This vertical, nonlinear dimension of the signifying chain is made up of signifiers that, for a variety of reasons, have been repressed from the chain and replaced by other signifiers serving as metaphors for these repressed signifiers. The repressed signifiers—only virtually present in the signifying chain—are described by Lacan as *points de capiton,* the "anchoring points" or "buttons" that keep upholstery attached to the framework of a piece of furniture (*E,* 503/154).

In the seminar of 6 June 1956 Lacan uses the text of Racine's *Athalie* to illustrate the ways in which certain key words (*mots-clés*) run beneath the surface of the play, allowing an attentive auditor or reader to grasp the ultimate meaning of the action (S 3, 300–301). He argues that the word *crainte* ("fear") serves as the the *point de capiton* of this text, precisely because it is "the point of convergence which allows the retroactive and prospective situating of everything that happens in this discourse" (S 3, 303–4). It is the signifier, *crainte,* that fixes the meaning of the relatively ambiguous speeches of the various characters in the play, but it can only be that to which everything else in the play relates because it is not itself a part of the signifying chain. If it were part of this chain, it would need grounding by reference to some other, "occulted" signifier.

The *points de capiton,* then, serve as the signifieds for the signifying chains of a subject's discourse, and Lacan maintains that "the schema of the *point de capiton* is essential in human experience" (S 3, 304). To fix the ultimate meaning of any discourse is to determine the signifiers that have been repressed by that discourse. In this way the psychoanalyst's careful attention to the analysand's discourse may lead to discovering the repressed signifiers that—unsaid within the signifying chain itself—nevertheless constitute the ultimate meaning of that discourse.

It is at this stage in Lacan's argument that we come to his radical rethinking of the classic psychoanalytic notion of the Oedipus complex. It is "the notion of the father" that serves as the preeminent *point de capiton* buttoning down the subject's signifying chain and thereby allowing it to take on a relatively fixed meaning (S 3, 304). However, Lacan's approach to this "notion of the father" marks his most apparent structuralist move, fusing as it does Freudian psychoanalysis and the structural anthropology of Claude Lévi-Strauss. Having situated the human being in an essential relation to an absent but structurally present system of language, Lacan now takes the almost inevitable next step of identifying this language system with the background "language" of structural anthropology, the "language" in terms of which particular human behaviors exhibited in social settings are intelligible. In the mid-1950s, of course, Lacan was largely limited to Lévi-Strauss's great book of 1949, *The Elementary Structures of Kinship,* but the anthropologist's radical rethinking of the meaning of kinship relations is in remarkable harmony with Lacan's own rethinking of the significance of the Oedipus complex.[60]

Lévi-Strauss's fundamental claim is that the apparently chaotic and virtually random systems of kinship and marriage taboos in cultures around the world in fact exhibit a rigorous and ultimately simple logic. According to this logic, a kinship system—essentially identifiable with a particular elaboration of the incest taboo (which taboo "has the universality of bent and instinct, and the coercive character of law and institution")[61]—is a means for regulating the "exchange of women" in a way that, by contributing to social stability, actually constitutes the bedrock of culture.[62] The prohibition of incest can accomplish this lofty end, because it is "less a rule prohibiting marriage with the mother, sister or daughter, than a rule obliging the mother, sister or daughter to be given to others. It is the supreme rule of the gift, and it is clearly this aspect, too often unrecognized, which allows its nature to be understood." From this Lévi-Strauss can conclude: "It is no exaggeration, then, to say that exogamy is the archetype of all the manifestations based on reciprocity, and that it provides the fundamental and immutable rule ensuring the existence of the group as a group."[63]

Returning to the analogy between structural linguistics and anthropological investigations of kinship systems (first explored in the article of
1945 discussed earlier in this chapter), Lévi-Strauss offers at the end of
The Elementary Structures of Kinship the following, rather shocking, explanation of a series of apparently unrelated prohibitions among the
Andaman Islanders: "These prohibitions are all thus reduced to a single
common denominator: they all constitute a *misuse of language,* and on
this ground they are grouped together with the incest prohibition, or
with acts evocative of incest. What does this mean, except that women
themselves are treated as signs, which are *misused* when not put to the
use reserved to signs, which is to be communicated? In this way,
language and exogamy represent two solutions to one and the same
fundamental situation."[64]

Without worrying about the details of Lévi-Strauss's position, Lacan
in "Function and Field" immediately turns to its essence:

The marriage tie is governed by an order of preference whose law concerning
the kinship names is, like language, imperative for the group in its forms, but
unconscious in its structure. In this structure, whose harmony or conflicts
govern the restricted or generalized exchange discerned in it by the social
anthropologist, the startled theoretician finds the whole of the logic of combinations: thus the laws of number—that is to say, the laws of the most refined
of all symbols—prove to be immanent in the original symbolism. At least, it
is the richness of the forms in which are developed what are known as the
elementary structures of kinship that makes it possible to read those laws in
the original symbolism. And this would suggest that it is perhaps only our
unconsciousness of their permanence that allows us to believe in the freedom of
choice in the so-called complex structures of marriage ties under whose law we
live. (*E*, 276–77/66)

We see here the very nucleus of structural explanation: Lévi-Strauss
"startles" Lacan with the conclusion that an infinitely large range of
human behaviors can be explained as variant possibilities of a combinatorial system. This system can itself be reduced to the most basic laws
of number: addition and subtraction, positive and negative.[65] Crucial
to such a theory is the claim that the logic of combinations governs and
perhaps even determines actual human behaviors without the agents in
these behaviors being in any way conscious of such a logic. It is along
lines such as these that Lacan further enriches his concept of the unconscious, adding to the more properly "linguistic" notion of the
transindividual portion of discourse, which serves as his initial explica-

tion, the fundamentally structuralist idea that much of what is unconscious goes beyond the merely linguistic to serve as the ground for the intelligibility of all human behavior.

Armed with this richer conception of the unconscious, Lacan immediately sets to work to revise the psychoanalytic notion of the Oedipus complex. He writes: "This is precisely where the Oedipus complex—insofar as we continue to recognize it as covering the whole field of our experience with its signification—may be said, in this connection, to mark the limits that our discipline assigns to subjectivity: namely, what the subject can know of his unconscious participation in the movement of the complex structures of marriage ties, by verifying the symbolic effects in his individual existence of the tangential movement towards incest that has manifested itself ever since the coming of a universal community" (E, 277/66). What Freud had understood as a struggle between instinct and the demands of civilization, a struggle in which instinctual renunciation and culturally stipulated identifications are the normative outcomes,[66] Lacan describes as an entry into the "unconscious participation" in the background "language" making "civilized" behavior possible and intelligible. The child, in passing through the Oedipus complex, learns the language of familial relations and thereby adopts a position within the culture of his family by taking on a *name*, itself made intelligible by the language of kinship. It was Lévi-Strauss who first showed how strictly our behaviors are determined by the logic of kinship relations, and Lacan unites this anthropological insight with the traditional psychoanalytic emphasis on the resolution of the Oedipus complex. Central to Lacan's theoretical maneuver is the fact that psychoanalysis situates the development of the Oedipus complex at precisely the period in which children are most effectively acquiring the language of their parents (beginning from about the age of two-and-a-half years). For Lacan, successful negotiation of oedipal conflicts is quite literally a matter of learning to speak properly. The "primordial Law," which Freud and many anthropologists have seen as the incest taboo, "is revealed clearly enough as identical with an order of language" (E, 277/66).

The name that the child learns to speak properly and to take as his own through the resolution of the Oedipus complex is "the *name of the father*" (*le nom de père*). Paternity in its cultural significance has little to do with biological origins, Lacan notes in "On a Question Preliminary to Any Possible Treatment of Psychosis," and is strictly a function of "the symbolic context" (E, 556/199). It is the child's acceptance of a

particular signifier which confers upon him an identity (that bound up
with the father's name [*nom*]) and also signifies the child's recognition
of the prohibition of incest (the father's "no" [*non*])[67] and of the father's
standing as "the figure of the law" (*E, 278/67*).

In "The Neurotic's Individual Myth" Lacan elaborates his notion of
the father, stressing in particular its symbolic significance: "The father
is the representative, the incarnation, of a symbolic function which
concentrates in itself those things most essential in other cultural structures: namely, the tranquil, or rather, symbolic, enjoyment, culturally
determined and established, of the mother's love, that is to say, of the
pole to which the subject is linked by a bond that is irrefutably natural."[68] It is the failure of the real father fully to live up to "the symbolic
value crystallized in his function" that is "the source of the effects of the
oedipus complex which are not at all normalizing, but rather most
often pathogenic."[69] Thus, it is the *béance* between the symbolic and the
real that is at the root of the neuroses (and even psychoses) with which
the psychoanalyst is confronted.

Crucial to Lacan's account is the fact that this new identity is essentially a "function of symbolic identification" (*E, 278/67*). The name of
the father situates the *je,* the subject (in contrast to the *moi*), in a relation
to other subjects: "I am my father's child." However, this symbolic
identity is inherently distinct from, and almost certainly at odds with,
the imaginary identity of the *moi,* forged in the series of narcissistic
identifications growing out of the infant's first self-recognition in the
mirror. Thus, the gap between the subject and the *moi* is reintroduced
here in Lacan's theorizing of the Oedipus complex: the *moi* is basically a
product of pre-oedipal relations with imaginary others, while the subject
is fundamentally a product of oedipal relations articulated in a symbolic
system.[70]

The consequences of this account for a general theory of the human
being are striking and important. In chapter 2, I argued that Lacan sees
the very origins of our identity as opening up a *béance* or gap between
the lived experience of our bodies and the *mois* that are constructed for
us by imaginary relations. What "Function and Field" adds to this
general picture of the human being is yet another gap, this time
between the imaginary *moi* and the subject constituted by a web of
symbolic relations.[71] We are, then, triplex creatures, doubly split from
ourselves. It is no wonder that we are not completely comfortable with
ourselves and that we find ourselves racked by neuroses and psychoses.

According to psychoanalytic theory, failures to negotiate the Oedipus complex successfully lead to various forms of neurosis and even psychosis,[72] and Lacan proceeds to argue that an analysand's use of his father's name is a fundamentally important feature of the psychoanalytic dialogue. This is particularly the case, because—although the name belongs preeminently to the symbolic register of the subject's experience—the name of the father is inextricably bound up with imaginary identifications (leading to the aggressive tendencies characteristic of the oedipal child) and with real relations between parent and child. Thus, Lacan writes:

It is in the *name of the father* that we must recognize the support of the symbolic function which, from the dawn of history, has identified his person with the figure of the law. This conception enables us to distinguish clearly, in the analysis of a case, the unconscious effects of this function from the narcissistic relations, or even from the real relations that the subject sustains with the image and the action of the person who embodies it; and there results from this a mode of comprehension that will tend to have repercussions on the very way in which the interventions of the analyst are conducted. (*E*, 278/67)

In the analysand's use of the father's name, then, we have an indirect access to the analysand's being as one subject in a symbolic system (*je*), as a congeries of imaginary identifications (*moi*), and even as a body witnessed in the act of speaking. As we shall see, such access provides the basis for a Lacanian typology of mental disorders.

In Lacan's later work the account sketched here becomes the basis for a much more elaborate examination of the process by which gender identity is constructed. While this is a major issue in chapter 7, it is important to mention here that Lacan's notions of the *name of the father* and of the symbolic paternal function are ultimately bound up with his theory of the phallus. In his paper of 1958, "The Signification of the Phallus," Lacan introduces the key idea that the phallus is essentially a signifier and not an imaginary construct or a real bodily organ: "For the phallus is a signifier, a signifier whose function in the intrasubjective economy of analysis might lift the veil from that which it served in the mysteries. For it is to this signifier that it is given to designate as a whole the effect of there being a signified, inasmuch as it conditions any such effect by its presence as signifier" (*E*, 690/285).[73] In effect, the phallus is the ultimate *point de capiton*, the signifier that fixes the meaning of the signifying chains of every subject's discourse, by virtue of its being "veiled" or repressed. The phallus is present beneath every signifier as the signifier that has been repressed, and as such every signifier in effect is a metaphor substituting for the phallus.[74]

As such a signifier, the phallus is not anything that any man or woman could possible "have" (hence, it must not be confused with the penis). Indeed, this is the key to Lacan's reinterpretation of Freud's notion of castration.[75] Precisely because no one can *have* the phallus, it becomes that which all want to *be*. The phallus then serves to signify as well that fullness of being, that complete identity, the lack of which is the fact of our ineluctable want-of-being. To the extent that all of our speech is a metonymic attempt to cover over this fundamental want-of-being, all human speech is figuratively linked to the phallus as the central *point de capiton* of our discourse. And, as Lacan notes later in "The Signification of the Phallus," it is most basically the repression of the phallus as signifier that serves to constitute the unconscious as a language (*E, 693/288*).

Language and Suffering   Given the extent of the symbolic in our lives according to Lacan's theory of language, it is clear that the recognition we desire is largely to be achieved by and within language itself, through the speech of the other to whom we direct our demands. Thus, we seek in the other's speech some recognition of the fact that we exist as desiring subjects outside of language and its conventionally defined roles, as well as a recognition of the fact that our identities are not simply exhausted in the imaginary constructions of our fantasy lives.

Naturally, this approach to language and desire has direct consequences for the practice of psychoanalysis, where the scene is precisely that of the intersubjective dialogue. It is, for example, the analysand's demand for recognition addressed to the analyst that motivates his continual willingness to engage in free association in accordance with the fundamental rule of psychoanalysis. Recognition is held out as the promised "gift" to be presented on the occasion of the analysand's full assumption of his history. Lacan approaches this point in the following passage from "Function and Field":

What is at stake in an analysis is the advent in the subject of that little reality that this desire sustains in him with respect to the symbolic conflicts and imaginary fixations as the means of their agreement, and our path is the intersubjective experience where this desire makes itself recognized.

From this point on it will be seen that the problem is that of the relations between speech and language in the subject. (E, 279/68)

Thus the special domain explored by psychoanalysis—the territory of "mental disorders" in particular—can be mapped out in terms of peculiarities confronted by the analyst in the analysand's speech. In "The Agency of the Letter" Lacan concludes a list of figures of style and tropes by commenting: "Can one really see these as mere figures of speech when it is the figures themselves that are the active principle of the rhetoric of the discourse that the analysand in fact utters?" (E, 521/ 169). To understand the analysand is to understand his speech, and this in turn means to understand the particular rhetoric that shapes and colors that speech. Thus, the art of the psychoanalyst is in a fundamental sense an applied rhetoric.

In "Function and Field" Lacan sketches a minimal typology of mental disorder by reviewing what he describes as three "paradoxes" in the relation between the analysand's speech and language.

The first paradox is that lying at the heart of madness (la folie). In the delirium of a psychotic one finds, on the one hand, a form of speaking that "has given up trying to make itself recognized" (E, 279/68), a solipsistic exploitation of the reserves of language without regard for the intersubjective dialectic of speech. On the other hand, precisely because of this solipsism, psychotic delusions exhibit a stereotypical quality that demonstrates the fact that the subject here "is spoken rather than speaking" (E, 280/69). Traditional religious themes, for example, intertwine with more or less conventionally condemned sexual practices in the Memoirs of Senatspräsident Dr. Daniel Paul Schreber (which serve as the basis for Freud's most important theoretical treatment of psychosis),[76] as well as in such works of literature as the theatrical poetry of Antonin Artaud.[77] The paradox of psychosis is that the psychotic's speaking manifests a fundamental "absence of speech" (E, 280/69), where speech properly involves some degree of creative dialogue.

The second paradox of speech and language defines the symptoms characteristic of the various neuroses. "The symptom is here the signifier of a signified repressed from the consciousness of the subject" (E, 280/69), and it is thus "speech functioning to the full, for it includes the discourse of the other in the secret of its cipher" (E, 281/69). The paradox of the neurotic's speech is that it is speech not only unconscious of its repressed content but also largely unconscious of the very fact of its being spoken. It is the task of the psychoanalyst, then, to help the neurotic analysand unfold not only the hidden meaning of his symptomatic discourse but also the hidden fact that there is a rhetoric of these symptoms. This is the burden of the stylistically most spectacular paragraph in "Function and Field": "Hieroglyphics of hysteria, blazons of phobia, labyrinths of the *Zwangsneurose* [obsessions]—charms of impotence, enigmas of inhibition, oracles of anxiety—talking arms of character, seals of self-punishment, disguises of perversion—these are the hermetic elements that our exegesis resolves, the equivocations that our invocation dissolves, the artifices that our dialectic absolves, in a deliverance of the imprisoned meaning, from the revelation of the palimpsest to the given word of the mystery and to the pardon of speech" (*E,* 281/69–70). Although subsequent Lacanian theorists have done much to elaborate a typology of neurosis,[78] the evocative model displayed here is perhaps more typical of Lacan's own approach to traditional issues of psychiatric classification.

The third and last paradox defining a category of mental disorder "is that of the subject who loses his meaning in the objectifications of discourse" (*E,* 281/70). This is the fate of most of us caught up in the objectifying jargon of contemporary "scientific civilization." If asked to speak about ourselves—for example, in the context of a psychoanalytic session—we are at first likely to fall into the stereotypical, quasi-scientific psychological descriptions with which we are regularly bombarded by the media. We are in effect given by our culture a means of "communication" by which we can avoid a genuine "speaking" about ourselves. We are speaking about ourselves without speaking about ourselves: this is the paradox of modern "alienation." To the extent that we accept these descriptions as accurate, we are accepting an account of ourselves as others, as objects of a "scientific" theory, and we thereby fail to live up to our being as subjects. With his skill in finding linguistic examples, Lacan offers the following striking confirmation of this thesis: "To give an exemplary formulation of this, I could not find a more pertinent terrain than the usage of common speech—pointing out that the '*ce suis-je*' of the time of Villon has become reversed in the '*c'est moi*' of modern man" (*E,* 281/70). Lacan's point here is that, in medieval French, the speaker clearly takes on the role of subject—"Ce suis-je," "I am this one"—while in modern French, the speaker has been transformed into an object (the *moi* conveniently bringing us back to Lacan's account of the *moi* as an alienated identity)—"C'est moi," "It is me."

Lacan's essay "On a Question Preliminary" augments this typology by distinguishing between three different technical terms used by Freud to characterize ways in which the human subject rejects or otherwise disposes of unpleasant realities or psychical contents (*E*, 557–58/200–201):

1) The neurotic's behavior is fundamentally shaped by the repression (*refoulement*, *Verdrängung*) of certain signifiers from his conscious discourse.[79] These repressed signifiers, now unconscious, are to be found in the Other, and the neurosis takes the form of a question addressed to the Other (see S 3, 196), asking about these signifiers. Since the repressed signifiers are nevertheless present in the Other—in the unconscious—psychoanalytic treatment of neurosis in effect works towards the analysand's discovery of these signifiers, towards his answering the question of his neurosis.

2) The alienation suffered by the modern, scientific subject is largely a product of negation or denial (*dénégation*, *Verneinung*),[80] a systematic *méconnaissance* of the signifiers constituting the subject's discourse that parallels the mechanism for the formation of the *moi*. Here, psychoanalytic treatment aims at the subject's coming to genuine self-knowledge, itself largely a matter of her simply listening to what she is saying.[81]

3) With respect to the psychotic, Lacan argues that his discourse is a product of the foreclosure (*forclusion*, *Verwerfung*) of certain "primordial signifiers." In contrast to repression or negation—both of which involve the preservation of the signifiers rejected, either in the Other or in the elements of conscious discourse that are negated—foreclosure involves the utter expulsion and destruction of the signifiers at issue. As has often been observed,[82] Lacan is here extending more or less casual usage by Freud into a rather precise theory. According to this account, foreclosure is specified as follows: "What is at issue when I speak of *Verwerfung*? It concerns the rejection of a primordial signifier into an external obscurity, a signifier which will be lacking from then on at this level. This is the fundamental mechanism that I suppose to be at the base of paranoia. It is a matter of a primordial process of exclusion of a primitive inside, an inside which is not the inside of the body, but that of a first body of the signifier" (S 3, 171). In an important contribution to the theory of psychosis, Lacan argues that it is in "the foreclosure of the Name-of-the-Father in the place of the Other, and in the failure of the paternal metaphor, that I designate the defect that gives psychosis its essential condition, and the structure that separates it from neurosis" (*E*, 575/215). To foreclose a signifier as

central to human experience as the *name of the father* is to cut loose the signifying chains that constitute the subject's discourse, depriving them of their *point de capiton,* and it is the failure of his discourse to achieve any sort of fixed signification that is characteristic of the psychotic's delirium.[83] It is also this failure of signification that makes psychosis so resistant to successful psychoanalytic treatment.

Chapter Four
From the Symbolic to the Real

The final section of "Function and Field" bears the title "The Reso-
nances of Interpretation and the Time of the Subject in Psychoanalytic
Technique." As his title indicates, Lacan offers here something of a
recapitulation of the themes of sections 1 and 2: the interpretation of
the analysand's empty speech and the implications for analytic technique of a careful attention to speech and language. This recapitulation
takes these themes into a new key, however, emphasizing most particularly the role of time in the linguistic unfolding of the analytic dialogue
and probing what can only be called time's "philosophical" dimensions.
It is here too that something like Lacan's alternative to a theory of
psychoanalytic "cure" emerges, although we must bear in mind the fact
that the notion of cure carries with it the quasi-medical connotations to
which Lacan objects in the work of most English and American psychoanalysts.

I have already stressed Lacan's claim that psychoanalysis is, among
other things, a practice in which a certain kind of human subject comes
into being, is "realized." It is this claim that is deepened in the final
pages of "Function and Field," where Lacan simultaneously pursues the
role of the symbolic in constituting this subject and lays the foundation
for seeing the symbolic as but one facet of the human being, other
facets being arranged under the now familiar registers of the imaginary
and the real. Paradoxically, it is Lacan's total immersion in the role of
the symbolic that leads his reader to grasp the essential fact that there is
more to man and woman than the register of linguistic and quasi-
linguistic systems might seem to allow.

Speech and the Realization of the Subject

The section opens with a brief commentary on Freud's celebrated
case of the "Rat Man."[1] Lacan's purpose is unclear until the third page
of the section, where he finally notes: "But it is not a question of
imitating him [Freud]. In order to rediscover the effect of Freud's

speech, it is not to its terms that we shall have recourse, but to the principles that govern it" (*E, 292/79*). We see here Lacan's familiar move toward a deeper study of the role of speech and language in the psychoanalytic dialogue, and we might well expect a return to the structuralist issues engaged previously. However, Lacan immediately surprises (and even shocks) his reader: "These principles are simply the dialectic of the consciousness-of-self, as realized from Socrates to Hegel, from the ironic presupposition that all that is rational is real to its culmination in the scientific view that all that is real is rational. But Freud's discovery was to demonstrate that this verifying process authentically attains the subject only by decentering him from the consciousness-of-self, in the axis of which the Hegelian reconstruction of the phenomenology of mind maintained it" (*E, 292/79–80*). In short, the principles structuring the analyst's interventions in the psychoanalytic dialogue—indeed, the principles structuring this dialogue itself—are to be found in the dialectical process through which self-consciousness evolves. Lacan suggests rather casually here that this process involves a transition from taking logic to be the basic criterion for the real (epitomized in Socrates's faith in the law of noncontradiction) to the "scientific" faith that even the most apparently absurd events can be explained rationally. At the level of self-consciousness, this transition might be reflected in the maturing adult's gradual realization that genuine self-understanding comes only after an arduous confrontation with aspects of character long repressed or denied. This process of coming to self-consciousness has as its end, however, the distinctively Freudian (and anti-Cartesian) notion that genuine consciousness of self cannot be attained within the frame of phenomenological introspection but demands a frame of reference outside consciousness. This Freudian frame is, of course, the unconscious, and Lacan is here simply reiterating his familiar claim that what he terms the human subject (realized perhaps most fully in the course of the psychoanalytic dialogue) is distinct from the center of consciousness we call the ego or *moi*. This claim is echoed at the beginning of his enigmatic paper of 1955, "La chose freudienne, ou Sens de retour à Freud en psychanalyse" ("The Freudian Thing, or The Meaning of the Return to Freud in Psychoanalysis") (*E, 401–36/114–45*). Here Lacan maintains that as a result of Freud's discovery of the unconscious "the very center of the human being was no longer to be found at the place assigned to it by a whole humanist tradition" (*E, 401/114*).

Every positing of a "center" in a field of knowledge carries with it the implicit presumption that a "totality" can inevitably be arranged around such a center. In other words, to define a thing as having a center is to define a system in principle closed, within which that thing and its relations to other things can be exhaustively determined.[2] It is precisely this assumption of totality with respect to the human subject that Lacan is attacking in the names of Freud and Hegel:

> But if there still remains something prophetic in Hegel's insistence on the fundamental identity of the particular and the universal,[3] an insistence that reveals the measure of his genius, it is certainly psychoanalysis that provides it with its paradigm by revealing the structure in which that identity is realized as disjunctive of the subject, and without appeal to any tomorrow.
>
> Let me simply say that this is what leads me to object to any reference to totality in the individual, since it is the subject who introduces division into the individual, as well as into the collectivity that is his equivalent. Psychoanalysis is properly that which reveals both the one and the other to be no more than mirages. (E, 292/80)

Psychoanalysis destroys the analysand's illusions that his identity can be fully captured in the imaginary construct called the *moi,* and it does this quite simply by showing how this imaginary identity is riddled with gaps both created and covered over by the variety of symbolic systems into which he was born.[4] (Lacan's claim that the same analysis holds for human "collectivities" lays the foundation for a Lacanian approach to social thought, political theory, and ideology, topics that must remain outside the scope of this study.)[5] The notion of totality is a dream of the imaginary *moi,* and the realization of the subject in the psychoanalytic dialogue has the effect of destroying this dream. This happens as a result of the analysand's coming to realize the division within him, a division that Lacan suggests is fundamentally reflected in Hegel's notion of the "unity" of universal and particular in the same subject.

Crucial to this claim is the fact that, for Lacan, the identity of universal and particular is something that is achieved only within language and only within the "primary language" of desire that psychoanalysis teaches the analysand to speak.

> In order to free the subject's speech, we introduce him into the language of his desire, that is to say, into the *primary language* in which, beyond what he tells us of himself, he is already talking to us unknown to himself, and, in the first place, in the symbols of the symptom.

In the symbolism brought to light in analysis, it is certainly a question of a language. This language . . . has the universal character of a language that would be understood in all other languages, but, at the same time, since it is the language that seizes desire at the very moment in which it is humanized by making itself recognized, it is absolutely particular to the subject. (*E*, 293–94/81)

The same can be said of any person's use of language: while the language itself is inherently universal, the fact of its being spoken by a particular person in a particular place and time is no less inherently a fact of language as speech. As he had done in section 2 (*E*, 279/68), Lacan again associates the particularity that disrupts language's universality with human desire, which, insofar as it is human, always aims ultimately at recognition by particular others. In effect, the practice of psychoanalysis has as its goal precisely the analysand's coming to know that his desire speaks a language which is, in crucial respects at least, at odds with the "universal" language that makes human communication possible. Once "introduced" to this primary language of desire, the analysand is in a position to begin to exploit the special resources of this language in the telling of his history. Much of the last section of "Function and Field" is devoted to clarifying ways in which the analyst can facilitate the analysand's assumption of this primary language.

I have already reviewed Lacan's distinctions between need, demand, and desire, but these distinctions are deepened now as he explores the technical implications of his reorientation of psychoanalytic theory toward speech and language. A fundamental difference between biological need and linguistically articulated demand concerns their aims: where the aim of need is a change in the organic status of the animal or person who needs (for example, the satisfaction of thirst), the aim of demand is "a transformation of the subject to whom it is addressed" (*E*, 296/83). Linguistic articulation not only makes demand an essentially intersubjective phenomenon, it also highlights the performative power of language to effect changes in the world outside the speaker.[6] Demand introduces "the effect of a signifier" into the real.[7] Lacan's insistence on this point introduces a further elaboration of the nature of language, since he can now argue that, at least from a psychoanalytic point of view, what distinguishes human language from the simpler systems of "communication" that we share with other animals (what Lacan calls *langage-signe*) is precisely the fact that human languages, unlike animal sign systems, are essentially performative. That is, while it is not false to think of language in terms of information theory, as involving "a signal by which the sender informs the receiver of something by means of a certain code" (E, 296/83), it is wrong to think that such a model fully captures the range of effects that language has upon us.[8] What information theory fails to grasp is simply the performative dimension of language, the fact that language changes us.

Moreover, language changes us in the most fundamental of ways. Human language is not merely performative; its performance in fact serves to define subjectivity itself. The "highest function of speech" is to transform the other to whom speech is addressed into "a new reality" (E, 298/85). Rather than seeing this "highest function" as something over and above the basic functioning of speech (which might be taken to remain communication), however, Lacan insists that this "is in fact the essential form from which all human speech derives rather than the form at which it arrives" (E, 298/85). What makes this performative aspect of language possible is the conjunction of a number of features that together serve to distinguish human language from animal symbol use.

1) An animal's use of symbols can be distinguished from language in that it exhibits a "fixed correlation of its signs to the reality that they signify" (E, 297/84). It is precisely this lack of a fixed, indeed natural, connection between signifier and signified that characterizes human language. It will be remembered that Saussure goes so far as to define language in terms that necessitate the essentially arbitrary, conventional, and thus impermanent relation between signs and their referents. It is this flexibility, even ambiguity, of language that allows the same signifiers to play both descriptive and performative roles. Naturally, the psychoanalyst must be alert to the particular ambiguities that flourish in the speech of each analysand.

2) Lacan offers a second characteristic of human language by quoting one of his critics: " 'Human Language (according to you) constitutes a communication in which the sender receives his own message back from the receiver in an inverted form.' This was an objection that I had only to reflect on for a moment before recognizing that it carried the stamp of my own thinking—in other words, that speech always subjectively includes its own reply" (E, 298/85). This claim goes back to Lacan's earlier insistence that demand always has as its most important aim recognition by the other. When a speaker says, for example, "I love you," the response expected and certainly demanded is precisely the same message, "I love you," where only the referents of the pronouns

have been reversed. The speaker in effect calls into existence an intersubjective dialogue in his speaking, and the psychoanalyst must take this virtual dialogue into account in the course of her interventions in the analysand's discourse.

3) From the point of view of information theory, human language contains many elements that are simply redundant and unnecessary, and this is powerful evidence that the simple communication of information is not the primary function of language. Lacan writes:

> It can be asserted that a substantial portion of the phonetic material is superfluous to the realization of the communication actually sought.
>
> This is highly instructive for us, for what is redundant as far as information is concerned is precisely that which does duty as resonance in speech.
>
> For the function of language is not to inform but to evoke. (*E*, 299/86)

It is because of its "redundancies," Lacan suggests, that the speaking of a language can actually constitute the performance of an action. Those aspects of an utterance that do not serve in any way to carry information, that do not play any role in "representing" the world external to language—aspects such as repetition, mumbling, pauses, as well as intonation and phrase contour—effectively define the range of appropriate responses to that utterance. They "evoke" an entire world of legitimate linguistic expectation conjured up by the utterance. Most crucially, these redundant aspects of speech serve to evoke and thereby to construct the other to whom one speaks, whose basic features are circumscribed by the form of the utterance addressed to her. In "Variantes de la cure-type" Lacan sharpens this point by distinguishing between true discourse (*discours vrai*) and true speech (*vraie parole*), arguing that it is in the latter than an intersubjective context is performatively specified: while discourse is concerned with the accurate description of things, speech focuses on the performance of mutual human recognition (*E*, 351–52). In the psychoanalytic session, the analysand limns a role for the analyst by means of the performative elements of his speech, and the analyst must take this script into account before taking an active part in the drama of the dialogue.

4) We come now to a final feature distinguishing human language from animal symbol use, a feature that sums up the importance of all the others in the context of the psychoanalytic dialogue. If it is the performative dimension of speech that defines human subjectivity, this is made possible by the fact that our initial linguistic approach to an

other takes the form of a question. At one level, the question is "Do you love me?" Yet this question masks an even deeper question—"Who or what am I?"—which the analysand in particular addresses to the analyst both early on and throughout the duration of the analysis.[9] We have already seen that the analysand's empty speech becomes full—and the analysand assumes his true role as psychoanalytic subject—when this speech takes the form of an intersubjectively intelligible narration of his past in the form of a history of origins. The analytic dialogue has achieved an important part of its purpose when the analysand can successfully narrate an answer to the question, "Who or what am I?"—an answer that manages to cast the analysand himself as a subject who has a history. It should also be remembered, however, that this narration can take the form of a story with plot only when some sort of conclusion begins to be anticipated in the course of its telling. In short, the story of the analysand's origins can be told only in the light of his end and ultimately only in the light of his anticipated death.

Lacan introduces these difficult but important issues in a passage that sums up the difference between the human and the animal by emphasizing something tantamount to a linguistic determinism.

What I seek in speech is the response of the other. What constitutes me as subject is my question. In order to be recognized by the other, I utter what was only in view of what will be. In order to find him, I call him by a name that he must assume or refuse in order to reply to me.

I identify myself in language, but only by losing myself in it like an object. What is realized in my history is not the past definite of what was, since it is no more, or even the present perfect of what has been in what I am, but the future anterior of what I shall have been for what I am in the process of becoming. (E, 299–300/86)

My speech inevitably objectifies me by making my present merely the product of a past on the way to a future, and yet, by taking at least the implicit form of a question, my speech also opens itself up to the other who can transform me simply through an act of recognition. Neither of these dimensions of human speech is present in the animal's use of symbols.

This dialectic of linguistic objectification and transformation through recognition by the other lies at the very heart of the psychoanalytic dialogue. The analysand in effect strives to objectify himself by telling his life history; the analyst in effect strives to prevent this objectification, at the same time encouraging the process of self-narration, and necessarily uses the possibility of withholding or conferring recognition as the means of achieving this aim. This is what Lacan means when he suggests that "speech is in fact a gift of language" (*E*, 301/87) and characterizes the analyst's responsibility to the analysand in these terms: "Henceforth the decisive function of my own reply appears, and this function is not, as has been said, simply to be received by the subject as acceptance or rejection of his discourse, but really to recognize him or to abolish him as subject. Such is the nature of the analyst's *responsibility* whenever he intervenes by means of speech" (E 300/87). How the analyst replies to the analysand's questions, how she responds to each of his self-narrations, will determine whether the analysand is caught as an object in the symbolic network woven in the course of the psychoanalysis or emerges as a fully fledged human subject capable both of assuming his status as the hero of a narration and of narrating the tale that grants him this status.

Truth in Speech

Lacan summarizes this description of the psychoanalytic process in an important passage:

Analysis can have for its goal only the advent of a true speech and the realization by the subject of his history in his relation to a future.

Maintaining this dialectic is in direct opposition to any objectifying orientation of analysis, and emphasizing this necessity is of first importance if we are to see through the aberrations of the new tendencies being manifested in psychoanalysis. (*E*, 302/88)

If the aim of the psychoanalyst is to keep the dialectic of the analytic dialogue going, if the aim is to forestall the ever-present possibility of giving in to some objectifying characterization (for example, the analysand's narrating a life history on the theme, "I am an obsessional neurotic"), Lacan nevertheless insists that the discourse of the analysand must ultimately come to manifest the truth.[10] Clearly the truth in question here is also integrally tied to the analysand's full acceptance of his essential temporality. What, then, is it that makes an utterance true?

In "The Freudian Thing"—the "thing" in question here being quite precisely *truth*—Lacan adopts a Heideggerian account of truth, understanding truth as essentially a state or process of disclosure.[11] The disclosure at issue for Lacan is that manifested in the act of speech, and thus it is the fact that we are speaking beings that leads to truth's playing a shaping role in human reality. "It all began with a particular truth," Lacan writes, "a disclosure, the effect of which is that reality is no longer the same for us as it was before" (E, 408/120). That truth is to be understood in terms of the signifier's advent and effect upon the real, in terms of the dependence of the signified upon the signifier, is the main burden of the remarkable prosopopoeia of "The Freudian Thing," in which truth speaks of itself (or rather herself), announcing at the start that "I am the enigma of her who vanishes as soon as she appears" (E, 408/121).[12]

The key to Lacan's account here is that the temporality that is the truth of the human subject is the one shape of identity that is neither objectifying nor alienating. Unlike the imaginary identity conjured up in one's relation to mirror images and unlike the symbolic identity determined by one's place in the symbolic systems that constitute his cultural community, one's identity as a temporal being—as "one who thus has been" (E, 255/47) and "will have been thus" in relation to a future (see E, 300/86 on the future anterior)—partakes in the real. Indeed, it is the human being's inherent temporality that makes possible both those imaginary processes by which mirror images are transformed into ideals for imitation by the young ego and those symbolic processes by which the systems of language are incarnated in the temporally relative utterances of speech. If we were not beings capable of living the present as a synthesis of past and future, such complex processes would be inconceivable.

Is true speech, then, simply discourse that reflects the inevitability of temporality? Following Heidegger's analysis of "care" (Sorge) in Being and Time, Lacan is certainly in a position to distinguish an "authentic" realization of temporality in the subject from an "inauthentic" and alienating realization. Discussing the connection between temporality and care, Heidegger writes:

The items of care have not been pieced together cumulatively any more than temporality itself has been put together 'in the course of time' out of the future, the having been, and the Present. Temporality 'is' not an *entity* at all. It is not, but it *temporalizes* itself. Nevertheless, we cannot avoid saying, 'Temporality "is" . . . the meaning of care', 'Temporality "is" . . . defined in such and such a way'; the reason for this can be made intelligible only when we have clarified the idea of Being and that of the 'is' in general. Temporality temporalizes, and indeed it temporalizes possible ways of itself. These make possible the multiplicity of Dasein's modes of Being, and especially the basic possibility of authentic or inauthentic existence.[13]

The inauthentic realization of temporality would accept it as a positively definable characteristic of the subject, not unlike (for example) the characteristic of being an efficient certified public accountant. In attributing a particular character to temporality and then embracing this character in his own self-narration, the analysand would remain caught in an alienating identity and would not speak the truth. The authentic realization of temporality, in contrast, would recognize the fundamental nothingness of temporality and, thus, the inescapable emptiness, *béance*, gap, or gulf around which the human subject builds a false identity. This inauthentic identity is, as we have seen, designed to preserve a basic self-*méconnaissance* and, in this way, to forestall authentic self-knowledge.

Thus, characterizing Freud's therapeutic goal in the case of the Rat Man, Lacan writes: "This is the goal of bringing the subject to rediscover . . . in this history, together with the fateful constellation that had presided over the subject's very birth, the gap [*béance*] impossible to fill, of the symbolic debt of which his neurosis is the notice of nonpayment" (*E,* 303/89).[14] Lacan will circle back once again at the end of "Function and Field" to explore the deepest significance of this *béance* at the center of the subject, this gap opened up by the subject's temporality, a *béance* ultimately inseparable from a recognition of the subject's mortality. At this stage in his text, however, he turns once again to particular questions of psychoanalytic technique and their relation to problems in psychoanalytic theory.

Truth and the *moi* Lacan proceeds, then, to a rather obvious point, but one which opens out onto a rich theoretical field: "In order to know how to reply to the subject in analysis, the procedure is to recognize first of all the place where his *ego* is, the *ego* that Freud himself defined as an *ego* formed of a verbal nucleus; in other words, to know through whom and for whom the subject poses *his question*. So long as this is not known, there will be the risk of a misunderstanding concerning the desire that is there to be recognized and concerning the object to whom this desire is addressed" (*E,* 303/89). It is no doubt obvious that the analyst must determine the situation of the analysand's ego or

moi, but Lacan's approach to this issue reveals his profound commitment to the nuances of speech and language in the constitution of the
human subject. To recognize the analysand's *moi* is to learn "through
whom and for whom the subject poses *his question.*" The analysand is
essentially—from the perspective of analysis—a question-asker, but
this question is always asked in a certain way (reflecting the one in the
past "through whom" the subject has come to the question of identity)
and of a certain other (reflecting the one—perhaps in the past, perhaps
in the future, certainly in the present in the person of the analyst—"for
whom" this question is asked). In short, the analysand's question of
identity—"Who or what am I?"—is a question that can be grasped
only by understanding that neither its linguistic form nor the context
of its utterance is really determined by the analysand. This apparently
fundamental question in fact originates from a complex "nucleus"
within the subject—namely, the subject's *moi*—which must not be
identified with the subject himself.

   This notion is clarified when Lacan explicitly sketches an account of
the tripartite structure of the human subject:

It is therefore always in the rela::ion between the subject's ego [*moi*] and the 'I'
[*je*] of his discourse that you must understand the meaning of the discourse if
you are to achieve the dealienation of the subject.

   But you cannot possibly achieve this if you cling to the idea that the ego
[*moi*] of the subject is identical with the presence that is speaking to you. (*E,*
304/90)

The Lacanian subject is the uneasy coexistence of three distinct moments. There is, first of all, the real "presence that is speaking to you,"
the speaking body, the subject of the actual act of enunciation. Secondly, there is the symbolic subject indicated by the *je* of the speaking
body's discourse, the subject of the statement actually uttered.[15] The
third moment of the subject, distinct from both the speaking body and
the *je,* is the imaginary *moi* constructed (as we have seen) early in
childhood to give the subject an identity that it really lacks. Lacan
often uses the image of "fading" to describe the situation of the speaking body as it slides beneath the chain of signifiers that it utters in
constituting the subject as *je.*[16]

   While this passage offers a succinct summary of fundamental theoretical issues, Lacan uses it as a springboard toward a critique of contemporary psychoanalytic theory and practice. As we have seen, Lacan was

particularly troubled by a tendency he saw in the ego psychology developed by émigré analysts in the United States to eliminate the Freudian theory of the unconscious in favor of a developmental psychology growing out of the later Freudian "topography" of the psyche in terms of ego, id, and superego.[17] His objections to ego psychology take two different forms. On the one hand, he argues from the beginning of "Function and Field" that such an emphasis on developmental psychology makes the linguistic dimension of the psychoanalytic dialogue take a back seat. The ego psychologist, armed with a powerful theory, may be tempted to downplay the actual utterances of the analysand as revelatory of his truth in favor of an alienating prior theoretical modeling of analysands of this type. Such a tendency leads to regarding language itself as a "wall" separating the analysand from the analyst[18] and to disregarding the importance of language as the only evidence for the truth of the subject's situation. Lacan puts this point rather gently in saying that "we must be attentive to the 'un-said' that lies in the holes of the discourse, but this does not mean that we are to listen as if to someone knocking on the other side of a wall" (*E*, 307/93).

On the other hand, and perhaps equally importantly, Lacan objects that ego psychology is in the process of turning psychoanalysis into a kind of "two-body psychology," in which the dialogue between analysand and analyst establishes "a phantasmic communication in which the analyst teaches the subject to apprehend himself as an object" (*E*, 304/91). Here, again, we see Lacan's worry that the power of the theory in ego psychology will lead to precisely the quasi-scientific, alienating objectifications that psychoanalysis ought to be helping subjects in the modern world escape. Even more dangerously, such an approach to the dynamics of the psychoanalytic session tends to cast the analyst in the role of the model, the analysand's conformity to whom is defined as "mental health." The goal of analysis in such a theory would be the analysand's willing adaptation to his cultural environment, as evidenced by his successfully contributing to society (as does the analyst in "curing" the analysand of his failure to adapt).[19]

Lacan argues that this tendency grows out of taking Freud's later model of the psyche as a theory of the mind completely separable from the dialectical context of psychoanalysis in which the theory is in fact rooted. Theory ought, in fact, to grow out of a sustained reflection on the dynamic involved in the actual practice of psychoanalytic treatment. Nowhere is this separation of theory from practice clearer, Lacan suggests, than in the ego psychologists' "deformed" interpretation of

Freud's celebrated aphorism on the intention of psychoanalytic practice, "Where id was, there ego shall be [*Wo Es war, soll Ich werden.*]."[20]
Lacan returns to this gnomic text a number of times in the course of his
work, but in "Function and Field" his discussion focuses strictly on the
American ill-treatment of Freud's words. Thus, he writes: "And this
deformed usage of Freud's formula that all that is of the *id* must become
of the *ego* appears under a demystified form; the subject, transformed
into a *cela* [that is, an object, a thing, but not the *id,* which is *ça* in
French], has to conform to an *ego* in which the analyst will have little
trouble in recognizing his ally, since in actual fact it is to the analyst's
ego that the subject is expected to conform" (*E,* 305/91). Lacan's own
reading of Freud's aphorism, in marked contrast to this, can be found
in "The Freudian Thing" (*E,* 416–18/128–29). Here, he begins by
stressing the fact that Freud's German leaves out the definite articles
before *Es* and *Ich,* thus indicating that the aphorism does not deal
directly with the id (*das Es*) or the ego (*das Ich*). Leaving these theoretical entities behind, Lacan is able to translate Freud by using *ça* for *Es*
and *je* for *Ich* and by coining a reflexive form of *être* (*s'être*) to take the
place of *c'était* (with the *ça* elided). The result is the following: " 'There
where it was,' I would like it to be understood, 'it is my duty that I [*je*]
should come to being' ['*Là où c'était, peut-on, là où s'était, voudrions-nous
faire qu'on entendit, c'est mon devoir que je vienne à être.*']" (*E,* 417–18/
129). In short, the imperative inherent in psychoanalysis is that the
analysand assume his truth by bringing into being a fully worked out
self-narrative in the first person (*je*), and in this way Lacan writes the
late Freudian topography out of Freud's famous aphorism.

Two years later, in "The Agency of the Letter," Lacan offers a gloss to
a somewhat less tendentious translation of Freud:

The end that Freud's discovery proposes for man was defined by him at the
apex of his thought in these moving terms: *Wo Es war, soll Ich werden.* I must
come to the place where that was. [*Là où fut ça, il me faut advenir.*]
   This is one of reintegration and harmony, I could even say of reconciliation
(*Versöhnung*).
   But if we ignore the self's radical ex-centricity to itself with which man is
confronted, in other words, the truth discovered by Freud, we shall falsify
both the order and methods of psychoanalytic mediation. (*E,* 524/171)

If the goal of psychoanalysis is "reintegration and harmony," the analyst
nevertheless must never lose sight of the human being's "radical ex-

centricity to itself." These apparently conflicting concerns are to be united in psychoanalytic practice by means of the now familiar notion of temporality.

Transference, Punctuation, and Interpretation Returning to "Function and Field," we find an admirable summary of these issues in a rhetorical question, where Lacan makes his own position unusually clear: "Does psychoanalysis remain a dialectical relation in which the non-action of the analyst guides the subject's discourse towards the realization of his truth, or is it to be reduced to a phantasmatic relation in which 'two abysses brush against each other' without touching, while the whole gamut of imaginary regressions is exhausted—like a sort of 'bundling' pushed to its extreme limits as a psychological experience?" (*E*, 307–8/93–94). We return again, then, to the familiar notion that the analyst's role in the psychoanalytic dialogue is to help the analysand's discourse realize his truth as a human subject and is not to encourage a rash of "imaginary regressions" that will lead to the ultimate *méconnaissance* in which the analysand identifies with the analyst. In order to clarify just how the analyst is to succeed in this, Lacan next turns his attention to the role of the analyst, as this role is constituted in the psychoanalytic dialogue by means of the analysand's transference, that is by his largely unconscious repetition of childhood situations and relationships in the situation and relationship defined by the psychoanalytic dialogue.[21]

What makes the temptations of ego psychology so powerful, what makes the analysand so willing to accept the false objectifications offered by psychological theory, is the fact that "the subject believes that his truth is already given in us and that we know it in advance" (*E*, 308/94). The analysand supposes the analyst to know the truth of the analysand's life, and thus in coming to the analyst he casts her in the role of "the subject-supposed-to-know" (*le sujet-supposé-savoir*) (*E*, 308 n.2/111 n.96). There is much that can be said about this feature—the very "support"—of the psychoanalytic relation of transference. For the purposes of achieving a deeper understanding of the role of the analyst in the analytic dialogue, however, what is most crucial is that this supposition on the part of the analysand guarantees that every behavior of the analyst will be charged with meaning. As Lacan points out in "Variantes de la cure-type," "what he answers is less important in its substance than the place from which he answers" (*E*, 347). While the analysand's supposition is clearly a product of his imaginary defining of expectations, it is simultaneously a fully real dimension of the analytic relationship and, as such, cannot be ignored by the analyst. This leads Lacan to the following important observation:

> Reality in the analytic experience does in fact often remain veiled under negative forms, but it is not too difficult to situate it.
>
> Reality is encountered, for instance, in what we usually condemn as active interventions; but it would be an error to define the limit of reality in this way.
>
> For it is clear on the other hand that the analyst's abstention, his refusal to reply, is an element of reality in analysis. More exactly, it is in this negativity insofar as it is a pure negativity—that is, detached from any particular motive—that lies the junction between the symbolic and the real. This naturally follows from the fact that this non-action of the analyst is founded on our firm and stated knowledge of the principle that all that is real is rational, and on the resulting precept that it is up to the subject to show what he is made of. (*E*, 309–10/95)

The analyst's silence throughout much of the analytic dialogue—a silence that we have already seen is often enough to foster aggressive behavior in the analysand—is taken by the analysand to be meaningful precisely because he takes his interlocutor to be one who knows and, thus, one who knows when it is appropriate to keep quiet. If the analyst is guided by the "scientific" assumption that the real is rational, a similar assumption lies behind the analysand's transference toward the subject-supposed-to-know as incarnated in the analyst.

If her silences are pregnant with assumed meaning, the analyst's active interventions in the analysand's discourse are, we may say, revealing deliveries of explicit meaning. The analyst acts only to celebrate the analysand's assumption of the truth: "The fact remains that this abstention is not maintained indefinitely; when the subject's question has taken on the form of true speech, we give it the sanction of our reply, but thereby we have shown that true speech already contains its own reply and that we are simply adding our own lay to its antiphon. What can this mean except that we do no more than to confer on the subject's speech its dialectical punctuation?" (*E*, 310/95). Once again, Lacan's text has circled back on itself and returned to a previous theme—that of "punctuation"—constructing for itself a new "lay" to its earlier "antiphon." Even the musical metaphors here—the analysand's antiphonal revelation of truth to which is added as counterpoint (this itself involving a notion of punctuation!) the analyst's secular lay—recall earlier metaphorical treatments of the analytic dialogue. Thus, Lacan has described the analysand's discourse as a multipart score (*E,* 253/45), which is played in its totality only by a psychoanalytic technique alive to the effects of speech and language (*E,* 291/79). Here, the analyst's active intervention is characterized as both the addition of a counterpoint and as the simple punctuation or interpretation of the original composition offered by the analysand.

To understand how intervention can simultaneously play both such an active and such a passive role, one must remember that active intervention is, for Lacan, ideally nothing more than a temporal breaking— punctuation—of the analysand's discourse. It adds to the analysis a formal recognition of the temporality that has been active in the analytic dialogue all along. Lacan writes: "The other moment in which the symbolic and the real come together is consequently revealed, and I have already marked it theoretically: that is to say, in the function of time" (*E,* 310/95). The temporal reality of the human subject underlies the temporal unfolding of the analytic dialogue, and it is the full realization on the part of the analysand of this temporality—in particular, the necessary imbrication of past and future with the present—that serves as a fundamental aim of psychoanalysis. Lacan suggests that there is no better way for the analyst to further this ultimate realization than to serve essentially as a temporal marker.

There are two domains within psychoanalysis where questions of time are of paramount importance. The first concerns the question of the total duration of a psychoanalysis.[22] Lacan insists that this issue can never be resolved in advance, that duration must remain essentially "indefinite" (*E,* 310/95), because any prediction of the likely end of analysis on the part of the analyst would only strengthen the analysand's transferential illusion that the analyst is all-knowing, thus "setting the analysis off on an aberrant path whose results will be impossible to correct" (*E,* 310/96).

The second and much more controversial domain where time is important to analysis concerns the length of individual psychoanalytic sessions. It will be remembered that it was on the issue of variable-length sessions that Lacan and his followers broke with the Société psychanalytique de Paris and organized the Société française de psychanalyse in 1953, so Lacan's report that year to the Congrès des psychanalystes de langue française in Rome was almost bound to deal with this "particularly ticklish" (*E,* 312/97) issue at some point.

What was really at stake in this controversy was the notion of analytic "neutrality." Crucial to Freud's conception of psychoanalytic tech-

nique is the demand that the analyst encourage the analysand's unfettered free association, and among other suggested rules for assuring this
Freud insists that the analyst must maintain the appearance of "emotional coldness"[23] or total neutrality. Any positive or negative indication by the analyst will only serve to deform the course of free association and thus restrict the analysand's freedom. The convention of the
forty-five- or fifty-minute analytic hour allows the psychoanalytic dialogue to be interrupted without the active intervention of the analyst
and is designed to preserve her neutrality.

Lacan recasts the controversy in terms of an opposition between the
notion of time as that within which the unconscious comes to reveal
itself in the course of the analysand's free association and the notion of
time as measured by the clock. Given the inevitable meaningfulness of
any intervention in the analysand's discourse, Lacan maintains that "the
suspension of a session cannot *not* be experienced by the subject as a
punctuation in his progress" (*E,* 313/98). It is absurd, then, to think
that analytic neutrality is preserved by the arbitrary cutting off of a
psychoanalytic session after fifty minutes. Sessions must be just as long
as it takes for some fragment of the truth to be spoken, and this ideal
duration cannot be predetermined. For some analysands at certain
points in their analyses, the sessions may need to be quite long; for
others at other points, the sessions may properly be ended after a rather
brief duration.[24] In any case, the actual length of sessions is an essential
and crucially important dimension of the dialectic of psychoanalysis,
and it is the one dimension over which the analyst asserts (and appears
to the analysand to assert) an actual control.

Thus, the time of the psychoanalytic dialogue is in effect the time in
which the narrated history of the analysand is received, gathered, and
recorded by the analyst, all three operations being founded on her
action of punctuating the analysand's discourse by ending sessions and
by, ultimately, bringing the analysis itself to a close. In performing
these rather humble and almost "scribal" functions, the analyst is nevertheless doing what can be done in allowing the truth to be realized in
the subject: "But above all he [the analyst] remains the master of the
truth of which this discourse is the progress. As I have said, it is he
above all who punctuates its dialectic. And here he is apprehended as
the judge of the value of this discourse" (*E,* 313/98). Lacan goes so far
as to compare the analyst's acts of controlling time in the analytic
dialogue to the adding of punctuation to sacred texts, where both
actions serve to resolve the ambiguity, for better or worse, of the

discourses involved. "It is a fact, which can be plainly seen in the study of the manuscripts of symbolic writings, whether it is a question of the Bible or of the Chinese canonicals, that the absence of punctuation in them is a source of ambiguity. The punctuation, once inserted, fixes the meaning; changing the punctuation renews or upsets it; and a faulty punctuation amounts to a change for the worse" (*E,* 313–14/98–99). Lacan's thesis about the importance of punctuation can be easily illustrated. A sequence of words, even if it is grammatically correct, remains dependent for its ultimate meaning on the points at which pauses are introduced into it. In the absence of such punctuation, signification remains indeterminate, and multiple conflicting meanings remain virtually present.[25] The sequence of words "I am a child like father" might, for example, be understood as a comment either about the speaker's father—"I am a child, like Father"—or about the speaker himself—"I am a childlike father." Only the punctuation of this word sequence allows a firm meaning to be grasped.[26]

Thus the meaning of an analysand's speech is ultimately fixed by the interpretative intervention of the analyst. While this intervention is clearly active—for example, taking the form of ending a day's session— it is not something capriciously initiated by the analyst. Rather, the movement of punctuation comes about as a response to the meaning *anticipated* by the analyst in the course of her close attention to the analysand's speech. This anticipated meaning is always already present in the analysand's speech, the linear sequence of which continually resolves ambiguities retroactively (only to generate others). As Lacan remarks in the seminar of 6 June 1956, "a signifying unity presupposes a certain closed circuit [*une certaine boucle bouclée*] which situates its different elements" (S 3, 298). Thus, the analyst's punctuation of the analysand's narrative simply marks in time a signification that this narrative would have achieved for itself *après-coup* (by "deferred action").[27] In this respect, the analyst's active intervention is passive as well. This passivity is emphasized in "Variantes de la cure-type," where Lacan argues that the analyst's knowledge (*savoir*) is in effect "a learned ignorance" (*une docte ignorance*): the ability to ignore what she knows and to avoid speaking (*E,* 349, 357–62).

The analyst's interpretation of the analysand's discourse is also in itself a performative use of language. This interpretation, precisely by introducing a "closure" to the analysand's associative discourse brings into existence "something new," namely the signification that was only virtually present in this discourse. We see here one of the ways "in which the signifier effects the advent of the signified, which is the only conceivable way that interpretation can produce anything new."[28] Of course, it is only by producing something new that interpretation— and the psychoanalytic dialogue as a whole—can be said to have any effect on the analysand and his suffering. As we have already seen, what is at stake here is quite literally the production of a new subject, since the analyst's responsibility grows from her power "to recognize" or "to abolish" the analysand as subject (E, 300/87). Thus, it is the performative dimension of the analyst's contribution to the analytic dialogue that makes this dialogue potentially therapeutic.

Lacan closes his treatment of time in psychoanalysis by insisting, in an uncharacteristic concession to his critics, that "I am not here to defend this procedure [of varying session-length], but to show that it has a precise dialectical meaning in its technical application" (E, 315/100). In a footnote added in 1966 (on the occasion of the publication of the Écrits), Lacan makes the further admission that "whether a damaged stone or a cornerstone, my strong point is that I have never yielded over this" (E, 300 n.1/112 n.106), suggesting that the issues involved in the session-length controversy remain live issues, worthy of continued debate.[29]

Thus, the psychoanalytic dialogue is best construed as a monologue by the analysand, in itself largely indeterminate in meaning, which is given a more determinate meaning by the punctuation that the analyst brings to it. For Lacan, it is primarily session endings that serve as appropriate punctuation marks for this dialogue. The truth of the human subject—that is, the realization of his ineluctable temporality and the consequent realization of the falsity of all the imaginary and symbolic masks by means of which he has tried to avoid this troubling truth—this truth is eventually captured in the discourse as narrated by the analysand and punctuated by the analyst, and it is at this point that the series of analytic sessions may be terminated. Curiously, Lacan ends his discussion by comparing his conception of analytic technique to teaching tactics common in Zen Buddhism (E, 315–16/100–101). The analyst's sudden ending of sessions is comparable to the Zen master's use in teaching of bizarre questions and apparently irrational responses. The analyst's interventions serve to reduce the analysand's faith in the imaginary and symbolic illusions that have sustained his self-méconnaissance, just as the Zen student's faith in rationality is reduced by the master's behavior. Moreover, within the progress of a psychoanalysis, the fundamental truth that the subject realizes is the nothingness that constitutes human temporality, just as the Zen student comes to realize the nothingness (*śūnyatā* or "emptiness") that constitutes all things.[30]

Death and the Psychoanalytic Cure

It may appear that Lacan considers the analyst to be in complete control of the psychoanalytic dialogue. Despite insisting that the analyst is "the master of the truth" revealed in the analysand's discourse, and despite stressing that the analyst works on the same side of "the wall of language" as the analysand (at the level of speech rather than at the level of some unknown and inaccessible reality of the analysand), Lacan nevertheless does not minimize the difficulties facing the analyst. Far from being "the master of the situation," the analyst continually faces the analysand's opposition, in a variety of forms, to progress in the analytic dialogue, opposition that the psychoanalytic tradition has dubbed "the negative therapeutic reaction" (*E,* 316/101).[31] Without naming his opponents, Lacan suggests that a popular psychoanalytic understanding of this reaction ties it to "a primordial masochism," itself characterized as "a pure manifestation" of the "death instinct" that Freud had introduced into psychoanalytic theory in *Beyond the Pleasure Principle* (1920). The problem with such an account is that it really fails to explain anything, since it in no way shows why moments of insight into his truth should provoke the analysand into hostility toward the analyst and the process of psychoanalysis. However, the account offered at least does have the virtue of bringing in the death instinct, which Lacan describes as "this culminating point of Freud's doctrine" (*E,* 316/101).

What Lacan intends to "demonstrate" in the final pages of "Function and Field" is "the profound relationship uniting the notion of the death instinct to the problems of speech" (*E,* 316/101). It must be stressed that Lacan reads *Beyond the Pleasure Principle* (as he so often reads Freud in general) more for evocative suggestions than for clear indications of theory. Here he weaves an elaborate philosophical tapestry around a few hints in Freud's text and at the same time plays down precisely the pessimistic biologism that has struck many other readers of Freud's book.[32] Thus, after reviewing the problematic status of the death instinct in psychoanalytic theory, emphasizing in particular that "it is not a question of biology" (*E,* 317/102), Lacan comes to the heart of his position: "The death instinct essentially express[es] the limit of the historical function of the subject. This limit is death—not as an eventual coming-to-term of the life of the individual, nor as the empirical certainty of the subject, but, as Heidegger's formula puts it, as that 'possibility which is one's ownmost, unconditional, unsupersedable, certain and as such indeterminable (*unüberholbare*)', for the subject— 'subject' understood as meaning the subject defined by his historicity" (*E*, 318/103). The reference to Heidegger here brings us back to the familiar theme of temporality and to the idea that the meaningfulness of life as well as of speech is necessarily anticipatory, that is, essentially forged in relation to the human subject's future. Just as my utterance can be understood by a listener only by anticipating what I am likely to say next, so too the events of a subject's life come to have meaning only through their relationship to a future point in that life that is somehow essential and revelatory of meaning.

Death is such an essential and revelatory future moment, not because it is a nonarbitrary end point of life, but because it is the one part of the subject's life that cannot be taken away from the subject: one's death is unavoidably one's own. In the passage of *Being and Time* immediately following that quoted by Lacan, Heidegger elaborates precisely this point, although his language preserves the phenomenological emphasis that Lacan is in the midst of purging from his own work: "As such, death is something *distinctively* impending. Its existential possibility is based on the fact that Dasein is essentially disclosed to itself, and disclosed, indeed, as ahead-of-itself. This item in the structure of care has its most primordial concretion in Being-toward-death. As a phenomenon, Being-toward-the-end becomes plainer as Being toward that distinctive possibility of Dasein which we have characterized."[33]

Within the context of the psychoanalytic dialogue, this Heideggerian theme determines the aim of the analysand's self-narration. In telling the analyst the story of his life, the analysand is basically trying to frame an answer to the question, "Who am I?" The answer toward which the analytic dialogue tends—what Lacan terms "true speech"—is the realization in this subjective self-narrative of his essential being-toward-death. The realization of his temporality is the full realization—that is, the full "making real" in his self-narration—of the fact that he is a mortal creature. It is in the light of this realization of mortality that the events of his life, as well as their being brought together into the whole of this life, take on an authentic and unequivocal meaning. Summing up the real import of Freud's teaching, Lacan remarks that life "has only one meaning, that in which desire is borne by death."[34]

For this mortal meaning to be disclosed as the ultimate signification of the analysand's self-narration, mortality must be intimated in the analyst's interventions in this narrative. This is in part naturally achieved, thanks to the disruptive, "session-killing," effects of her punctuating intervention. Lacan goes further, however, to urge in a number of texts that the analyst make death (*la mort*) present in the analytic dialogue by playing dead. Developing an analogy between the analytic situation and a game of bridge, Lacan argues that the analyst is to be seen as the dummy (*le mort*) in the game, keeping silent no matter how she is dealt with by the analysand.[35]

Given this account, there is no need to postulate a "primordial masochism" to explain the analysand's opposition to the disclosure of his truth in the psychoanalytic dialogue. Rather, this opposition is properly understood as a denial of the real constituted by death. In a similar manner, Lacan argues, the young child's acquisition of speech serves as a means of successfully denying the real obstructions in the way of his constant pleasure. The *"Fort! Da!"* game described by Freud—significantly enough, in *Beyond the Pleasure Principle*—was, as we have seen, devised by Freud's grandson as a way to cope with weaning, and Lacan argues (clearly using Freud's text as little more than a springboard to his own theories) that this text is to be taken as emblematic of the acquisition of language (*E*, 318–19/103).

What we now need to understand—and this is part of what the analysand comes to understand in the course of the analytic dialogue—is that the interlacing of language and mortality brings us back to the Lacanian concept of desire, since "the moment in which desire becomes human is also that in which the child is born into language" (*E*, 319/ 103). When biological need is articulated as demand, what is left over constitutes desire, and, as we have seen, desire is thus made dependent upon language for its existence, even though it is precisely that which cannot be adequately expressed in language. When Freud's grandson begins to play the game of alternating phonemes—*Fort! Da!*—"his action thus negatives the field of forces of desire [*Elle négative ainsi le champ de forces du désir*] in order to become its own object to itself" (*E*, 319/103). The toy, which the little boy would make disappear over the edge of his bed, was taking the place of his mother, and the act of making it disappear was a kind of destruction of her. In the place of the mother—constituting a presence in her absence—the boy puts the sound, *"Fort!,"* a sound picked up from the family. In doing this, "the child begins to become engaged in the system of the concrete discourse of the environment" (*E*, 319/103). Thus, the child's first utterances are both private objects for his own manipulation and cultural legacies, so that Lacan can write: "*Fort! Da!* It is precisely in his solitude that the desire of the little child has already become the desire of another, of an *alter ego* who dominates him and whose object of desire is henceforth his own affliction" (*E*, 319/104). This is an affliction that psychoanalysis comes to "cure," or at least relieve, and Lacan suggests that Freud's therapeutic technique is able to accomplish this aim only because of the intimation of mortality at the heart of language itself.

In the previous chapter I introduced Lacan's use of Alexandre Kojève's lectures on Hegel's *Phenomenology of Spirit* in an effort to clarify Lacan's fusion of Hegelian themes with Saussure's structuralist account of language. Now, at the conclusion of his major theoretical statement, Lacan returns to Kojève's Hegel, bringing many of the threads of "Function and Field" together in a single aphorism: "Thus the symbol manifests itself first of all as the murder of the thing, and this death constitutes in the subject the eternalization of his desire" (*E*, 319/104). Desire is eternalized—that is, made essentially unsatisfiable—as part of the same process by which the symbolic world of language substitutes itself for the world of objects. Lacan's text here echoes that of Kojève, who writes:

In Chapter VII of the *Phenomenology*, Hegel said that all *conceptual* understanding (*Begreifen*) is equivalent to a *murder*. Let us, then, recall what he had in view. As long as the Meaning (or Essence, Concept, Logos, Idea, etc.) is embodied in an empirically existing entity, this Meaning or Essence, as well as this entity, *lives*. For example, as long as the Meaning (or Essence) "dog" is embodied in a sensible entity, this Meaning (Essence) *lives*: it is the real dog, the living dog which runs, drinks, and eats. But when the Meaning (Essence) "dog" passes into the *word* "dog"—that is, becomes *abstract* Concept which is *different* from the sensible reality that it reveals by its Meaning—the Meaning (Essence) *dies*: the *word* "dog" does not run, drink, and eat; in it the Meaning (Essence) *ceases* to live—that is, it *dies*. And that is why the *conceptual* understanding of empirical reality is equivalent to a *murder*.[36]

In "murdering" the real world of objects and thereby constituting a reality inherently structured by the system of language, the human subject undergoes a transformation from a biological organism with needs that can be simply satisfied to a human being with unavoidable and fundamentally frustrating desires.

Such a situation clearly has immense consequences for the concept of human freedom, and Lacan approaches this issue (again very much under the sway of Kojève) along the path of Hegel's dialectic of master and slave in the *Phenomenology of Spirit* (1807).[37] In this, Lacan is almost certainly influenced by Sartre's example in *Being and Nothingness*,[38] although he comes much closer than Sartre to sharing Hegel's critique of the Cartesian *cogito*. Hegel argues that self-consciousness emerges as the result of a life-and-death struggle between two consciousnesses. If this struggle does not lead to the death of at least one of these protagonists, it is because one of them has yielded to the other and has accepted slavery as the price for living. The master/slave dialectic, then, reveals the surprising truth that it is the slave who realizes a genuine self-consciousness, because he is able to find himself in the product of his labor.[39] The master, in contrast, is left in the position of a pure consuming consciousness, utterly dependent upon the slave's labor and living in a world that is fundamentally alienating, because it is really that of the slave. The master's freedom to consume, then, turns out to be dependent upon the slave's freedom to attain self-consciousness, and it is precisely this self-consciousness that the master cannot attain.[40]

It is this Hegelian argument that lies behind a particularly dense paragraph in "Function and Field." Lacan writes: "Man's freedom is entirely inscribed within the constituting triangle of the renunciation that he imposes on the desire of the other by the menace of death for the enjoyment of the fruits of his serfdom—of the consented-to sacrifice of his life for the reasons that give to human life its measure—and of the suicidal renunciation of the vanquished partner, depriving of his victory the master whom he abandons to his inhuman solitude" (E, 320/104). In Lacanian terms, it seems there are but three possibilities for us as human subjects, all of which involve renunciation. Like the master, we can enjoy the satisfaction of our needs, at the cost of our humanity. Like the slave, we can realize our humanity, our self-consciousness, our truth as temporal beings, but only at the cost of remaining eternally caught up in desire, eternally unsatisfied. Finally, following the example of neither master nor slave, we can give in to death, thereby renouncing both our animality and our humanity. In any event, it is death that triangulates our options.

Within this highly restricted domain of human freedom, it is clear in which direction Lacan is asking us to direct ourselves. If the goal of psychoanalysis is the analysand's assumption of the truth of his history as a human subject, and if this truth is to be identified with the essential temporality of the human being, then the fully analyzed analysand is most comparable to Hegel's slave, who has authentically assumed his being-toward-death: "So when we wish to attain in the subject what was before the serial articulations of speech, and what is primordial to the birth of symbols, we find it in death, from which his existence takes on all the meaning it has. . . . To say that this mortal meaning reveals in speech a center exterior to language is more than a metaphor; it manifests a structure" (E, 320/105). It is our relation to our death that is authentically ours and can be denied only imperfectly by our imaginary identifications with ideal images or by our acceptance of symbolic roles. It is death that gives human life meaning and that thus serves as the ex-centric center of our speaking and of our living.

Death and desire are thus intimately related in Lacanian theory: indeed, the subject's assumption of his mortality is itself also the assumption of his desire. Throughout his work of the 1950s Lacan repeatedly emphasizes that the ultimate aim of psychoanalysis as a therapeutic technique is precisely the analysand's "avowal" of his desire.[41] Desire is avowed only when the analysand assumes the full truth of his being a subject, and this assumption of subjectivity entails a new relationship between the subject and desire. Analysis liberates the subject from the alienation or neurosis resulting from the unconscious play of desire by bringing to the level of conscious realization the effects of desire on human beings. In "The Direction of the Treatment" Lacan makes this point in an aphorism: "Desire merely subjects what analysis makes subjective" (E, 623/260). Thus, analysis works against both the analysand's falling victim to playing an alienating role as defined by the symbolic systems into which he is born and his flight to an imaginary moi identity. The former danger is, Lacan believes, that to which ego psychology, with its ethics of adaptation, particularly contributes. The latter danger is that which Lacan claims is more likely to come up in analytic practice. As early as "Some Reflections on the Ego" (written in 1951), he explicitly identifies the moi (here termed the "ego") as a force of "resistance to the elusive process of Becoming, to the variations of Desire."[42] In the name of leading the analysand to assume this desire, Lacan stresses the need for the subject to be liberated from the moi's illusory identity, going so far as to encourage "the disintegration of the imaginary unity constituted by the ego [moi]."[43]

Such a dramatic recommendation forcefully raises the question of just what kind of "cure" for human suffering is promised by Lacanian psychoanalysis. As it happens, this question is not at all clearly resolved by Lacan during the 1950s. On the one hand, he writes of his own experience "of the suffering we relieve in analysis."[44] On the other hand, "Variantes de la cure-type" argues that psychoanalysis be defined strictly as "the treatment that one expects from a psychoanalyst" (*E,* 329), leaving entirely out of the account just what it actually is that the analyst accomplishes in this treatment. In the same article (one of the very few of his writings that did not originate in an oral presentation), Lacan reminds his readers of the fact that even Freud admitted that the cure (*la guérison*) is a surplus benefit of psychoanalytic treatment (*la cure psychanalytique*) (*E,* 324–25), not something essentially aimed at by the analyst in the course of the treatment.[45] This apparent resistance to the idea of cure in Lacanian theory is rather starkly expressed in the text by which Lacan founded the École freudienne de Paris in 1964, where he insists that training analyses are not to be restricted to those candidates with medical degrees, "pure psychoanalysis not being in itself a therapeutic technique."[46]

If psychoanalysis is not essentially therapeutic and if the assumption by the analysand of his desire is not guaranteed to be a cure for his suffering, then what exactly is the psychoanalyst doing?[47] Throughout his work, Lacan's consistent answer to this question is that psychoanalysis is effectively an ethical discipline,[48] a discipline as a result of which the analysand emerges as a responsible, ethical agent, that is, as a fully human being. In this discipline, the analyst plays the role of "the moral master, the master who initiates the one still in ignorance into the dimension of fundamental human relationships and who opens for him what one might call the way to moral consciousness, even to wisdom, in assuming the human condition."[49] Such a position may suggest that the analyst is herself in possession of moral wisdom. Indeed, the requirement that would-be psychoanalysts undergo analysis themselves as the fundamental component of their training would seem to be justified if analysis does lead to such wisdom. It is important to note, however, that Lacan remains unalterably opposed to anything that might lead the analysand to take the analyst as a model to be imitated. If the analyst does possess moral wisdom, part of this wisdom will be the "learned ignorance," the unwisdom, required to assist the analysand in his assumption of his own truth and to foreclose the possibility of her becoming a model. If the analyst is a master of sorts, this is required in order that she may better serve.

What, then s the content of this ethical wisdom? Lacan devoted the entire semina of 1959–60, *L'éthique de la psychanalyse* (The ethics of psychoanalys to this question, and in the final session of the year he summarized t essential ethical teaching of psychoanalysis in a para-

dox: "I propose that the only thing of which one can be guilty, at least
in the analytic perspective, is to have given up on one's desire [*c'est
d'avoir cédé sur son désir*]" (S 7, 368). The "common man" is one who
betrays his desire on a regular basis, giving it up either for the sake of
some social, symbolic good (thereby settling for his identity as a *je*) or
for the sake of his own imaginary satisfaction (thereby retreating to the
moi). The "hero," in contrast, is precisely the one who does not give up
on his desire, despite countless social incentives to do so, the one who
has authentically "acted in conformity with his desire."[50] What the
psychoanalyst offers the analysand is the opportunity to recognize and
to assume his own desire, so that he can then act in conformity with
this desire. What the psychoanalyst holds out is the faith that there is
an authentically satisfactory (though not necessarily "satisfying") identity to be achieved in the *béance* between the *je* and the *moi*. Action in
conformity with desire serves "to re-establish a more human relationship"[51] between the analysand and the analyst but also between the
newly realized human subject and the other people in his world. As
Lacan remarks in a typically anti-American aside in "The Freudian
Thing," "the terms of psychoanalytic intervention . . . make it sufficiently clear, I think, that its ethic is not an individualist one" (*E*, 416/
127). The human subject produced by the dialectic of psychoanalysis is
one almost painfully aware of the extent to which his subjectivity exists
only as a complex structure, as "an inmixing of an otherness."

The fact that death lies at the heart of the psychoanalytic dialogue
guarantees that the dialectic of analysand and analyst is not reduced
simply to the level of an individual's coming to grips with his mortality. As a quasi-Hegelian slave caught up in desire, the analysand
emerges from the analytic dialogue in essential relation to others. Indeed, the notion of cure that remains largely implicit in "Function and
Field" is precisely the notion of encouraging a kind of self-narration
that in the full assumption of the narrator's being-toward-death, allows
him to act in the world of others with authentic self-knowledge, free of
the various forms of *méconnaissance* that typically alienate the self from
others.[52] This leads Lacan to a final, technical point: "The question of
the termination of the analysis is that of the moment when the satisfaction of the subject finds a way to come to realization in the satisfaction
of everyone—that is, of all those whom this satisfaction associates with
itself in a human undertaking" (*E*, 321/105).[53] This is not a matter of
the analysand's adaptation to the demands of his environment, in the
sense that ego psychology understands the notion of adaptation as

integral to the psychoanalytic cure. Rather, this passage suggests that the termination of analysis ultimately may depend as much upon a subjectively informed reorganization of society as upon the individual's adjusting to a preexisting social order. It is this vaguely utopian hint that helps ground Lacan's suggestion that "of all the undertakings that have been proposed in this century, that of the psychoanalyst is perhaps the loftiest" (*E*, 321/105).

"Function and Field" comes to a close with a brief coda, in which Lacan dramatically paraphrases a fragment of the Bṛhadāraṇyaka Upaniṣad,[54] simultaneously alluding to T. S. Eliot's *The Waste Land* and reemphasizing his own fundamental theme, that "the gift of speech" is the "privileged field" of psychoanalysis (*E*, 322/106–7). In the Upaniṣad, Prajāpati, the god of thunder, rumbles three times, and each rumble is understood by a particular class of disciples to mean something different. What the thunder says each time is "*Da!*" thereby foreshadowing or echoing Freud's grandson in *Beyond the Pleasure Principle*. What the *deva*s understand by this is "*Dāmyata*, master yourselves"; what the men understand by this is "*Datta*, give"; what the *asura*s understand by this is "*Dayādhvam*, be merciful." And Prajāpati insists that all have heard and understood him properly.

This conclusion evokes many things in the context of Lacan's appearance in Rome. Not least, it calls to mind the ambiguity with which Eliot invested this fragment of the Upaniṣads when he used it as the closing benediction of *The Waste Land*,[55] an ambiguity that no doubt also marked Lacan's call in 1953 for an almost spiritual renewal of the practice and theory of psychoanalysis. Clearly it is also meant to be understood as an exemplary instance of the essentially dialectical existence of speech in which any word spoken gains its meaning only in relation to the other to whom it is addressed. As we saw in chapter 1, the response to Lacan's manifesto on the part of the international psychoanalytic community clearly confirmed the truth of this Lacanian point. It is the decade between "Function and Field" and Lacan's final "excommunication" from the International Psychoanalytic Association, a decade full of teaching and institutional strife, that provides Lacan's Rome report with its full significance.

Chapter Five

The Psychoanalyst as Textual Analyst

Despite the facts that Lacan was essentially a psychoanalyst, that his teaching seminars were meant primarily for analysts in training, and that his published writings were grounded in a close reading of Freud's texts through the prism of his own experience as a psychoanalyst, in the United States Lacan's work came first to the attention of literary critics. Indeed, nearly a decade after his death, in this country Lacan remains read much more often in academic departments of literature than in psychoanalytic institutes, and the vast majority of the many articles and books in English dealing with Lacan are written from the perspective of literary criticism.[1] On the one hand, this fact about the intellectual appropriation of Lacan is largely due to the enthusiastic response of North American literary critics to recent French theoretical writings in general; Lacan has come to be read in circles of literary theoreticians trained on the works of Roland Barthes and Jacques Derrida. On the other hand, Lacan's position in current literary criticism is to a great extent a product of the contingent fact that the first mature essays of his published in English—"The Insistence of the Letter in the Unconscious" (1957) and "Seminar on 'The Purloined Letter' " (1956)—both appeared in the influential literary critical journal, *Yale French Studies,* in 1966 and 1972, respectively,[2] and included rather direct discussions of literary texts and figures of speech.

As a matter of fact, Lacan's seminars of the 1950s included a great deal of literary commentary. Using his thorough knowledge of ancient literature and of the French classics, Lacan was able to illustrate quite casually with literary examples his points about the importance of language and speech to the proper theorizing of the psychoanalytic experience. In the course of the 1950s, Lacan's use of specific literary texts underwent a profound development. Where he began by using these texts simply to illustrate points of psychoanalytic theory, he ended the decade by using literary texts and psychoanalytic concepts in tandem to develop something approaching a new aesthetics. It is to three examples of extended literary analysis that I turn in the present chapter.[3]

Poe's "Letter"

In 1966 Lacan chose to open the mammoth collection of his writings, *Écrits*, with "Le seminar sur 'La Lettre volée' " ("Seminar on 'The Purloined Letter' ") (*E*, 11–61).[4] This text had its origins in the seminar of 1954–55, devoted in general to the role of the *moi* in Freudian theory and technique (see S 2, 207–40/175–205). For its appearance in the *Écrits*, the version first published in 1957 was augmented by a twenty-page trio of introductory texts provocatively printed after the seminar's text. To introduce his writings to the general public by beginning with a commentary on Edgar Allan Poe and by elaborating an already difficult text with an extensive and obscure introduction suggests that Lacan thought of this text as doing more than simply developing a psychoanalytic reading of Poe's tale. Indeed, the reader who comes to the "Seminar" expecting some sort of psychobiographical approach to Poe, some sort of account of the way "The Purloined Letter" reveals the character of its author's neurosis, is bound to be surprised by Lacan's commentary.[5] Not only does he not treat the literary text as a symptom of Poe's illness, but he does not even approach the tale directly with the aim of writing a commentary on it. Rather, Lacan uses Poe's text essentially to introduce his own theory of the role of the signifier—and thus of speech and language—in the constitution of human subjectivity. "The Purloined Letter" is offered as an emblem of the radical truth that Freud's discovery of the unconscious brought to the human sciences, and in this way the tale is read as both an illustration of and a commentary on Lacan's distinctively linguistic reading of Freud.

That Lacan's approach to Poe's tale is by means of a highly theoretical reflection on psychoanalytic practice is made clear in his opening paragraphs. Here he describes the "lesson of this seminar" in terms of showing how imaginary features of experience manifest the human being's "capture in a *symbolic* dimension." The fragments of our imaginary *moi* identity "reveal only what in it [our experience] remains inconsistent unless they are related to the symbolic chain which binds and orients them" (*E*, 11/28). In other words, the central point of the

"Seminar" is that it is the symbolic chain of signifiers and its laws that determine the effects of subjectivity relevant to psychoanalytic theory; products of the imaginary "figure only as shadows and reflections in the process" (*E,* 11/29). In short, Lacan is again pursuing his fundamental theory that "it is the symbolic order which is constitutive for the subject" (*E,* 12/29).

The status of "The Purloined Letter" in the "Seminar" appears somewhat marginal at first. Lacan claims, however, that he will illustrate the truth revealed in the work of Freud "by demonstrating in a story the decisive orientation which the subject receives from the itinerary of a signifier" (*E,* 12/29), suggesting that Poe's tale is offered here not simply as a privileged example of the truth brought by Freud but as an illustration carrying the force of demonstration. In fact, a careful reading of the "Seminar" reveals that the demonstrative force at issue here comes, not from Poe's text itself, but from the particular way in which Lacan reads and analyzes this text.[6]

The key to Lacan's reading lies in his systematic distinction between "a drama, its narration, and the conditions of that narration" (*E,* 12/29) as found in Poe. While these three dimensions of the tale could not exist without one another, Lacan discusses them separately so as to bring out several distinct theoretical points. Beginning with the drama, he notes that it is constructed in the form of two scenes, the second of which is a precise structural repetition of the first (*E,* 12/30).

The first scene, which Lacan does not hesitate to describe as "the primal scene" (*E,* 12/30), takes place in the royal apartments, where the Queen finds herself surprised by the King as she peruses the contents of a letter, which it is important he not see. In her effort to keep this letter from the King's attention, the Queen simply places it, open but upside down, upon a table. At this moment the Minister D—— appears, immediately perceiving the situation and grasping how it might be turned to his advantage. Producing another letter, the Minister manages to substitute it for the Queen's letter, taking the latter with him as he leaves the royal couple. All of this is carefully noticed by the Queen, while the King remains utterly unaware of anything but the Minister's official concern with public affairs.[7]

The second scene takes place some eighteen months later in the Minister's office at his hotel. In the meantime, the Prefect of police and his officers have thoroughly but fruitlessly searched the Minister's hotel, going over every inch of space within it with any number of elaborate techniques designed to find the letter's hiding-place. The private detective Dupin calls on the Minister and, with the intent of looking carefully for the purloined letter, wears a pair of green glasses. The Minister greets Dupin while "pretending to be in the last extremity of *ennui*," and Dupin carries on a conversation of no particular import while he searches the room for evidence of the letter. Spotting a "much soiled and crumpled" letter resting in a card-rack dangling from the center of the Minister's mantelpiece, Dupin realizes that this is the missing letter (despite its bearing "*very* conspicuously" D——'s own black seal and despite its being addressed "in a diminutive female hand" to the Minister himself). After engaging the Minister in a long conversation, Dupin makes his exit, leaving behind as if forgotten his snuffbox. Returning the next morning to pick up this snuffbox, Dupin arranges for a commotion outside the windows of the hotel to distract the Minister, and in this moment of distraction he successfully takes the letter, substituting for it a facsimile bearing within it a nasty quotation from the French tragedian, Crébillon.[8]

Lacan argues that this second scene is a repetition of the first scene in the sense that both scenes involve three fundamental positions, which effectively determine the actions of those persons who occupy them (*E*, 14–15/31–32). The first position, occupied initially by the King and then by the police, is that of "a glance that sees nothing." This glance makes it possible for both the Queen and the Minister to keep the letter hidden. The second position, occupied by the Queen and then the Minister, is that of "a glance which sees that the first sees nothing and deludes itself as to the secrecy of what it hides." It is the delusion that follows from this glance that makes possible the theft of the letter, first by the Minister and then by Dupin. The third position, occupied by the successful thieves, is that of a glance that "sees that the first two glances leave what should be hidden exposed to whomever would seize it." These three positions essentially define the "intersubjectivity" in terms of which the various characters' actions can be shown to be meaningfully chosen.[9] Thus, the second scene repeats the first, not simply because it involves the theft of the letter, but because the two thefts are motivated by a precisely similar intersubjective structure. Lacan's point here is, crucially, that the actions of the individuals involved are explained in terms of a repeating intersubjective structure and not in terms of the desires, purposes, or interests of those individuals.

What we have here, then, Lacan suggests, is a startling example of what Freud described in *Beyond the Pleasure Principle* as the compulsion to repeat (*Wiederholungszwang*), which Lacan renders in French as *l'automatisme de répétition* (repetition automatism) (*E*, 15–16/32). Freud had been struck by the fact that many neurotic symptoms (and, indeed, many symptomatic behaviors characteristic of everyday life) manifest themselves repetitively. Insofar as these symptoms essentially repeat in a disguised way fundamentally traumatic experiences (the memories of which have been repressed into the unconscious), the continual repeating of such painful experiences is apparently inexplicable by the pleasure principle, the principle that all mental events are regulated by the more or less mechanical lowering of intrapsychical tension.[10] The central argument of *Beyond the Pleasure Principle* aims to explain the repetition compulsion as a consequence of the generally "conservative" nature of the instincts, a conservatism that introduces the notion of the death instinct into Freudian theory.[11]

The first stage in seeing how Lacan relates his analysis of "The Purloined Letter" to these Freudian speculations is to note that the drama's second scene repeats the structure of the first scene without this repetition's being in any way a result of the operation of the pleasure principle. That the Minister assumes the position of the Queen is in no way explained by appeal to levels of tension within his psychical apparatus. Rather, it is explained by appeal to a three-position structure of intersubjectivity. Lacan himself points up the radical character of such a form of explanation by reminding his readers that this is just another way of putting his fundamental formula, "*the unconscious is the discourse of the Other*" (*E*, 16/32): to grasp the character of an individual's unconscious is to grasp the structure of the intersubjective relations (relations between self and Other) constituting him as a subject. Lacan argues further, however, that repetition automatism "finds its basis in what we have called the *insistence* of the signifying chain" (*E*, 11/28), and to introduce this specifically linguistic dimension of his analysis Lacan turns from the drama of Poe's tale to its narration.

"The Purloined Letter" features several layers of narration, the entire tale being narrated by an unnamed friend of Dupin. What Lacan focuses on in the "Seminar" is the way that each of the two scenes of the drama is narrated in the course of a different kind of dialogue, this dialogic contrast constituting the symbolic drama that sustains the reader's interest. What makes these dialogues different is "the opposite use they make of the powers of speech" (*E*, 18/34): in effect, the dialogues contrast two very distinct analyses of the relation between language and speech.

The "primal scene" of Poe's drama is narrated in the course of a dialogue between the Prefect of police and Dupin.[12] What Lacan emphasizes here is that the Prefect's telling of the Minister's theft of the letter from the Queen is itself an indirect narration: the Prefect tells Dupin (and his friend, Poe's narrator) the story as told to him (apparently) by the Queen herself. Central to the functioning of this narration is the presupposition that the content of the narrative neither loses nor gains anything in its retelling, that the Prefect's narration is essentially a "report" guaranteed to retransmit with "exactitude" the Queen's message, and that his speech in this case is perfectly transparent (*E,* 18–19/ 34–35). In other words, the first dialogue rests on a model of language as simply the communication of information and ignores the possibility of any speech's bearing a noninformational, performative dimension.

The scene of Dupin's retrieval of the letter from the Minister's hotel is narrated by Dupin himself in a dialogue with his unnamed friend. The most striking characteristic of this dialogue from Lacan's perspective is that Dupin prefaces his narrative with an extensive and erudite methodological digression, explaining how he managed to find the letter when all the police's efforts to do so had failed.[13] Comparing himself to a schoolboy skilled at winning in the guessing game of "even and odd," Dupin argues that success in detection depends upon a "*thorough* identification" between the detective's intellect and that of his opponent. Such "identification" demands that one get beyond one's own ways of reasoning, limited as they are by the individual's purposes and ingenuity, and focus attention on the structural relations defining the intersubjective field in which the act of detection occurs. Fundamental to Lacan's discussion is the claim that Dupin's narration acts within and, in effect, enacts "the register of truth," by revealing the very process of disclosure to us, while simultaneously hiding from us its application to the present case (*E,* 20–21/35–37). Invoking the name of Martin Heidegger, Lacan returns to the German philosopher's account of truth, noting that in Poe's tale "we rediscover a secret to which truth has always initiated her lovers, and through which they learn that it is in hiding that she offers herself to them *most truly" (E,* 21/37). Put another way, it is in Dupin's performance of the processes of detection and disclosure that "truth here reveals its fictive arrangement" (*E,* 17/ 34): it is through performative speech's ability to create something new that truth is brought onto the scene.

Having introduced this Heideggerian notion of a truth that simultaneously discloses and hides itself, Lacan is able to shift the domain of

his analysis from the manifest surface of Poe's text to its latent meaning. From Poe's drama and its narration, Lacan now turns to consider
"the conditions of that narration" (E, 12/29), the final and most important level of his study. Noting that Dupin's explanation of his methodology fails to enable the reader to solve the mystery of his discovery of the
purloined letter, Lacan turns his attention to a number of paradoxical
questions suggested by the very concept of a missing letter, thus introducing into his analysis recognizably Lacanian preoccupations about the
signifier. The paradoxes of the missing letter revolve around two questions: in what place does a letter exist (E, 23–25/38–40), and to whom
does a letter belong (E, 27–29/41–43)?

To the first of these questions, Lacan answers that Poe's tale makes it
clear that a letter must have "the property of *nullibiety*" (E, 23/38), that
is, a signifier is "nowhere" in the real, and this is made apparent by the
fact that, although they search everywhere in the Minister's hotel for
the letter, the police cannot find it. "Being by nature symbol only of an
absence," a signifier is simultaneously present and absent wherever it
goes, unlike real objects, which are inevitably in their places (E, 24–
25/39–40). In this way the signifier bears with it "the register of
truth." As Lacan remarks in the seminar of 16 April 1955, "it is truth
which is hidden, not the letter. For the policemen, the truth doesn't
matter, for them there is only reality, and that is why they do not find
anything" (S 2, 236/202). It is important to note, however, that the
truth of the letter does not reside simply in its meaning, and this is why
Poe never discloses the contents of the purloined letter: "It is not only
the meaning [*sens*] but the text [*texte*] of the message which it would be
dangerous to place in circulation" (E, 26/41). In other words, the
signifier as a material object is itself implicated in the signifier's symbolic truth—it is the signifier's materiality that allows it to transform
the human world performatively—and this suggests that the signifier is
unlike any other object (S 2, 232/198), inasmuch as it is simultaneously real and symbolic.

At this point, the second paradoxical question comes into play, since
it appears that the signifier, as being "nowhere," cannot legitimately
"belong" to anyone. If its truth is not exhausted in its function as
bearing meaning, and if its material existence is such that it is truly
present only as absent, is there any sense in which a signifier (for
example, a letter) could be possessed either by its sender or by its
recipient? Lacan's answer to this question, as we should expect by now,
leads him to discount the importance of human individuals in the

whole process by which a signifier passes from one person to another (a process typically misrecognized as "communication"). This point is perhaps put most clearly in his brief description of precisely how the letter "performs" in relation to the Queen: "From then on, to whatever vicissitudes the Queen may choose to subject the letter, it remains that the letter is the symbol of a pact, and that, even should the recipient not assume the pact, the existence of the letter situates her in a symbolic chain foreign to the one which constitutes her faith" (*E*, 28/42). The Queen's brief "holding" of the letter utterly transforms her intersubjective position, her status vis-à-vis all the other characters in Poe's tale, and it accomplishes this transformation regardless of the particular content of the letter and of the identity of the letter's sender. Thus, Lacan concludes: "Our fable is so constructed as to show that it is the letter and its diversion which governs their [the story's subjects] entries and roles. If *it* be "in sufferance," *they* shall endure the pain. Should they pass beneath its shadow, they become its reflection. Falling in possession of the letter—admirable ambiguity of language—its meaning possesses them" (*E*, 30/44). Although Lacan goes on to elaborate this point by considering in detail the ways the Minister and Dupin in turn find themselves transformed by their brief "holdings" of the letter (*E*, 30–41/44–53), the heart of Lacan's analysis remains that it is the signifier's "priority" over the signified (*E*, 28–29/42) that lies at "the very foundation of intersubjectivity" (*E*, 20/35).

It is this claim that brings us back to the Freudian notion of repetition automatism and to Lacan's attempt to show that this phenomenon "finds its basis in what we have called the *insistence* of the signifying chain" (*E*, 11/28). Maintaining that the subjects caught up in a relation of intersubjectivity "model their very being on the moment of the signifying chain which traverses them," thus taking their turns in the endlessly repeating intersubjective structure, Lacan drives home the moral of the "Seminar" in a much-quoted paragraph: "If what Freud discovered and rediscovers with a perpetually increasing sense of shock has a meaning, it is that the displacement of the signifier determines the subjects in their acts, in their destiny, in their refusals, in their blindness, in their end and in their fate, their innate gifts and social acquisitions notwithstanding, without regard for character or sex, and that, willingly or not, everything that might be considered the stuff of psychology, kit and caboodle, will follow the path of the signifier" (*E*, 30/43–44). This moral is rather dramatically recalled in the introductory material added to the "Seminar" for its appearance in the *Écrits*, where Lacan compares the human subject to a computer. Here, he argues that the laws of unconscious overdetermination of human symptomatic behavior can be identified explicitly with the laws of probability, which render intelligible a variety of phenomena apparently resulting from chance (see *E*, 59–60, as well as 29/43).[14]

If repetition automatism, the Freudian compulsion to repeat, is to be explained in this way as a product of the signifier's movement along a signifying chain, it remains for us to remember how the signifier also brings death into the dynamic of human desire and action. It is on this note that Lacan brings the "Seminar" to a close by allowing the purloined letter, the signifier itself, to remind his (its) readers that the signifier is in its very essence "that presence of death which makes of human life a reprieve obtained from morning to morning in the name of meanings whose sign is your crook" (*E*, 39/51): " 'You think you act when I stir you at the mercy of the bonds through which I knot your desires. Thus do they grow in force and multiply in objects, bringing you back to the fragmentation of your shattered childhood' " (*E*, 40/52). What the signifier is urging us to do is to confront the simple fact of our destiny as subjects permanently and unavoidably subjected to the signifier, and Lacan alludes playfully to Heidegger—from whom, as we saw in the previous chapter, much of his account of death is derived— in his final summation of the signifier's and the "Seminar" 's message: " 'Eat your Dasein' " (*E*, 40/52).[15]

Hamlet and Desire

Some five years after the seminar devoted in part to "The Purloined Letter," Lacan returned to a large-scale attempt at literary criticism in his seminar of 1958–59, the general topic of which was *Le désir et son interprétation* (Desire and its interpretation).[16] In the seven sessions held between 4 March and 29 April 1959, Lacan focused his attention on Shakespeare's *Hamlet*, using the greatest tragic drama of the English language to illustrate some of the more difficult features of his own theory of human desire.[17]

Hamlet, because it is a text that has provided grist for the mills of psychoanalysts from Freud on,[18] offers Lacan the perfect opportunity to contrast his approach to literature with that of other analysts. Dismissing much psychoanalytic literary interpretation as "hogwash [*calembre-daines*]" (*D*, 5:16/20), Lacan explicitly attacks the kind of psychoanalytic criticism that reduces works of literature to symptoms of their authors' neuroses: "To seek in works of art traces that provide information about the author is not to analyze the bearing of the work as such" (*D*, 3:15). To approach the work of art as such, however, involves not only the formal study of the work's structure; rather, it is essential that the analyst come to understand the special character of the relation between the work and its audience. Hence, in the case of a play like *Hamlet*, which most audiences find deeply moving, it is incumbent upon the literary analyst to grasp the way in which the play's structure challenges each audience member's own relation to his or her own desire (*D*, 3:16). In other words psychoanalytic literary criticism ought to take seriously the performative effect of a work of art on its audience, the way the work's structure directly changes the members of its audience.[19]

Lacan's treatment of *Hamlet* accomplishes this only in an indirect way: while arguing that the play reveals to its audience the tragic character of all human desire, he leaves it largely to us to elaborate precisely how this revelation is supposed to transform the audience. His strategy here—which he identifies as that characteristic of all genuine psychoanalytic interpretation by praising Ernest Jones's pursuit of the same strategy—is a matter of transforming a merely psychological account of the play into something else: "Not by making reference to a more profound psychology, but by implying a mythic arrangement, supposed to have the same meaning for all human beings" (*D*, 2:23). A work of art has the power to take a particular character, situation, or act and to highlight in this particular something of universal importance. It is this move from the particular to the universal that psychoanalytic criticism should not only explain but enact in its own move from the psychological to the mythic. In accomplishing this, such criticism will in fact be mirroring psychoanalytic practice itself, since "it is one of the clearest lessons of the analytic experience that the particular is that which has the most universal value" (*D*, 1:12).

Early in his seminar Lacan announces that "what distinguishes the tragedy of Hamlet, prince of Denmark, is that it is the tragedy of desire" (*D*, 2:18). At the beginning of the final session devoted to the play, he repeats this claim, but with the crucial addition that "from one end of *Hamlet* to the other, all anyone talks about is mourning" (*D*, 7:32/39). Indeed, the key to understanding Lacan's reading of the play lies in grasping the intimate connection between desire and mourning, a connection which he relates directly to the castration complex. Introducing his approach to *Hamlet*, Lacan explicitly claims that he is using Shakespeare's play "to reinforce our elaboration of the castration complex and to grasp how this is articulated in the concrete detail of our experience" (D, 1:8). If the "Seminar on 'The Purloined Letter' " emphasizes that human destiny is permanently subjected to the signifier, the *Hamlet* seminar deepens this claim with an analysis of such subjection in terms of castration.

"The drama of Hamlet is the encounter with death" (D, 4:26), Lacan remarks: Hamlet, of course, encounters death in the form of his father's ghost in the first act of the play and eventually encounters his own death in the bloodbath of the play's final scene. More crucially, Hamlet is forced, through the course of the play, to encounter and to come to grips with a form of death that lies at the heart of desire: the death of narcissism accomplished through the subject's giving up his claims to be or to have the phallus. It is the symbolic castration involved in this process—a castration marked by the phallus as a signifier being repressed (or "veiled") and replaced by "the name of the father"—that Shakespeare's play presents on the stage.

As is generally the case with his seminars, Lacan's path to *Hamlet* makes its approach through a return to particular texts by Freud. Before turning to Lacan's treatment of the play itself, then, it will prove useful to sketch the Freudian background of this treatment. Here Lacan emphasizes, not Freud's brief remarks on the play found in *The Interpretation of Dreams*, but two later theoretical essays, which Lacan persuasively argues need to be read together.

In a very brief essay of 1924, "The Dissolution of the Oedipus Complex,"[20] Freud focuses his attention on the process by which the oedipal situation—the child's complex of incestuous desires directed toward the parents—is dissolved or destroyed in the course of childhood development, to be replaced by the period of sexual latency. What Lacan emphasizes in Freud's account is that the Oedipus complex proves weaker than the child's narcissistic interest in his own body (D, 7:36–40/45–48). For example, Freud argues that the young boy comes to realize that both ways of satisfying his oedipal desires will entail castration: to love his mother is to open himself up to the father's castrating punishment, but to be the object of his father's love (that is, to assume his mother's position) requires his castration as well. Freud concludes: "If the satisfaction of love in the field of the Oedipus complex is to cost the child his penis, a conflict is bound to arise between his narcissistic interest in that part of his body and the libidinal cathexis of his parental objects. In this conflict the first of these forces normally triumphs: the child's ego turns away from the Oedipus complex."[21] While Freud goes on from this to explore the replacement of desire by identification in the post-oedipal phase, Lacan's interest remains directed toward desire. If the Oedipus complex is to be dissolved by a return to narcissism, it nevertheless remains the case that narcissism itself must be abandoned for desire. The child's desire for his parents must ultimately be transformed into desire for other persons; narcissism can only serve as a stage along the way to the subject's authentic assumption of desire.

Lacan maintains that this move from narcissism to desire requires the intermediary work of mourning: the child can move on from the parents as objects of desire to new objects of desire only by mourning adequately the loss of his own status as the unique focus of the parents' (and indeed of all others') desires. In short, the child dissolves the Oedipus complex by giving up his own claim to be the phallus, the imaginary object of the Other's (and the mother's) desire, that extraordinary object that fully satisfies all possible desire, but such a traumatic loss can be surmounted only through a rich and complete process of mourning. This theme of mourning the phallus leads Lacan to one of Freud's important metapsychological essays, "Mourning and Melancholia," first published in 1917.[22]

Freud argues that mourning is essentially a process by which the ego comes to grips with the loss of a desired object in reality, and this process involves a rather slow and sustained "reality-testing."[23] The aim here is to detach libido from the lost object "bit by bit," by forcing the ego to confront gradually the fact that the desired object no longer exists. Thus, "memories and expectations" focused upon the object are successively considered by the ego as it mourns, and the gap between these past and future images of the object and the object's present nonexistence poses a challenge to the ego's own narcissism: "The ego, confronted as it were with the question whether it shall share this fate, is persuaded by the sum of the narcissistic satisfactions it derives from being alive to sever its attachment to the object that has been abolished."[24] We see here the connection between mourning and the dissolution of the Oedipus complex, both of which are accomplished through the medium of narcissism, and this strengthens Lacan's claim that mourning is involved in the overcoming of oedipal desire.

Crucial, however, both to Freud's account of mourning and to Lacan's extension of this account is the claim that the process of mourning cannot satisfactorily rest in narcissistic satisfaction. Indeed, Freud's basic argument in "Mourning and Melancholia" is that what makes melancholia (or certain kinds of depression) pathological and thus distinguishes it from mourning is precisely that the melancholic subject remains rooted in narcissism: both conditions involve a process of detaching libido from a lost object, but the "normal" result of mourning is a "displacement" of this libido to a new object with narcissism serving only as an intermediate stage.[25] Thus, the successful issue of mourning is the finding of a new object of desire to replace the lost object in a way that closely parallels the finding of a new object of desire to replace the parents in the successful dissolution of the Oedipus complex. It is on these grounds that Lacan maintains that the resolution of the Oedipus complex is made possible through the successful mourning of the phallus.

Hamlet is a play about desire precisely because it displays in a graphic way the process by which mourning the lost phallus allows for the constitution of a new object of desire. It is "the tragedy of desire" because it displays as well the terrifying consequences of the narcissism that results from mourning too long postponed. From this perspective, then, Shakespeare's play is structured along the lines of three well-articulated themes: Hamlet's symbolic castration, his regression to narcissism, and the process of mourning through which he manages to assume his own identity as a desiring being and hence to act.

As the standard psychoanalytic account of Hamlet insists, the key to grasping Hamlet's curious inability to act lies in understanding his position vis-à-vis each of his parents. However, where Ernest Jones, for example, argues that Hamlet is simply caught in the grip of the Oedipus complex, confronted by the fact that "the thought of incest and parricide combined is too intolerable to be borne,"[26] Lacan stresses the idea that Hamlet is actually face to face with the unavoidable human reality of symbolic castration.

Hamlet is completely dependent upon his mother's desire, in effect replaying the role of the pre-oedipal child in his desire to be the phallus that the mother lacks. Hamlet is equally dependent upon his father for the oedipal knowledge that he cannot in fact be the phallus; indeed, Lacan will argue that the message brought by the ghost of Hamlet's father is that symbolic castration is an ineluctable fact of human existence.

From the second scene of act 1, Shakespeare makes it clear that Hamlet is dominated by his mother's desire: in response to her request that he remain at home, rather than going to Wittenberg, Hamlet

replies, "I shall in all my best obey you, madam" (*Hamlet,* 1.2.120).
This position of dependency upon the mother's desire reaches its dramatic peak in the confrontation scene between Hamlet and the queen at
the end of act 3. The scene begins as an extraordinarily brutal attempt
by Hamlet to force his mother to recognize and acknowledge her own
guilt for her husband's murder. This attempt is both motivated by
Hamlet's loyalty to his father's ghost and undermined by the ghost's
appearance to Hamlet alone in the course of the scene. Her son's
apparently insane behavior in speaking of a presence invisible to her,
taken in conjunction with his unthinking murder of Polonius, leads
Gertrude to the despairing conclusion that Hamlet is mad. In an effort
to dispel this belief, Hamlet confesses his own feigned madness to the
queen, but in doing so he simultaneously reveals the true extent to
which his desire is modeled upon hers. The scene's climax comes in
Hamlet's response to his mother's question, "What shall I do?":

> Not this, by no means, that I bid you do:
> Let the bloat king tempt you again to bed,
> Pinch wanton on your cheek, call you his mouse,
> And let him, for a pair of reechy kisses,
> Or paddling in your neck with his damned fingers,
> Make you to ravel all this matter out,
> That I essentially am not in madness,
> But mad in craft.
>
> (*Hamlet,* 3.4.182–89)

This is a passage tailor-made to show Hamlet as possessed with an
incestuous and oedipal desire for his mother, as the standard psychoanalytic reading of the play demands. What Lacan stresses, however, is
that the desire revealed here "is far from being his own. It is not his
desire for his mother; it is the desire of his mother" (*D,* 3:20).

In short, what the confrontation scene reveals is that Hamlet's desire
remains completely at the mercy of what his mother desires. Despite
his efforts to make Gertrude give up her desire for Claudius for the sake
of his father's memory, Hamlet's response shows how he ends up surren-
dering totally to precisely this desire. Indeed, the very way he speaks in
this passage shows how completely he himself is in the grip of her
desire, forced to express her desire even as he makes his demand upon
her (see *D,* 3:20–21). As Lacan notes, Hamlet remains under the sway

of his mother's desire until the very end of the play, his failure to act
showing that he himself does not choose between Claudius and his
father any more than does Gertrude (*D*, 5:12–13).

Commenting on the confrontation scene, Lacan notes:

> There is no moment where, in a more complete way, the formula that *the desire
> of man is the desire of the Other* is more evident, more accomplished, completely
> annuling the subject.
>
> Hamlet addresses himself here to the Other, his mother, but beyond her
> herself—not with his own will, but with that of which he is for the moment the
> support, namely that of the father, and as well that of order, decency, and
> modesty. . . . In front of his mother, he carries on this discourse beyond her
> herself; then falls back, that is, he falls back to the level of the Other, before
> whom he can only capitulate. (*D*, 3:23)

Not only is Hamlet's desire that of the Other, but everything he
manages to do in the course of the play—even his acceptance of Claudius's wager, which leads to the final resolution of the action—is done
at a time set by someone other than himself. Hamlet's desire is dependent upon the desire of the Other, but he is also "constantly suspended
in the time of the Other, throughout the entire story until the very
end" (*D*, 5:14/17; see *D*, 5:13–16/17–20).

Hamlet's position with respect to his father, the late king murdered
by his brother and heir, Claudius, is itself ambivalent. In the first of his
great soliloquies, Hamlet reveals his imaginary fascination with his
father,

> So excellent a king, that was to this
> Hyperion to a satyr, so loving to my mother
> That he might not beteem the winds of heaven
> Visit her face too roughly.
> (*Hamlet*, 1.2.139–42)

In this idealized portrait, we see again a striking manifestation of
Hamlet's own incarnation of his mother's desire, further evidence of his
wish to emulate the perfect king and lover his father's memory now
models for him, and further proof of his desire to become the imaginary
phallus that his mother desires. Yet when Hamlet meets with his
father's ghost at the end of act 1, what the ghost reveals to him is the
bitter truth of his murder by Claudius, a murder the outcome of which

(Gertrude's hasty marriage to Claudius) shows Hamlet that even what appeared the most perfect love was absolutely false (*D*, 4:31).

This bitter rent in Hamlet's idealized image of human love is marked by the demand that the ghost makes upon Hamlet: "Revenge his foul and most unnatural murder" (*Hamlet*, 1.5.25). From the very moment that he learns the truth about his father's death and swears to kill Claudius in revenge, Hamlet finds himself confronted with "the crime of existing" (*D*, 1:15). It is a crime, of course, that Claudius continues to exist, but so long as he fails to avenge his father's death, so long as he puts off the one act that will balance the scales of justice, Hamlet too is "guilty of being," as he shows in the great soliloquy, "To be or not to be" (*D*, 1:15). In this way, Hamlet's father both destroys his son's own imaginary goal—that is, he devastates the illusion of human fulfillment under which Hamlet's desire has developed—and leaves him with a duty to act, a duty the nonsatisfaction of which confers guilt upon Hamlet. It is in this domain that castration enters the tragedy of Hamlet.

From another angle, however, the "crime of existing" is the very core of the existential fact of our mortality: Hamlet, confronted by his father's ghost, is face to face with death, and throughout its various twists "the drama of Hamlet is the encounter with death" (*D*, 4:26). Existing is a crime to the extent that we pursue various tactics to avoid accepting the fact of our mortality: to the extent that our lives are played out in pursuit of countless imaginary satisfactions, to the extent that our identities are dominated by culturally force-fed signifying chains, we are guilty of leading lives of illusion with the aim of denying the essential nothingness that marks us as mortal beings. It is precisely this that the ghost reveals to Hamlet, and it is precisely this knowledge that makes Hamlet the hero that he is.

What is at stake, then, when Lacan identifies castration as the fundamental theme of *Hamlet*, is nothing less than the truth of human life. In the fourth session of the seminar Lacan summarizes this truth in the formula, "there is no Other of the Other," noting that this is "the great secret of psychoanalysis" (*D*, 4:30–33). Comparing the ghost's revelation to Hamlet with the lifting of "the veil that weighs upon the articulation of the unconscious chain," Lacan stresses that this veil itself plays a fundamental role in that it allows the subject to speak (*D*, 4:30). Speech is made intelligible only because certain key signifiers (*points de capiton*) have been repressed from the signifying chain and replaced by metaphors that in turn make possible meaning itself. To unveil such repressed signifiers, then, would be to run the risk of destroying the points of reference that make speech intelligible. In unveiling the truth of human mortality, the ghost of Hamlet's father in effect gives up the secret surrounding the most important *point de capiton,* the phallus as imaginary fullness of being, complete identity, and immortality.[27] The secret spilled by the ghost is, of course, simply that there is no such thing as the phallus in the real: if we look to imaginary Others for the filling of the want-of-being that we recognize in ourselves, we must come to realize that the Other is castrated as well. It is precisely this knowledge that Hamlet's father presents to Hamlet in the first act of Shakespeare's play. The ghost is powerless, and knowledge of this situation—because it gives Hamlet only one possible response to the state of affairs in which he finds himself— makes Hamlet essentially powerless as well.

Lacan sums up this dimension of his reading of *Hamlet* by stressing that the special value of Shakespeare's play is that it reveals to us the fact that even the Other to which we turn for our identity is castrated, a notion that he puts algebraically as "S($\cancel{A}$)" (the signifier of the Other with the bar).[28] Since this Other "is not being, but the place of speech, where the ensemble of the system of signifiers rests, that is, a language," the castration of the Other is necessarily symbolic and lies in the fact that a particular signifier is lacking in the Other (*D,* 4:31). This missing or hidden signifier is, of course, the phallus (*D,* 4:32), and the fact that it is missing from the Other means that we cannot find it for ourselves by appeal to the Other: in the end, the Other cannot constitute our identity for us. In other words, "in the signifier there is nothing that guarantees the dimension of truth founded by the signifier" (*D,* 6:20/25), and as speaking beings our castration lies precisely in this lack of a guaranteed truth or meaning.[29] Thus, "the truth of Hamlet is a truth without hope" (*D,* 4:31), "a truth without truth" (*D,* 4:32), and the Other's castration discloses the truth that castration is the ineluctable state of the human condition.

This means that Hamlet's apparent dependence upon the Other's desire and his remaining always at "the hour of the Other" are both fundamentally illusions that he has (in some sense) taken upon himself:

For Hamlet there is no hour but his own. Moreover, there is only one hour, the hour of his destruction. The entire tragedy of *Hamlet* is constituted in the way it shows us the unrelenting movement of the subject toward that hour.

Yet the subject's appointment with the hour of his destruction is the common lot of everyone, meaningful in the destiny of every individual. (*D*, 6:20/25)

In short, it is mortality and the inability of the symbolic system of language to render compensation for this mortal condition that are the defining features of castration, both in human beings in general and in the case of Hamlet in particular. What makes Hamlet unusual is that, thanks to the ghost's revelation, he quite literally knows this "truth without hope."

Most of the time that we see Hamlet on the stage he is engaged either in mourning the death of his father or in denouncing his mother and uncle for their insufficient mourning. As the play progresses, we see him cut himself off more and more from his relations with other people, not only his mother and uncle, but Rosencrantz and Guildenstern his old friends, and, most importantly, Ophelia his beloved. In effect, Hamlet's mourning moves him deeper and deeper into a position of narcissism, a position in which he is unable to focus desire on any object other than himself. As Lacan puts it, "Hamlet just doesn't know what he wants" (*D*, 6:26); he lacks a desired object, apparently being unable to displace his desire from his dead father to a new object. Thus his mourning is transformed into the pathological condition that Freud describes as melancholia.[30] Such a regression to narcissism and to a profound melancholia is perhaps the only possible response to the shattering revelation of castration brought to Hamlet by the ghost of his father.

Nevertheless, if there is any hint of hope in *Hamlet,* it comes in the fact that Hamlet does finally manage to assume his own identity as a desiring being; the death of Ophelia provides a new occasion for mourning and at the same time an opportunity to revive Hamlet's desire. Speaking generally of the role of ritual in mourning, Lacan suggests that "ritual introduces some mediation of the gap [*béance*] opened up by mourning. More precisely, ritual operates in such a way as to make this gap [*béance*] coincide with that greater *béance,* the point *x,* the symbolic lack" (*D,* 7:32/40). Through the rituals of mourning, the lost object is introjected by the subject, reconstituted as an imaginary part of the subject itself. While there are many dangers here—the most apparent of which is the extension of the narcissism involved here into melancholia—this process of imaginary reconstitution does hold out the promise of filling to a certain extent the want-of-being inherent in the subject as a result of symbolic castration. To get beyond the trauma of castration, as well as the narcissism to which this trauma gives rise, it is necessary for the subject to accept some object as in a rough way equivalent to the phallus, which the subject can neither have nor be. This object is the object of fantasy, which, Lacan says, "takes the place of what the subject is—symbolically—deprived of" but "satisfies no need" (D, 5:11/15) and which, in Lacan's later algebra comes to be symbolized as "a" (the *objet petit a* or *objet a*).[31] While fantasies can be generated in any number of ways, the process of mourning provides a particularly rich context for the production of fantasies and hence for the production of substitute objects for the phallus.

Clearly alluding to Freud's "Mourning and Melancholia," Lacan argues that the death of another person opens up "a hole in the real" for the subject. This hole in the real "sets the signifier in motion" in a search throughout the system of the Other for the all-powerful signifier that will make up for the lost object (D, 6:30/37–38). Because this signifier is the phallus, unavailable either to the subject or the Other, "swarms of images, from which the phenomena of mourning arise, assume the place of the phallus" (D, 6:30/38) in an attempt to fill or at least cover over the hole in the real left by the loss of the object.[32] What the signifier cannot accomplish—"it is the system of signifiers in their totality which is impeached by the least instance of mourning" (D, 6:30–31/38)—the system of the imaginary attempts by means of fantasy. In cases of adequate and successful mourning, an imaginary object is constituted that is able to take the place of the lost object, and to the extent that this occurs such a fantasy object can also substitute for the phallus. In short, successful mourning mourns not only the object lost but also the human condition of castration.

What this means, among other things, is that the fantasied objects of desire are in fact substitutes for the phallus. All human desire is inherently fetishistic, then, given Freud's account of the fetish as a substitute for the castrated penis.[33] From this, Lacan can maintain that "all objects of the human world have this character" of being fetishes (D, 5:11/15), insofar as such objects are themselves parts of the world only as involved in human desire.[34] With respect to Shakespeare's *Hamlet,* what this means is that Hamlet can regain his subjectivity as a desiring being—and thereby regain an active involvement in the human world—only through reconstituting in fantasy an object that can substitute for the phallus that he knows is missing. This is why Lacan insists, at the end of the first session of the seminar, that "the play of

Hamlet tells how something comes to be equivalent to that which is lacking" as a result of castration (*D*, 1:17).

It is Ophelia, Lacan argues, who is thus fetishized at the climax of the tragedy, coming to play the role of the *objet petit a* in Hamlet's revived desire (*D*, 5:9/15). Ophelia is "quite simply what any girl [*toute fille*] is," a "vision of life ready to blossom, of life bearing all lives": "This image of vital fecundity illustrates for us, more than any other creation, the equation I have already mentioned in my course, *Girl =Phallus*" (*D*, 4:35). Thus it is precisely as "any girl" that Ophelia takes the place of the phallus, but for this process to occur Hamlet must first reconstitute her in fantasy as a desired object. It is this that is at stake in the great graveyard scene with which the final act of *Hamlet* opens.

Hamlet in effect learns how to mourn adequately by watching Laertes, Ophelia's brother, as he mourns at her open grave. In fact Laertes goes so far as to leap into Ophelia's grave: "Hold off the earth awhile, / Till I have caught her once more in mine arms" (*Hamlet*, 5.1.236–37). It is as the jealous witness of this scene of profound grief, forthrightly acted upon, that Hamlet comes forward and jumps into Ophelia's grave so as to engage in hand to hand combat with Laertes. Laertes is here playing the role of Hamlet's imaginary double—in the play's final scene the buffoonish lord Osric even says of Laertes that "his semblable is his mirror" (5.2.118). Laertes is the other appearing in Hamlet's mirror as both model to emulate and rival against whom to struggle (*D*, 6:24–26/31–32 and 28/35). In his jealous rage, what Hamlet learns from Ophelia's brother is both how to mourn and how to love: dragged away from his struggle with Laertes, Hamlet cries out, "I loved Ophelia. Forty thousand brothers / Could not with all their quantity of love / Make up my sum" (5.1.256–58). What Lacan particularly emphasizes, however, is that in learning to mourn, and thus learning to love, what Hamlet most crucially accomplishes is the reconstitution of his identity. This is marked by the cry with which Hamlet appears to the company assembled around Ophelia's grave, a cry that comes, Lacan maintains, at "the moment when he once again seizes his desire" (*D*, 3:25):

> What is he whose grief
> Bears such an emphasis? whose phrase of sorrow
> Conjures the wand'ring stars, and makes them stand

Like wonder-wounded hearers? This is I,
Hamlet the Dane.
(*Hamlet*, 5.1.241–45)

At the very moment that Hamlet finally acts on his own he also
assumes his identity as "the Dane," that is, as his father's son. He
accepts, in effect, the name of the father as a substitute signifier for the
phallus, and this act of acceptance makes it possible for him to enter
into the work of mourning, the outcome of which will be the fantasy
object, Ophelia, the object of Hamlet's now hyperbolic love.

We have already seen how the process of mourning manages to
produce an imaginary object meant to fill the hole in reality left by the
loss of the mourned object. Lacan wants to insist on two fundamental
features of this object that enter into reestablishing the subject's identity. On the one hand, this object is constituted as "an impossible
object" (D, 6:29/36): having died, Ophelia can no longer satisfy Hamlet's desire. Lacan claims that "the very structure at the basis of desire
always lends a note of impossibility to the object of human desire" (D,
6:36), precisely because this object is always essentially a fetishistic
substitute for the phallus, which has had to be given up.[35] On the other
hand, the very fact that the fantasy object is impossible makes it not
merely the object of desire but the *cause* of desire. Lacan elaborates this
by reference to the graveyard scene in *Hamlet*: "Laertes leaps into the
grave and embraces the object whose loss is the cause of his desire, an
object that has attained an existence that is all the more absolute
because it no longer corresponds to anything in reality. The one unbear-
able dimension of possible human experience is not the experience of
one's own death, which no one has, but the experience of the death of
another" (D, 6:29-30/37). If desire is essentially marked by a lack, a
gap between need and demand, then the sort of object best qualified to
open up such a gap and to maintain it in the midst of all sorts of partial
satisfactions is nothing other than an object that is inherently impossible and, thus, always and inevitably lacking. Here again, we see the
necessity of the work of mourning in shaping the human subject's
identity as a desiring being.

Once Hamlet has successfully mourned Ophelia, thereby reconstituting her as a fantasy object, he is able to turn away from his narcissistic
obsession with himself. Even so, his final act of revenge comes only at
"the moment when he has made the complete sacrifice . . . of all
narcissistic attachments, i.e., when he is mortally wounded and knows

it" (*D*, 7:42–43/51). It is only when the indubitable knowledge of his mortality comes to Hamlet that he is fully able to accept the human fact of castration. In accepting this fact, he finds himself finally able to attack and to kill Claudius, who is no longer anything for Hamlet but a mortal man. Until he has given up his narcissism, Lacan argues, Hamlet is prevented from acting by the narcissistic fear that in striking the king—his mother's lover and thus that which she desires—he would be striking at the phallus, which remains the heart of his imaginary identity (*D*, 7:42/50). Thus, his mourning of Ophelia sets the stage for Hamlet's final realization that there is no real phallus, that there is no Other fully endowed with the all-encompassing power that symbols of power always promise, that any appearance of such a phallic Other is always an "apparition," a mere ghost, what Lacan calls a "phallophany" (*D*, 7:44). This realization is tantamount to the realization that his narcissism is doomed to inevitable failure, and it is this realization that makes it possible for Hamlet finally to act.

It remains to return to the idea suggested early in my discussion of the *Hamlet* seminar, that Lacan's approach to literary criticism entails some analysis of the way works of literature transform their audiences. The scattered remarks throughout the seminar that address this issue are summarized in the opening of the fourth session, where Lacan states: *"Let my desire be given to me {Qu'on me donne mon désir}*, such is the meaning that I have told you *Hamlet* has for all those critics, actors, and spectators who lay their hands on it" (*D*, 4:26). Shakespeare's play is "a kind of apparatus, a web, a bird-snare, where man's desire is articulated" (*D*, 2:24), where the fictional structure of truth is presented (most notably in the play-within-a-play; see *D*, 2:28), where it is revealed that we all are caught up in the "note of impossibility" that characterizes the structure of desire. In effect, when Lacan claims that *Hamlet* challenges each spectator's own relation to his or her desire (*D*, 3:16), he is suggesting that the play forces us to cry out for our desire—"Let my desire be given to me." In asking us to model our actions on those of Hamlet, by taking him as the tragic hero, the play's structure leads us as spectators to enter into the work of mourning: in mourning Hamlet, Ophelia, or Gertrude, we are brought to mourn the phallus as well. In this way, although Lacan himself never says it, the character of Hamlet—a character who, Lacan repeatedly insists, is not a real person (see *D*, 3:13–15)[36]—is offered to the audience as an *objet petit a*, a fantasy object in effect ready-made by Shakespeare so as to help us mend the hole in the real left by the symbolic castration of the phallus.[37] Thus, our experience of *Hamlet* should, ideally, help us come to a realization of our own castration and of the corresponding necessity to get beyond narcissism in order to act in the human world as desiring beings.

Antigone and Tragedy

The year after his analysis of *Hamlet,* Lacan returned to literary interpretation in his seminar, and again he took as his object a work of tragic literature, in this case Sophocles' *Antigone.* The three sessions on *Antigone* held between 25 May and 15 June 1960 form part of the seminar *L'éthique de la psychanalyse* (The ethics of psychoanalysis), and Lacan's interest here focuses on the ethical core of tragedy as a dramatic genre (S 7, 283–333). In striking contrast with his use of *Hamlet* as little more than an illustration of a great deal of psychoanalytic theory, what Lacan offers in these sessions is nothing less than a general theory of the "tragic effect," the effect of tragedy on an audience.

At the most fundamental level, then, the background to the seminar is Aristotle's famous remark in book 6 of the *Poetics* that the function of tragedy is "through pity and fear effecting the proper purgation [*katharsis*] of these emotions" (1449b 27–28). Indeed, Lacan opens his discussion with a review of the literature on katharsis, stressing the ambiguity of the Greek term, which evokes both the sacred notion of purification and the medical notion of purging (S 7, 286–89). What interests Lacan most in Aristotle's account (for the few details of which, Lacan points out, we must turn to book 8 of the *Politics*) is the explicit linkage made between the process of katharsis and pleasure. The purging of the passions is inherently pleasurable, Aristotle argues in his discussion of musical education in the *Politics*: those caught up in a religious or mystical frenzy can be "restored" by sacred melodies "as though they had found healing and purgation"; those who are simply by nature carried away by the emotions of pity or fear find their souls "lightened and delighted" by musical katharsis; and, in general, "the melodies which purge the passions likewise give an innocent pleasure to mankind" (*Politics,* 8:7, 1342a 6–16).[38] This relation between katharsis and pleasure suggests that one route toward grasping the essence of tragedy is to consider how katharsis must be linked to desire, and indeed Lacan argues that "*Antigone* makes us see in effect the target [*le point de visée*] that defines desire" (S 7, 290). Thus, if *Hamlet* is "the tragedy of desire," the seminar on Sophocles generalizes this position so as to show how tragedy as a genre is constituted in relation to desire.

Perhaps the best way to pursue Lacan's argument here is to begin by reviewing briefly his basic interpretation of *Antigone,* using the particular example as a springboard to his more general theory of tragedy. Any commentator on Sophocles' play immediately faces a profoundly difficult task, a task made all the more awesome by the existence of a striking interpretation of the play by the German philosopher, Hegel. Hegel argues that each of the two central characters of the play— Antigone, daughter of Oedipus, and Creon, Oedipus's brother-in-law—personifies a different and conflicting order of ethics and law. Creon represents the public law of the city and emphasizes the right of the state over that of individuals within the political community. Antigone represents the private law of the family, the love between individuals that is itself the basis of the ethical community. When Creon forbids the burial of Antigone's brother, Polyneices, on the grounds that he was an enemy of the state, this public law comes into harsh conflict with the familial and sacred duty to bury one's own dead, and Antigone, in choosing to go ahead and bury her brother, stands for the priority of the individual to the state. What the tragic dénouement of the play reveals—the triple suicide of Antigone (after being buried alive), of Haemon (Creon's son and Antigone's lover), and of Eurydice (Creon's wife)—is that both of these conceptions of law or ethical duty are in fact one-sided and that each contains the germ of its dialectical collapse. Sophocles' play stands as "one of the most sublime and in every respect most excellent works of art of all time," Hegel insists,[39] precisely because it reveals the perils of such ethical one-sidedness and suggests the terms for a fully ethical reconciliation of public and private interest and duty.[40]

Given Lacan's own enthusiasm for certain aspects of Hegel's work— particularly his reflections on the struggle of master and slave and on the nature of language—we might expect Hegel's reading of *Antigone* to shape his approach to Sophocles. Yet Lacan dismisses Hegel, remarking that his poetics is the weakest part of his work and asking how anyone could possibly find any sort of dialectical reconciliation or synthesis of opposites at the end of the play (S 7, 292). Going further, Lacan argues: "It is not a matter of one right that is opposed to another right, but of a wrong [*un tort*] which is opposed—to what? To something other, which Antigone represents. I tell you it is not simply the defense of the sacred rights of the dead and of the family, nor, much less, is it what has been portrayed as a saintliness on Antigone's part. Antigone is borne by a passion, and we will try to learn what passion" (S 7, 297). Thus Lacan sees the dialectic of the play as working itself out between Creon's wrong and Antigone's passion, and he in no way tries to gloss over the play's utterly devastating conclusion. As we shall see, it is in the overriding image of desolation left by the play—and in particular by the image of Antigone—that Lacan finds the essence of the drama's kathartic effect.

Turning his attention first to Creon, Lacan emphasizes that Sophocles portrays him quite simply as an ordinary human being. This dimension of his character is brought out most strikingly in the confrontation between Creon and his son, Haemon, a confrontation in which Creon's love and pride quickly turn to hatred and threats (*Antigone*, 626–765). Lacan notes that Creon is here showing us a tendency typical of human beings when it is a matter of their own sense of the good: there is a weakness here, a giving in to alternative notions of the good or of happiness, which reveals the fact that Creon really does not know what he wants. "This point is extremely important in order to fix Creon's stature—we will see in what happens just what he is, namely what executioners and tyrants always are—in the final analysis, human persons. It is only martyrs who can be without pity or fear" (S 7, 311). In short, like Hamlet through much of Shakespeare's play, like most human beings caught up in imaginary identities and symbolically constrained roles, Creon is unable to assume his own desire.

Nevertheless, as leader of his city, Creon acts in a way meant to maximize the good of the community: here, it is clear that "he wants the good" and the good of all (S 7, 300). This is exemplified in his own defense of the prohibition of Polyneices' burial that he has ordered:

> For I believe that who controls the state
> and does not hold to the best plans of all,
> but locks his tongue up through some kind of fear,
> that he is worst of all who are or were.
> And he who counts another greater friend
> than his own fatherland, I put him nowhere.
> So I—may Zeus all-seeing always know it—
> could not keep silent as disaster crept
> upon the town, destroying hope of safety.
> Nor could I count the enemy of the land
> friend to myself, not I who know so well
> that she it is who saves us, sailing straight,
> and only so can we have friends at all.
> (*Antigone*, 178–190)[41]

Creon's fault lies not in the one-sidedness of his political philosophy but in his mistakenly taking the good of all as "the law without limits, the sovereign law, the law that overflows, that passes beyond the limit" (S 7, 301). Creon is guilty of an "error of judgment" (S 7, 300), an error not unlike that which any politician might make.

Lacan stresses that the Greek term for such an error—*hamartia*—is in fact that used by Aristotle in the *Poetics* to characterize the mistake or tragic flaw that distinguishes the tragic hero from ordinary individuals.[42] Lacan argues, however, that Aristotle's analysis reduces "the distinctive teaching of tragic rites" to the level of an ethics conceived of as the science of happiness (S 7, 300–301). In effect, Aristotle's analysis would make Creon the tragic hero of *Antigone,* when in fact it is Antigone herself who is the true heroine of the play. Thus, the ordinary human error of judgment, *hamartia,* cannot provide the impetus for the kathartic effect of tragedy.

Thus, it is precisely the fact that Antigone is revealed to us as "an inhuman being" (S 7, 306) that makes her the dramatic focus, the true heroine, of Sophocles' play. The term in relation to which Lacan characterizes Antigone is *Atē*: subjectively, this word designates the delusion or blindness sent to human beings by the gods and responsible for irrational behavior; objectively, the word designates the doom or disaster attendant upon such delusion. In Sophocles' play, the second choral ode (lines 582–625), which follows Antigone's defense before Creon of her illegal burial of Polyneices, is devoted specifically to *Atē*. Here the chorus attempts to understand Antigone's fate in terms of the cross-generational curses that characterize the entire family history and that led in particular to Oedipus's downfall. Everything, the chorus maintains, can be related to a single law (*nomos*) of human destiny: "Near time, far future, and the past,/one law controls them all:/any greatness in human life brings doom [*ektos atas*]" (*Antigone,* 611–614).[43] Speaking of this ode, Lacan insists: "This word [*Atē*] cannot be replaced. It designates the limit beyond which human life cannot too long go. The text of the chorus is on this significant and insistent—*ektos atas*. Beyond this *Atē* one can last only a short time, and it is there that Antigone wants to go" (S 7, 305). In other words, Antigone knows what she wants: hers is the drama of the all-too-rare human being who willingly assumes her own desire. "That Antigone thus leaves human limits behind, what does this mean for us, if not that her desire aims very precisely there—beyond *Atē?*" (S 7, 306). Moreover, "*Atē* is not *hamartia,* fault or error, it is not just a blunder" (S 7, 323). Where

Creon, in his human, all-too-human, weakness, makes a mistake and suffers the mortal consequences of this mistake, Antigone directly confronts and assumes as her own the profound otherness of desire, symbolized in the play by the uncrossable limit of *Atē*. Commenting on lines 1259–60, where the chorus itself declares that Creon now suffers because "he himself made a mistake [*autos hamartōn*]" and that this is "not an *Atē* of another [*ouk allotrian atēn*]," Lacan remarks: "*Atē*, which stems from the Other, from the field of the Other, does not concern Creon; it is in contrast the place where Antigone is situated" (S 7, 323).[44]

In this way Antigone stands out as a paradigm of the human being who assumes her own desire and who thereby recognizes the inherent Otherness of this desire and accepts the permanent intermixing of self and Other entailed by desire. It is precisely this that Creon cannot do, with the result that the drama of *Antigone* lies in the conflict between one who assumes and affirms desire and one who regularly gives up on and denies desire.

This conflict between Antigone and Creon is directly portrayed in Antigone's impassioned defense of her decision to bury Polyneices (*Antigone*, 441–525). The heart of this defense is taken by most critics, among them most notably Hegel, to be Antigone's invocation of the "unwritten laws" that contradict Creon's decree:

> For me it was not Zeus who made that order.
> Nor did that Justice who lives with the gods below
> mark out such laws to hold among mankind.
> Nor did I think your orders were so strong
> that you, a mortal man, could over-run
> the gods' unwritten and unfailing laws.
> Not now, nor yesterday's, they always live,
> and no one knows their origin in time.
>
> (*Antigone*, 450–57)

Noting that everyone "understands" what Antigone means here, Lacan stresses that "I have always told you that it is important not to understand in order to understand" (S 7, 323–24). He then goes on to argue that what she is really evoking here in the name of the unwritten laws is something "that is in effect of the order of law, but that is developed in no signifying chain, in nothing" (S 7, 324). In other words, Creon's decree concerning Polyneices owes the possibility of its existence to language, to a signifying chain in relation to which such terms as "criminal" and "hero," "enemy" and "patriot" can have some meaning. In contrast, Antigone focuses our attention on a more fundamental feature of human existence made possible by the "law" of language: namely, the uniqueness of each individual human being.

Thus, Lacan maintains that the key to grasping Antigone's defense lies not in her contrasting of divine and human law, and indeed not in her defense itself. Rather, this key is to be found in the explanation of her action that she gives just before she goes to her death, an explanation the logic of which has troubled commentators as astute as Goethe (see S 7, 297–98). In an apostrophe to Polyneices, Antigone speaks as follows:

> Had I had children or their father dead,
> I'd let them moulder. I should not have chosen
> in such a case to cross the state's decree.
> What is the law that lies behind these words?
> One husband gone, I might have found another,
> or a child from a new man in first child's place,
> but with my parents hid away in death,
> no brother, ever, could spring up for me.
> Such was the law by which I honored you.
>
> (*Antigone*, 905–14)

Lacan, reducing this argument to her claim that her brother is something unique—"My brother is what he is"—explicates the logic of Antigone's argument in terms of the effect of language on the human subject. He writes:

It is clear that Antigone represents by her position this radical limit, which, beyond all characterizations, beyond all that Polyneices was able to do both good and evil, beyond all that could be inflicted upon him, maintains the unique value of his being.

This value is essentially from language. Outside of language, it could not even be conceived, and the being of one who has lived could not be detached in this way from all that he conveyed as good and as evil, as destiny, as consequences for others, and as sentiments for himself. This purity, this separation of the being from all the characteristics of the historical drama through which he traveled, this is precisely the limit, the *ex nihilo* around which Antigone holds fast. This is nothing other than the cut [*coupure*] that the very presence of language establishes in the life of man. (S 7, 325)

It is only through language that we are able to separate an agent and his actions, a human being and his characteristics: it is language alone that allows us to conceptualize individuals as unique, that makes it possible for us to disregard the qualities these individuals have in common with countless other individuals. It is because we are speaking beings, marked by the cut of primal repression, that we are able to think of ourselves as having characteristics and thereby also think of ourselves as those unique beings to which such characteristics belong.

In this way Antigone clearly stands for the value of the individual as opposed to Creon's putting the good of all ahead of that of any individual. As Lacan says, Antigone's defense is essentially "the making present of absolute individuality" (S 7, 323). It is crucial, however, to note that Antigone's position promotes a notion of the value of uniqueness that is independent of any particular good quality, a value that comes quite literally from nothing (*ex nihilo*). Polyneices is worthy of her sacrifice, not because he was a good brother or soldier or friend, but because, quite apart from any particular characteristic, he *was*. To put such value on the simple fact of existence—perceived most clearly through the retrospection of mourning—is in effect to cast away the "historical drama" of human life, and thus Antigone's action situates her in a special position, "between life and death" (S 7, 326). As is the case with most Sophoclean heroes (Oedipus may be the exception), Lacan notes, Antigone is in the position of being "at the end of the race [*à bout de course*]" from the very beginning of the play (S 7, 317). Her love for Polyneices takes her quite literally out of the world of the living, and her status as simultaneously living and dead is perfectly captured in the punishment to which her action destines her: live burial.

Thus, Antigone's desire is made possible only by language, and it is through language that her desire effectively intermingles life and death. The image of Antigone as reflecting this web of conceptual linkages is at the center of the great *kommos* or lamentation sung by Antigone and the chorus as she goes off to her death (*Antigone*, 802–82). The *kommos* is introduced by a choral ode in praise of "love [*erōs*] unconquered in fight" (*Antigone*, 781–801), an ode that ends with an image of "desire made visible [*imeros enargēs*]": "Desire looks clear from the eyes of a lovely bride:/power as strong as the founded world./For there is the goddess at play with whom no man can fight" (*Antigone*, 795–801). It is with this image that Antigone returns to the stage on the way to her death, and Lacan argues that this is precisely the image that Antigone herself presents (S 7, 311). Within the structure of Sophocles' play, she is "desire made visible," and in this way the heroine's image becomes "the target that defines desire" (S 7, 290). It is Antigone's beauty, her visible manifesting of desire through the radical nature of her action, that gives us as members of the audience pleasure and that produces the kathartic effect that defines tragedy (S 7, 332–33).

The *kommos* itself is effectively an invocation of Antigone's radiant beauty, dominated by Antigone's comparison of her fate to that of Niobe, daughter of Tantalus, turned to stone on Mount Sipylus for having boasted of having more children than Leto, the mother of Apollo and Artemis.

> The rock
> it covered her over, like stubborn ivy it grew.
> Still, as she wastes, the rain
> and snow companion her.
> Pouring down from her mourning eyes comes the
> water that soaks the stone.
> My own putting to sleep a god has planned like hers.
> (*Antigone*, 826–33)

What Lacan emphasizes with respect to this striking example of the personage between life and death, at the end of the race, is that Antigone in effect wants this solitary death that she is living. From this perspective, Antigone's desire is for precisely the state of inanimation toward which Freud's death instinct propels all living beings. Antigone "incarnates" the "pure and simple desire for death as such," Lacan maintains (S 7, 328–29). Nevertheless, as an effect of her beauty we fail to recognize immediately that the desire made visible here is ultimately a desire for death. Indeed, "the effect of beauty is an effect of blindness" (S 7, 327).

What the chorus sees in Antigone is someone who lives by her own laws—she is *autonomos* (821)—someone whose fate is chosen by her own self-knowledge—she is *autognōtos* (875)—and they see these characteristics as responsible for her tragic end. What the chorus is blind to is the fact that her autonomous status is itself simply the relation of the human being to the *coupure*, or cut, introduced by the signifier (S 7,

328). As we have seen, it is this effect of language that makes it possible to separate the unique human being from his characteristics, and it is this separation in turn that makes it possible for Antigone to reject as worthless all of Creon's arguments concerning Polyneices' criminality. Regardless of his deeds, Polyneices has the ultimate value of individuality conferred by language. Thus, from Creon's perspective and from that of the community (as reflected by the chorus), Antigone takes a stand on the side of crime. To stand for the unique individual is to stand against the community, and this is precisely the going beyond *Atē* that Antigone unshakably pursues as she assumes her desire (S 7, 329).

Now it is a precisely similar stand on the side of crime that lies at the heart of Lacan's general theory of the tragic effect. Antigone's beauty, the image of her as desire made visible, is the "center of the tragedy," inasmuch as the entire action of the play is articulated around the zone between life and death that she so radiantly occupies (S 7, 290). Generalizing from this example, Lacan describes his own critical task as follows: "Tragedy is that which spreads forward in order to produce this image. In analyzing it, we go backward, we study how it was necessary to construct this image in order to produce this effect" (S 7, 318). In other words, what Lacan turns to at this point is the effect that beauty has on desire, understanding that it is the image of beauty that serves as the "target" defining desire (S 7, 290 and 299). It is this effect of beauty on desire that Lacan identifies as the katharsis that is essential to the tragic effect (S 7, 332).

The connection between beauty and crime is mediated by Lacan's reflections on Sade and, in particular, on the notion of the "second death imagined by Sade's heroes" (S 7, 291). What most impresses Lacan here is that the basic structure of fantasy in Sade's writings is one of "an eternal suffering": the victims are rarely put to death by their suffering, and "it seems on the contrary that the object of the torments must preserve the possibility of being an indestructible support" (S 7, 303). There is a parallel here between the separation in *Antigone* of the unique human being from his actions and characteristics—a separation made possible by the advent of language—and the Sadean separation of the victim from his various torments. Antigone's defense of the zone between life and death is, indeed, simply a variation of this Sadean theme.

Lacan continues his argument: "Analysis clearly shows that the subject detaches a double of himself, which is made inaccessible to destruction, in order to make him a support for what must be called in this case—borrowing a term from the domain of aesthetics—the games of pain. For it is a matter here of the same region as that where the phenomena of aesthetics frolic, a certain free space. And here lies the conjunction between the games of pain and the phenomena of beauty, never underlined" (S 7, 303). The aesthetic theory Lacan has in mind here is that of Kant (S 7, 304), for whom any judgment that an object is beautiful must be "disinterested" and thus independent of the actual existence of the object.[45] For an object to be described as beautiful, its representation must stimulate our cognitive powers into "a free play" experienced as delight, quite apart from any actual interest or desire that might be satisfied by the real object itself.[46] As Kant writes, "One must not be in the least prepossessed in favor of the real existence of the thing, but must preserve complete indifference in this respect, in order to play the part of judge in matters of taste."[47] If Antigone's beauty lies in her occupation of a region between life and death, Lacan's Kantian gloss adds that this is the region where ordinary pleasure is left behind for the sake of the disinterested delight we take in beauty. Lacan's Sadean gloss adds to this that beauty's region is that "between two deaths": between the "first death" of the living being and the "second death" of the unique individual separated from all his qualities.

Thus Antigone's "crime" is that of Sadean "second death," and the *Atē* beyond which she dares to go is in some sense the limit to human action imposed by nature. The separation of the individual from his qualities is—precisely because it is effected by language—something contrary to nature. Thus, just as it is to the extent that Sade's heroes do not respect the natural order that their actions become "crimes" (S 7, 302–3), so too Antigone's defense of the unique value of the individual is "criminal" insofar as she also introduces a break with natural law, a break marked by the *coupure* of language.

What, then, is the effect of beauty on desire? Lacan argues, building on his subtle reading of *Antigone* through Sade and Kant, that beauty's effect is the "disruption of every object" of desire (S 7, 291), and this disruption is the key to understanding Lacan's theory of katharsis. It must be emphasized that the "disruption" at issue here is not that involved in Freud's notion of the "overvaluation" of the sexual object leading to "idealization" in the experience of being in love:[48] far from idealizing the object of desire, the image of desolation left by tragedy effectively de-idealizes and, thus, renders real, this object.

The beauty at which desire aims is that of an image, but even as "one image among others" this image has the power to purify us and thus to give us pleasure (S 7, 290). This power rests in beauty's reflection of the utter Otherness involved in human desire, an Otherness that implicates language, life, and death in the very possibility of identifying a human individual as the object of love. The "disruption" of desire's object that beauty effects is, in fact, the transformation of a mere object of desire into a human being *loved*.

Antigone's "crime" is essentially the antisocial scandal of love.[49] Her response to Creon's claim that Polyneices was an enemy of the state is simply: "I cannot share in hatred, but in love" (*Antigone,* 523). In effect, all attributes of social welfare and community significance are sacrificed in Antigone's invocation of her brother's absolute uniqueness, a uniqueness that grounds her loving desire.

Similarly, Sophocles' play has the effect of presenting us with an image in which such sacrifice is concentrated, and the kathartic effect of tragedy in general lies in the power this kind of image has to purify us as members of the audience. Tragedy confronts us—indirectly, to be sure—with the "criminal" fact of our individuality, with our indisputably real existence, and it accomplishes this through the mediation of an imaginary image that itself reflects the mark of *coupure* brought to human life by symbolic systems. The effect of tragedy, then, is to jolt us out of our imaginary identities and symbolic roles and to force or at least to encourage us to assume our real identities as unique, mortal beings. This is to say that the "tragic effect" is brought to fulfillment with our assumption of the inherently tragic character of human life. And it must be emphasized that love itself is a primary symptom of this tragic dimension. Antigone stands out as a paradigm of the human subject who assumes the full weight of her desire, thereby recognizing the ineluctable Otherness of human individuality and accepting the inevitable, although generally misrecognized, intermixing of life and death, of self and Other, involved in the real structure of love.

Chapter Six
The Impossible Real

By the late 1950s Lacan's seminars had begun to range beyond topics of merely specialized interest to psychoanalysts-in-training. His eagerness to explore such literary texts as *Hamlet* and *Antigone* was complemented by an interest in classic philosophical texts. The seminar *L'éthique de la psychanalyse,* for example, included much discussion of Aristotle and Kant, and the seminar of the following year, devoted to the topic of transference, opened with an elaborate commentary of some eleven sessions on Plato's *Symposium.*[1] At about the same time as this apparent change in Lacan's own intellectual concerns, vicissitudes in his relations with the International Psychoanalytic Association began to have an effect on the composition of his audience at the seminars. With his effective "excommunication" from the IPA late in 1963, Lacan found himself closed out of the Hôpital Sainte-Anne, where his seminar had been conducted since its inception. At the invitation of Fernand Braudel and Robert Flacelière, he resumed the seminar in January 1964 in the auditorium of the École normale supérieure before an audience both larger and more heterogeneous than in the past.

This abbreviated seminar of 1964, *The Four Fundamental Concepts of Psychoanalysis,* which became the first of the seminars to be published, marks the beginning of a new and difficult phase in Lacan's teaching. With his audience expanding to include philosophers, literary critics, and historians, as well as psychoanalysts-in-training willing to defy the IPA, Lacan began to shift the central focus of his teaching away from the letter of Freud's texts. While at least a generalized reference to Freud is almost always implicit in his remarks, his weekly lectures now tend to range across a wide variety of texts and intellectual issues. Where his earlier seminars and the essays resulting from them had worked toward developing a psychoanalytic theory based on the actual practice of analysis, the seminars of the 1960s and 1970s stray over a baffling array of philosophical texts, logical paradoxes, and mathematical theorems, their relation to psychoanalytic practice or theory at times seeming quite remote. There is as well a complementary change in

Lacan's style of argument: for the fairly rigorous exposition and commentary of the earlier seminars, he now substitutes a complex web of
analogy and wordplay, often allowing a suggested similarity between
two different domains to serve as the key to a largely unelaborated
argument.

The analogical arguments favored during these years tend to reflect
Lacan's growing concern with the unconscious as essentially the cause of
rupture or inconsistency in human behavior and in conscious discourse.
In his effort to develop a theoretical discourse of such rupture, Lacan
turns in particular to the formal study of paradox. Thus, in his seminar
L'identification (1961–62), Lacan uses the paradoxes of set theory to
elaborate the logical puzzles inherent in the very notion of identity,[2]
while the classic Greek paradox of the liar (that of the Cretan who
announces that all Cretans are liars) figures regularly in Lacan's account
of the way in which truth inheres in the very act of speech (see, for
example, S 11, 121/133, 127–29/138–40; compare *E*, 807–8/305–
6). Similarly, beginning also about the time of the seminar on identification, Lacan attempts to model the human subject with the paradoxical Möbius surfaces of topology—the "interior 8," the Möbius strip,
the Klein bottle, and the crosscap—each of which calls into question
the apparently simple distinction between inside and outside (see, for
example, S 11, 142–43/155–56). By the 1970s the very discourse of
the seminars has almost merged with that of the mathematical model
Lacan uses to clarify the relations between the real, the symbolic, and
the imaginary: working with the topology of Borromean knots—knots
made up of interlocking circles such that the entire knot of circles
comes undone when any one of the circles is cut—Lacan spends much of
his time pursuing theorems of knot theory and their proofs, leaving the
psychoanalytic significance of these theorems largely implicit (see, for
example, S 20, 107–23, as well as much of S 22). What is both
exhilarating and frustrating about these later seminars is that Lacan
almost systematically avoids the kind of argumentative closure that
hearers and readers expect from complex exposition. His discourses on
that which ruptures discourse quite precisely exhibit and even enact the
very rupture in question.

Similarly, Lacan's concern with rupture leads to an ever-growing
delight in multireferential and multilingual wordplay. The seminars of
the 1960s and 1970s are punctuated with an astonishing number of
neologisms, portmanteau words, and more or less spectacular puns.[3] In
thus taking advantage of the material resources of what he playfully

calls *lalangue*—the auditory (and occasionally visual) similarities and differences that constitute the diacritical system of signifiers[4]—Lacan seeks to undercut any naive faith in the classic notion of language as a tool for communication. In accomplishing this, he is of course presenting us as well with the disjunctive and rupturing qualities of the unconscious. Perhaps the most baroque example of Lacan's wordplay can be found in the full title of the very late seminar of 1976–77, which appears in its published form as *L'insu que sait de l'une-bévue, s'aile à mourre*. Embedded in this untranslatable and virtually unintelligible slogan is Freud's German term for the unconscious, *das Unbewusst*, which Lacan renders as *l'une-bévue*, "the one-blunder" (or "the a-blunder") through which is known a sort of "unawareness" (*l'insu*). If we take this unawareness known by means of the unconscious as the subject of the slogan, its verb, *s'aile à mourre*, might be translated as "takes wing to *mourre*," *la mourre* being a game of chance very much like the game of "even and odd" featured in the "Seminar on 'The Purloined Letter.' " However, we may also take the puzzling expression *s'aile à mourre* as being in apposition to "the unawareness known by the one-blunder," in which case this unawareness is clearly identified with love: as Lacan himself notes, *s'aile à mourre* is simply *c'est l'amour* (S 24).[5] *L'amour* is of course also *la mort*, and thus Lacan's title brings together the central psychoanalytic notions of love (*l'amour*), death (*la mort*), and chance (*la mourre*) in a punning definition of the unconscious: *The unawareness known by the one-blunder, that's love/that's death/that's chance!*

Given the intrinsic difficulty of Lacan's later work and the surprising fact that rather little of it is readily available even in French (at least in authorized versions), I do not aim here or in the final chapter of this study to provide the relatively systematic analysis of particular texts offered in earlier chapters. Instead I want to highlight a few new developments in Lacan's teaching of the 1960s and 1970s, developments that in some respects clarify or elaborate and in other respects genuinely transform his theories of the 1950s. In the present chapter I focus my attention on the emergence of the real (*le réel*) as a major theoretical category in Lacan's later work, a category rather shockingly dislodging the symbolic and the imaginary from the center of his attention. (In his seminar of 1974–75, devoted to the topological relations between the real, the symbolic, and the imaginary, the heretical character of Lacan's reflections is signaled by his title, *R. S. I.*, which is a rough homonym of *hérésie*.)

In 1973 Lacan characterizes the real as "the mystery of the speaking body," "the mystery of the unconscious" (S 20, 118), and as such it is clear that the real has come to stand at the very heart of his psychoanalytic reflections. In a sense this had been the case as early as "Function and Field," but the real of the human subject in Lacan's earlier work was largely assimilated by him to Heidegger's notion of *Dasein* as being-toward-death. By the 1960s Lacan is more likely to discuss the real in terms of the general thematic of rupture than in terms of Heideggerian existentialism.[6] Here the key notion with which he associates the real is that of *impossibility* rather than death or temporality (see, for example, S 11, 152/167). In his provocative television interview of 1973 Lacan identifies the real as "that which prevents one from saying the *whole* truth about it" (T, 53/35). Saying "the whole truth" is impossible, not simply because words ultimately fail to reflect the multifaceted character of the real, but because the very fact of language has so ruptured the real that there is no "whole" to be described. All language allows us to speak of is the "reality" constituted by the system of the symbolic; as we saw in chapter 3, human speech inevitably takes as its referent, its fundamental signified, the human discourse constructed through speech. Because "there is no metalanguage," the real perpetually eludes our discourse; "yet it's through this very impossibility that the truth holds onto the real" (T, 9/7). The real, then, stands "behind" the reality constituted in and by our use of language and only hints at its operative presence in the variety of failures or ruptures or inconsistencies that mark this symbolic reality. Lacan's earlier insistence that language has a performative effect on the world, that words in an important sense make things (and, most notably, those things that are human subjects), is now translated into a problematic, linguistic idealism: "The world is merely the fantasy through which thought sustains itself—'reality' no doubt, but to be understood as a grimace of the real" (T, 17/10). The real, the grimace of which is reality, is, as we have already noted, the unconscious.[7] One way, then, to approach Lacan's later work is to see him as trying to make a philosophically and scientifically satisfying case against the claims of linguistic idealism by showing that any such closed idealistic system simply cannot handle the paradoxical ruptures that crisscross it. Just as Kant argued against idealism in the *Critique of Pure Reason* for the sake of a realism of noumena, or "things-in-themselves," which were in principle unknowable,[8] so too Lacan can be seen as working against a structuralist idealism for the sake of a realism of "the mystery of the unconscious."

The distinction between the real and reality allows Lacan to mark a sharp contrast between psychoanalysis and psychology. Where psychoanalysis involves "an essential encounter" with "a real that eludes us" (S 11, 53/53), academic psychology routinely focuses on situations "in which it is we who make reality" (S 11, 130/142). What Lacan has in mind is psychology's dependence upon tests and experiments, none of which do anything more than elaborate the presuppositions already incorporated in the tests and experiments. Speaking of Pavlov's famous experiments, for example, he notes that "we interrogate the animal about our own perception," thus proving "absolutely nothing about the supposed psyche of the unfortunate animal" (S 11, 207/228).[9] More generally, we may say that psychology and both the natural and the social sciences presuppose the fundamentally closed and systematic character of reality. While the scientific worldview remains open-ended in its details, it effectively constitutes itself through the assumption that the system as a whole is a system; that is, that reality (as approached by the sciences) is in principle closed and that everything within reality is in principle capable of being explained by science.

In contrast, psychoanalysis as a praxis is devoted to trying "to treat the real by the symbolic" (S 11, 11/6), thereby utilizing the system of the symbolic to rupture its own closure. What is at stake here is in fact a fundamental epistemological question: How can we know the real, if everything that can be categorized and explained within the framework of a scientific theory belongs to reality? How can any discourse reflect an authentic knowledge of the real? I have already suggested that the distinctive character of Lacan's own late discourse is itself meant to serve as an answer to this very question. In *Télévision* he dismisses traditional epistemology as unable to break out of the reality constituted by discourse (*T*, 58–60/40–41). Lacan does at least suggest, however, that certain branches of mathematics and of logic manage to escape the closure of scientific discourse, approaching the real by means of the study of paradox.

In order to see more clearly just what Lacan thinks we can know about the real, I now turn to his accounts of the role of the real in fantasy and desire, in the Freudian concept of the drive, in the intersubjective structuring achieved by vision, and finally in the concept of sublimation involved in the very notion of ethics. The principal texts at issue in this chapter are the following: a paper delivered in 1960, "The Subversion of the Subject and the Dialectic of Desire in the Freudian Unconscious" (*E*, 793–827/292–325), which develops material first introduced in the seminar of 1957–58 (S 5)[10] and elaborated in the seminar of 1958–59 (S 6);[11] "Kant avec Sade" (*E*, 765–90), an essay originally written in 1962 as a preface for a deluxe edition of the works of Sade but based in large part on the seminar of 1959–60, *L'éthique de la psychanalyse* (S 7); and the seminar of 1964, *The Four Fundamental Concepts of Psychoanalysis* (S 11).

Jouissance and the *objet petit a*

As its title suggests, "The Subversion of the Subject and the Dialectic of Desire" elaborates Lacan's ongoing critique of the classical concept of a unified, Cartesian subject. In many respects the lecture simply repeats, in a manner suitable to the audience of philosophers to whom it was delivered, leading themes of his work of the 1950s, emphasizing in particular the way in which Freud's concept of unconscious desire radically undermines the philosophical tradition's largely unquestioned reliance on a theory of consciousness as the center of the human subject. The lecture exhibits a slight shift of tone, however, which ultimately has immense theoretical implications. Lacan here argues that "the structure of the subject" is manifested as "discontinuity in the real" (*E*, 801/ 299), and in this and subsequent texts he is more likely to speak of the human being as a *coupure* (cut), a *faille* (fault), a *fente* or *refente* (slit), or a *béance* (gap) than to speak (as he typically does in the 1950s) of these forms of discontinuity as characteristics of the human subject. The shift here is perhaps subtle, but in effect Lacan is working his way toward a fully structuralist account of the subject, a theory that identifies subjectivity with structured relations between various terms and that consequently denies that there is any sort of substantial subject existing independently of such structured relations. It is precisely the concept of the subject as a sort of Aristotelian "substance" that is ultimately subverted in "The Subversion of the Subject."

Lacan defends his thesis that the subject is a discontinuity by returning to his familiar claim that the unconscious is structured like a language. In effect this means that the unconscious is "a chain of signifiers that somewhere (on another stage, in another scene, [Freud] wrote) is repeated, and insists on interfering in the breaks [*coupures*] offered it by the effective discourse and the cogitation that it informs" (*E*, 799/297). From this it follows that the question, Who is speaking?, is always an appropriate response to human discourse. Our naive assumption is that the speaker—what Lacan calls "the subject of the enunciation [*énonciation*]"—can generally be identified with "the subject of the statement [*énoncé*]," the *je* or I that designates the speaker. Such an identification, however, would transform a fragment of the real (the speaking body) into a signifier, an element of the system of the symbolic. Moreover, as Lacan notes in the present text, the majority of statements uttered by a human subject lack any signifier of that subject (*E*, 800/298). When, for example, someone tells me that "It's raining cats and dogs," it is not only reasonable but almost necessary that I ask (myself at least), Who is this who tells me such a thing? In place of the unified subject of Western philosophy, then, we find instead "the place of the 'inter-said' (*inter-dit*), which is the 'intra-said' (*intra-dit*) of a between-two-subjects" (*E*, 800/299): the subject exists simply as the discontinuity between intention and meaning introduced by the fact that speech always occurs in relation to another speaker. The result of this is that we cannot put ourselves fully into language; saying everything is forbidden (*interdire*). This is of course another way of expressing Lacan's notion of castration, as he makes clear at the conclusion of his lecture when he asserts that "what analytic experience shows is that, in any case, it is castration that governs desire, whether in the normal or the abnormal" (*E*, 826/323).

The subversion of the substantial subject and its replacement by a complex structure of relations is best illustrated by the graph Lacan uses as the armature of his argument in "The Subversion of the Subject" (*E*, 817/315) (see figure 1). This "graph of desire" is meant to articulate the relations that constitute the identity of the subject: the fundamental trajectory is that from the barred subject—$\mathcal{S}$—to the *moi* ideal (*l'idéal du moi*)—I(A)—and represents the process by which the human subject takes on an identity through his interaction with the Other (*Autre*, with a capital A). In particular the graph illustrates the structure of the process by which the Other's question—What do you want?—is translated into its all-too-human form—What does the Other want of me?—thereby motivating the subject to constitute an identity (*E*, 815/312). [12] What the graph reveals is that identity is a matter of complex relations at all levels, the imaginary, the symbolic, and the real. Thus, the vector from the signifier to the voice—passing from *s*(A) through A—represents the level of conscious discourse. Here A is the synchronic system of the signifier, the Other as language, while *s*(A) is the "punctuation" that allows the signifiers to take on a meaning through the retroactive effect of temporality. (It will be remembered that it is the chain of signifiers in which a signifier is found that ultimately serves as the signified of that signifier.) What we have here

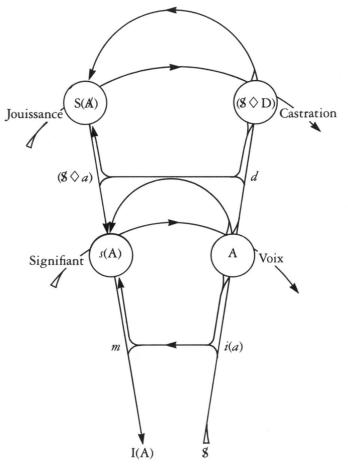

Figure 1. "Graph of Desire"

then is the familiar register of the symbolic as it is articulated in time, the register that results in the subject's discourse taking on a meaning (*sens*). The vectors subordinate to that of conscious discourse, those revolving around the *moi*—*m*—and the ideal *moi (moi idéal)*—*i(a)*— essentially repeat the imaginary doubling that Lacan had discussed in his early papers on the mirror stage and aggression.

What is new in the graph of desire is the upper vector, which runs from *jouissance* to castration by means of the signifier of the barred Other—S(A̶)—and the algorithm of the drive, in which the barred subject finds itself in relation to linguistic demand—($\lozenge$ D). This vector represents the level of the unconscious signifying chain, the unconscious as that which ruptures the unity of the Cartesian subject and its conscious discourse. The upper half of the graph may be taken as a schematization of the familiar dialectic of need, demand, and desire— here symbolized by *d*—the result of which is the fact that "through the effects of speech, the subject always realizes himself more in the Other," that "the subject is subject only from being subjected to the field of the Other" (S 11, 172/188). Such subjection is at least part of what is at issue in Lacan's notion of castration. As we have already seen with reference to his reading of *Hamlet*, however, the more shocking dimension of the subject's relation to the Other lies in the fact that the Other has no more of an identity than does the subject: the Other, too, is essentially castrated; hence, the signifier of the barred Other, S($\cancel{A}$). If the subject exists as divided by the effects of speech, the Other too is divided between the various signifiers that constitute it. Lacan writes: "Any statement of authority has no other guarantee than its very enunciation, and it is pointless for it to seek it in another signifier, which could not appear outside this locus in any way. Which is what I mean when I say that no metalanguage can be spoken, or, more aphoristically, that there is no Other of the Other" (*E*, 813/310–11). Identity, whether that of the subject or of the Other, is always situated in the gap of relationship between one and another: there is no fixed center grounding the existence of anything in the human world.

While we are still dealing with the register of the symbolic here, what the graph now reveals is the way in which the very existence of speech and language in effect castrates the human subject. This castration, Lacan suggests, involves a fundamental but obscure relation between the chain of signifiers and the register of the real. The real is obliquely indicated in the graph at two points: in the undifferentiated realm of *jouissance* that provides the grounding of the unconscious signifying chain and in the structure of fantasy (*le fantasme*) relating the barred subject to a special sort of object in the real—($\lozenge$ *a*)—and taking the place of *jouissance* in the subject's structure. The graph shows how *jouissance* (ultimate sexual enjoyment or bliss)[13] is prohibited from entering the subjective structure. What takes its place is *plaisir* (pleasure), which may be understood as the sort of satisfaction of desire that is inseparably connected to fantasy. In effect, then, the graph presents us with an elaboration of the familiar Lacanian theme that human subjectivity is constituted through giving up the ultimate in satisfac-

tion, an ultimate previously symbolized (as we have seen) by the phallus and now designated by the term *jouissance*.[14] It is the undifferentiated, unlimited, excessive character of *jouissance* that is tamed by the
subject's structure and replaced by the moderate satisfactions toward
which human desires aim (see *E*, 821/319).[15] (Lacan's notion of
jouissance here bears more than a family resemblance to Georges
Bataille's influential theory of eroticism as involving essentially the
notions of excess and transgression.)[16]

Toward the end of "The Subversion of the Subject" Lacan characterizes desire as "a defence [*défense*], a prohibition [*défense*] against going
beyond a certain limit in *jouissance*" (*E*, 825/322). I will return in
chapter 7 to the notion of *jouissance* as marking that fundamental "beyond" that envelops the functioning of the human subject, noting here
only that *jouissance* proper comes to be associated with women's sexuality in the later work of Lacan, while what is here contrasted with
jouissance as *plaisir* becomes in the later work the restricted notion of
phallic *jouissance*, characteristic of men's sexuality.

Turning now to desire, we must try to clarify the relations between
desire, fantasy, and the real. In the seminar of 1964 Lacan makes the
startling claim that "desire, in fact, is interpretation itself" (S 11, 161/
176), and what we are now in a position to see is that desire as such
simply offers a limited and limiting translation of that aspect of the real
designated by *jouissance*. Fundamental to Lacan's theoretical work of the
1960s and 1970s are the related claims that desire has as its cause
fantasy (or, more precisely, the structure of fantasy; see *E*, 814/312) and
that fantasy in turn is dependent upon, supported by, a real object—
what Lacan terms the *objet petit a* (the small *a* standing for *autre*, as
opposed to *Autre*)—although this fragment of the real is essentially
linked to the barred subject, divided by his relation to language, hence
the "algorithm" of phantasy, ($ ◊ a).[17] (In an extended sense, then, the
objet petit a can be described as the cause of desire; see, for example, S
11, ix.)

To say that desire is caused by fantasy is to say that the desiring
subject "sustains himself as desiring in relation to an ever more complex
signifying ensemble" (S 11, 168/185). If desire is what is left over as a
remainder when need is expressed by linguistic demand, it is nevertheless clear that desire is by that very fact necessarily bound up with the
signifying chain of language. That consciously articulated demand is
unable to express the remainder called desire is due to the fact that
something is present in the unconscious signifying chain that is not

strictly speaking symbolic. As Lacan notes in "The Direction of the Treatment," unconscious fantasy "is defined as an image set to work in the signifying structure" (*E*, 637/272). Desire's resistance to symbolization, then, is the effect of the imaginary dimension of fantasy, and this suggests that desire owes its existence—is caused by—the interference of the imaginary in the symbolic. Put in other terms, fantasy causes desire by breaking the continuity of the signifying chain of demand, by rupturing and making indefinite the closure of the symbolic system. In contrast to the law, which Lacan defines as "that which is determinate in a chain," a cause is always "something anti-conceptual, something indefinite," always the disruption present in "something that doesn't work" (S 11, 25/22). As a cause, then, fantasy shares in the impossibility of the real, and it comes as no surprise to see Lacan in 1965 describe fantasy as the "institution of a real."[18] It must be remembered, however, that the real that is fantasy is itself a matter of the rupture of the symbolic by the imaginary; that is, Lacan's theory of fantasy is just as structural and antisubstantialist as his theory of the subject.

In the graph of desire found in "The Subversion of the Subject" fantasy is marked by the "sigla" ($\mathbb{S} \Diamond a$), and this brings us to the second causal claim at issue here, namely that fantasy is dependent, and thus caused by, a real object, the *objet petit a* (or *objet a*). What Lacan's algebraic sigla indicates is that fantasy consists in the close relation between the barred subject and certain real objects: without these objects, fragments of the real, there could be no fantasy (and, hence, no desire). In a note to "The Direction of the Treatment" Lacan indicates that the sign $\Diamond$ "registers the relations envelopment-development-conjunction-disjunction" (*E*, 634 n. 1/280 n.26), contradictory relations to which Catherine Clément adds "the mathematical symbols for "greater than" (>) and "less than" (<), an absurd combination, well chosen to signify the essence of fantasy, namely, its impossibility."[19] Commenting on this sign in "Kant avec Sade" Lacan adds that it expresses as well "an identity which is founded on an absolute non-reciprocity" (*E*, 774), thus suggesting that what is impossible is to conceive independently of either the barred subject or its objects.[20]

If there is in this way something virtually inexpressible about the relational structure that constitutes fantasy, is it possible to say anything more about the object(s) to which the subject is related in fantasy? Perhaps the first thing that should be emphasized is that these objects play a crucial role in the subject's identity. Once the law of

language and the exigencies of speech have deprived the subject of the
all-powerful phallus and prohibited him from the free pursuit of
jouissance, the subject inevitably seeks a substitute to take the place of
the lost, all-satisfying object. The *objet petit a* is Lacan's name for that
something. In his seminar on *Hamlet* Lacan had described the process
involved here as one of mourning and argued that the replacement of
the phallus by the *objet a* was a crucial step in transforming a narcissistic
ego into a fully, maturely desiring subject. In "The Subversion of the
Subject" he adds that "the phantasy is really the 'stuff' of the 'I' [*Je*] that
is originally repressed" (*E,* 816/314). In other words the subject breaks
free from narcissism by melding his own being with that of the objects
on which his fantasies depend.

Now, these objects are associated with the erogenous zones, those
parts of the body where the distinction between inside and outside is
both marked and blurred by an anatomical border: "lips, 'the enclosure
of the teeth', the rim of the anus, the tip of the penis, the vagina, the
slit formed by the eyelids, even the horn-shaped aperture of the ear" (*E,*
817/314–15). (The zones described as erogenous are clearly connected
with the notion of instinct or drive, for which see the next section of
this chapter.) The actual objects, then, can be listed: "the mamilla,
faeces, the phallus (imaginary object), the urinary flow. (An unthinkable list, if one adds, as I do, the phoneme, the gaze, the voice—the
nothing.)" (*E,* 817/315). Each of these objects, Lacan claims, is a
partial representation of the function that produces it: thus, the feces
may stand for the set of processes associated with the rim of the anus
precisely because they are produced by those processes (see *E,* 817/315).
More crucial to the concept of the *objet a,* however, is the fact that each
of these objects is originally a part of the subject's body. In the seminar
of 1964 Lacan elaborates this point in response to a question: "The *objet
a* is something from which the subject, in order to constitute itself, has
separated itself off as organ. This serves as a symbol of the lack, that is
to say, of the phallus, not as such, but insofar as it is lacking. It must,
therefore, be an object that is, firstly, separable and, secondly, that has
some relation to the lack" (S 11, 95/103). In forming an almost symbi-
otic unity with such objects, the subject constitutes himself as a real
something over against the system of the symbolic and the various
chains of signifiers that determine his identity within the symbolic
register. As such the *objet a* serves as the "point of lack" at which "the
subject has to recognize himself" (S 11, 243/270).

We see here one of the many paradoxes that Lacan will explore throughout his later work: it is as points of lack, as nothings, that the objects in fantasy serve to constitute the subject's identity. He elaborates this point in "The Subversion of the Subject": "These objects have one common feature in my elaboration of them—they have no specular image, or, in other words, alterity. It is what enables them to be the 'stuff', or rather the lining, though not in any sense the reverse, of the very subject that one takes to be the subject of consciousness. For this subject, who thinks he can accede to himself by designating himself in the statement, is no more than such an object" (*E,* 818/315). Part of what Lacan seems to mean by this is that the *objet a* should not be confused with a simply imaginary object. By definition imaginary objects have specular images (indeed, they owe their origins to the mirror stage, which gives them their distinctive structural role in the constitution of the human subject). Thus, the *objet a* breast which is the cause of a particular fantasy must not be confused with the breast that might play a role in a given individual's imagined fantasy scenario. The lover's breast is an imaginary substitute (of which one can be fully conscious) for the real breast which is the cause of the subject's fantasy and desire. This real breast (of which one would generally not be conscious) in turn is (or, more properly, was) the mother's breast, that organ which once seemed inseparable from the subject's own being and which has now been lost forever. The difference here between the imagined object and the real *objet a* would emerge quite starkly in the negative response likely to be received if one were to ask an adult subject whether or not he would really like to suck at his mother's breast.

We saw in our review of the *Hamlet* seminar that Lacan argues that all human desire is essentially fetishistic. The grounds for this claim rest on his analysis that fantasied objects of desire are substitutes for the lost phallus, just as Freud had maintained that the fetish is a substitute for the castrated penis. By the time of "The Subversion of the Subject" Lacan has refined this position a bit, as we have seen, sharpening the distinction between the fantasied, imaginary objects of desire and the real *objet petit a* that causes desire and adding that the fetishistic dimension of desire is more strictly applicable to men—the man being "the weak sex in the case of perversion" (*E,* 823/320)—than to women. We might add that the fetishism present here occurs at two distinct levels, since the substitution of the *objet a* for the infinite *jouissance* of the lost phallus makes possible the subject's identity (his "stuffing"), while a further substitution of an imaginary fantasy object for the real *objet petit a* actually makes possible the subject's pursuit of human others in the intersubjective world. Thus, the subversion of the Cartesian subject announced in 1960 finds its completion in Lacan's vision of the human being as ruptured by the existence of language, as constituting an identity for itself in the face of this rupture by finding itself in unimaginable objects that are little more than "the slag [*la scorie*] of a phantasm" (*E, 780*), and as causally determined in its desiring by these fundamentally useless objects. So much for the unity, the dignity, and the freedom of the Cartesian subject, as well as for its countless heirs in the philosophical tradition reaching all the way to Sartre and beyond.

The Fading of the Subject

Having in this way disposed of the pretensions of the Cartesian subject, Lacan moves in the 1960s toward the surprising position that the method of psychoanalysis is radically Cartesian. In fact, it would not be going too far to maintain that the central theme of the seminar of 1964, *The Four Fundamental Concepts of Psychoanalysis,* is that a genuinely Cartesian method has as its inevitable consequence the overthrow, the decentering, of the Cartesian subject.

To understand the direction of Lacan's thought here it will be helpful to begin by considering the implications of his theory of fantasy. Lacan regularly describes the status of the subject caught up in the structure of fantasy—($ \lozenge a$)—by using the English term, "fading." We have already seen that the effect of language on the human subject, the "primal repression" or "castration" or "splitting" that results in the subject's becoming a barred subject ($), is to make the subject disappear or slip away beneath the signifying chain by means of which he is constituted within the register of the symbolic as a *je.* In "The Subversion of the Subject" the classic Freudian examples of dreams, slips of the tongue, and witticisms are taken as themselves "effects of 'fading' " in the sense that the subject fades away "by its occultation by an ever purer signifier" (*E, 800–801/299*). Thus the subject as caught up in fantasy is already in the process of fading beneath the chain of signifiers. This dimension of fading is complemented, however, by yet another fading of the subject, this time in relation to the *objet petit a* that causes his fantasy. The process described above, whereby the subject makes up for his loss of pure *jouissance,* for the symbolic castration of the phallus, by unconsciously "stuffing" himself (thereby creating himself) with such objects as feces and urine, is itself a process through which the subject fades away as something distinct from these *objets a*. Thus Lacan notes that he is attempting "to complete the structure of the phantasy by linking it essentially, whatever its occasional elisions may be, to the condition of an object . . . , the moment of a 'fading' or eclipse of the subject that is closely bound up with the *Spaltung* or splitting that it suffers from its subordination to the signifier." It is precisely this splitting of the subject by the signifier and his fading in relation to the *objet petit a* that is "symbolized by the sigla ($ \lozenge a$)" (*E,* 815–16/313).

An indication of the importance of this concept of fading to Lacan's theory of fantasy is found in "Kant avec Sade," where the subject's fading is tied directly to "the pleasure proper to desire" (*E,* 773–74). What Lacan argues here is that fantasy is the cause of the subject's pleasure (as well as the cause of desire) precisely to the extent that the subject experiences his own fading—either with respect to the signifier or with respect to the *objet a*—through his entertaining of the fantasy. The proof of this claim rests on "physiological experiment," which shows that pleasure and pain both end in the same limit (*terme*): "the fainting away [*évanouissement*] of the subject" (*E,* 774). That toward which pleasure tends, and thereby in relation to which pleasure can be given a teleological (or even a functional) account, is quite simply the subject's disappearance, the subject's fading in relation to other elements of the relational structure in which subjectivity is constituted. Something of this sort is found in the rather common experience of "losing oneself" in the course of such diverse activities as enjoying a film, participating in a sporting event, or reaching sexual orgasm.

Paradoxically enough it is in the light of the subject's fading that we can begin to grasp Lacan's position that psychoanalysis involves a Cartesian method. In the third session of the 1964 seminar Lacan rightfully remarks that Descartes's *cogito*—the claim that "I think; therefore, I am"—serves as a keystone in his philosophical system not so much because it establishes the ontological priority of consciousness but because it is one claim of which he can be *certain*. The Cartesian method is a method rooted in a quest for certainty, and certainty provides both the goal of the method and the modus operandi by which this goal is to be achieved (see S 11, 36/35). In the same way, "Freud's method is Cartesian," Lacan argues, "in the sense that he sets out from the basis of the subject of certainty. The question is—of what can one be certain?" What one can be certain of is, precisely, doubt: "Doubt is the support of his certainty" (S 11, 36/35). Lacan is here calling attention to the fact that the psychoanalytic method, quite apart from what it may yield in

terms of theoretical content, focuses on exactly the ruptures in consciousness, the failures of coherence, the inconsistencies marking every
human being's life in the world, all of which fall into the later Lacan's
register of the real. In thus focusing on disruption, psychoanalysis
treats as certain the claim that there is something—namely, the
unconscious—the truth and efficacy of which are preserved quite literally by the very existence of the conscious doubt that attends such
disruption. In this way, then, the fading of the subject, as a striking
disruption in consciousness, is simultaneously a compelling revelation
of the certainty of the unconscious.

In raising the issue of certainty Lacan is also raising more general
questions of epistemology, questions about the nature of human knowledge. In "The Subversion of the Subject" such questions first surface in
the context of the psychoanalytic theory of the instincts, and a review of
Lacan's radical rethinking of this theoretical terrain will do much to
clarify (among other things) the difficult relation between knowledge
and the real. Lacan introduces this topic with a discussion of terms (*E*,
803/301). The term translated as "instinct" in the standard English
edition of Freud is *Trieb*, a word quite naturally translated as "drive" or
"impulse."[21] Lacan's regular French translation is "the bastard term
'*pulsion*'," although he clearly prefers the punning *dérive*, which fuses
the notions of *drive* and *drift* (see also *T*, 42/28). What this discussion of
translation leads up to is an important critique of traditional "theory of
knowledge" using the French distinction between *savoir* and
connaissance, both of which can be translated as "knowledge," as a wedge
to distinguish Lacan's own position from that of the tradition. The
philosophical tradition has treated instinct as "*connaissance* that has the
astonishing property of being unable to be a *savoir*" (*E*, 803/301–2),
that is, as a natural, prelinguistic, and at least potentially conscious
experience that cannot be articulated fully in ordinary or scientific
discourse.[22] "But in Freud," Lacan insists, "it is a question of something quite different, which is a *savoir*, certainly, but one that involves
not the least *connaissance*, in that it is inscribed in a discourse, of which,
like the 'messenger-slave' of ancient usage, the subject who carries
under his hair the codicil that condemns him to death knows neither
the meaning nor the text, nor in what language it is written, nor even
that it had been tatooed on his shaven scalp as he slept" (*E*, 803/302).
We see here in quite dramatic terms that Lacan relates the concept of
Trieb, or drive, quite directly to the register of the symbolic: what is
taken by many commentators on Freud as little more than a biological

instinct becomes in Lacan the effect of a signifying chain inscribed on the subject's very body.[23] We might note in passing that the modern tradition of "theory of knowledge" (*théorie de la connaissance*) has tended to ground *savoir* in *connaissance*, ultimately following Aristotle's lead in finding certainty at the level of immediate experiences of a particular sort, while Lacan is clearly promoting an epistemology of *savoir* as something quite distinct from any *connaissance*.

Further on in "The Subversion of the Subject" Lacan develops the concept of the drive, characterizing it as "that which proceeds from demand when the subject disappears in it." By symbolizing it on the graph of desire with the sigla ($ \lozenge $ D), he emphasizes that the notion of fading provides a crucial point of similarity between fantasy and drive (*E*, 816–17/314). Moreover, the relation between drives and the symbolic is elaborated in a sentence that will provide much of the material for Lacan's reflections in *The Four Fundamental Concepts*: "Hence the concept of drive, in which [the subject] is designated by an organic, oral, anal, etc., mapping that satisfies the requirement of being all the farther away from speaking the more he speaks" (*E*, 816/314). In other words, it is the symbolic system, the chain of signifiers, that articulates the subject's body into erogenous zones with which the drives can be correlated. Indeed, it is only by means of signifying chains that stages of sexual development can be distinguished so as to be retroactively attributed to the subject's body. Hence, the drive is distinguished from "the organic function it inhabits" by "its grammatical artifice" (*E*, 817/ 314). This is an effect of language—and thus a *savoir*—that utterly escapes the *connaissance* of the driven subject, the subject set "adrift" by the symbolic register.

To see just how radical is Lacan's revision of the traditional reading of Freud, we must turn to his rather detailed commentary on the text of Freud's 1915 essay, "Triebe und Triebschicksale," translated into English as "Instincts and Their Vicissitudes."[24] In this essay Freud outlines a general conceptual framework for the understanding of instincts or drives by distinguishing four component aspects of every drive.[25] 1) Each drive has its source in a particular bodily process "whose stimulus is represented in mental life by an instinct," but the study of such sources "lies outside the scope of psychology" as a matter of biology. 2) Insofar as it is a kind of stimulus, a drive must exert an active pressure upon the psychical system; in the absence of any such pressure there simply is no drive or impulse. (In the case of the sexual drives this pressure is termed *libido*.)[26] 3) Each drive has as its aim satisfaction, and this satisfaction is obtained "by removing the state of stimulation at the source of the instinct." Since it is impossible to flee the stimulation of the drives, thanks to their origin within the organism, the satisfaction of each drive depends on some change in the body. 4) The aim of a drive, its satisfaction, is achieved through the appropriation of that drive's object, causing a bodily change that results in satisfaction. This process is facilitated by the fact that a number of different objects may satisfy one and the same drive (both water and wine may satisfy thirst for example), and, conversely, a single object may satisfy a number of different drives simultaneously (as is the case in complex sexual encounters). The fluidity of this relationship between a drive's aim and object is what makes possible the transformations of a drive, which Freud terms "vicissitudes."

About this complex analysis Lacan remarks in the thirteenth session of the 1964 seminar that it is not as "natural" as it may at first seem; indeed, he puts special emphasis on Freud's own description of the drive as a basic scientific "convention"[27] or, as Lacan prefers, following Jeremy Bentham, "a fundamental fiction" (S 11, 148–49/162–63). After reviewing Freud's fourfold analysis in some detail, Lacan concludes by comparing the whole account to a montage and in particular "in the sense in which one speaks of *montage* in a surrealist collage." He playfully elaborates this point with an image: "If we bring together the paradoxes that we just defined at the level of *Drang* [pressure], at that of the object, at that of the aim of the drive, I think that the resulting image would show the working of a dynamo connected up to a gas-tap, a peacock's feather emerges, and tickles the belly of a pretty woman, who is just lying there looking beautiful" (S 11, 154/169). What Lacan is stressing is the idea that Freud's concept of drive is in fact simply an assemblage of heterogeneous elements—some perhaps biological in their roots, but all clearly shaped by cultural or symbolic factors. It is precisely as a fiction, supported and determined by the register of the symbolic, that the drive holds together as a scientific concept. While this is the case with respect to each of the drives—for example, the possible choice of *Coca-Cola* as an object satisfying the drive of thirst is surely determined by a complex signifying chain— Lacan pays special attention to the notion of the genital drive in this respect. In a later session of the same seminar he argues that the genital drive is essentially constituted "in the field of the Other," that it is "subjected to the circulation of the Oedipus complex, to the elementary and other structures of kinship," and that, because of this, it is far from being a natural phenomenon of the biological organism (S 11, 173/189).

If we ask what it is in the drive that is natural, or, more properly, what belongs to the register of the real, Lacan's answer is that "what is fundamental at the level of each drive is the movement outwards and back in which it is structured" (S 11, 162/177). What he seems to have in mind is that each drive, although structured down to the finest detail by symbolic codes, nevertheless involves an almost indescribable movement out from the subject's body, toward some object, and back in toward the body again (see S 11, 162–65/178–81). There is, beneath all the cultural, symbolic encoding of the body, a real circuit between the body and its object, between more specifically those areas of the body where inside and outside meet and the *objets petit a* that partially represent the related bodily functions. Crucial to Lacan's account here is that the real object around which the circuit of the drive turns is not the symbolically determined object that ultimately (if only temporarily) satisfies the drive: the *objet petit a* must not be confused, for example, with a hamburger. Rather, the *objet a* "is introduced from the fact that no food will ever satisfy the oral drive, except by circumventing the eternally lacking object" (S 11, 164/180). The real object whose existence provides the support for the drive "is in fact simply the presence of a hollow, a void, which can be occupied, Freud tells us, by any object" (S 11, 164/180). As such, the real object in the drive is constituted only after the subject has been ruptured by the existence of speech and language: the drives are dependent for their real existence on the subject's symbolic castration, which launches the search for substitutes for the object forever lost.

The first radical consequence of this account is that Lacan's theory of the drives has nothing to do with any sort of developmental model of human sexuality. "There is no natural metamorphosis of the oral drive into the anal drive," he notes (thereby dismissing precisely the biological basis underlying Heinz Hartmann's attempt to unite psychoanalysis and developmental psychology in the theory of ego psychology); it is rather "by the intervention, the overthrow, of the demand of the Other" that the effects of so-called maturation are achieved (S 11, 164/180). It is the intervention of the field of speech and language that determines the "instinctual" drift of the drives in the life of the human subject. In particular, Lacan maintains in response to a question raised by Françoise Dolto, the so-called stages of development are in fact "organized" and given their meaning in the life of the subject by the fear of castration:

"The fear of castration is like a thread that perforates all the stages of development. It orientates the relations that are anterior to its actual appearance—weaning, toilet training, etc. It crystallizes each of these moments in a dialectic that has as its center a bad encounter" (S 11, 62/ 64). In other words, the chronology of the stages, the fact that they fit into a series of "stages," is a retrospective product of the "deferred action" of castration anxiety. Without the castrating intervention of the register of the symbolic, the drives of the human subject would not fit into the developmental sequence in which we claim to find them.

A second consequence of this account is that the concept of drive must be strictly distinguished from that of need. This again goes against the biologically oriented interpretation of Freud by emphasizing, for example, that food has essentially nothing to do with the satisfaction of the oral drive. "Even when you stuff the mouth—the mouth that opens in the register of the drive—it is not the food that satisfies it, it is, as one says, the pleasure of the mouth" (S 11, 153/ 167). This brings us back of course to the idea that it is the lost object, the *objet petit a*—the breast, in this example—that is fundamental to the existence of the drive. When Freud remarks that the object in the drive "is what is most variable about an instinct and is not originally connected with it,"[28] Lacan reads this as entailing that the drive's object is fundamentally useless and thus unrelated to any biological need (S 11, 153/168). Indeed, the drive's object is not even accessible to the subject (or to the subject's consciousness); it is essentially an object forever lost and is, as such, simply "impossible" (S 11, 152/167). Again, we see Lacan's insistence on grounding the concept of the drive in the register of the real, even if virtually all of the drive's manifestations are determined by the signifying chains of the symbolic.[29]

A third consequence of Lacan's account of the drive involves the intersubjective context within which the circuit from body to *objet a* occurs. We have already seen that the Other, as the locus of the symbolic, is fundamentally involved in permitting certain objects of need to attempt to substitute for the *objets petit a* of the drives. Lacan goes beyond this claim, however, to argue that every drive essentially involves the subject's constituting himself in relation to others who may occupy the position of the Other. He illustrates this most fully with the example of the scopic drive, the drive associated with the eye, with vision, and with the gaze (*le regard*). In essence, Lacan says, "what is involved in the drive is *making oneself seen {se faire voir}*. The activity of the drive is concentrated in this *making oneself {se faire}*, and it is by relating it to the field of the other drives that we may be able to throw some light upon it" (S 11, 177–78/195). Similarly, Lacan argues that there is a drive associated with the voice, and the activity here is *"making oneself heard."* With respect to the more familiarly Freudian oral and anal drives, Lacan is a bit less precise, but the parallel activities seem to be "making oneself be gobbled up" and "making oneself be shitted" (S 11, 177–78/195–96, 181–82/200), the former activity relating to masochism and the latter introducing the notions of the gift and of purification. In each of these cases what is most notable is that the subject's relation with the *objet a,* as well as with the particular symbolically approved substitute for this *objet a,* involves an activity by means of which the subject constructs himself (*se faire*) in relation to possible other subjects.

A final consequence of Lacan's account brings us back to the notion of the fading of the subject (here described with Ernest Jones's term "aphanisis"). In a rather difficult discussion of the relations between the subject and the Other, a discussion using concepts taken from set theory, Lacan argues that the subject fades in his being at the very moment that he finds himself given a meaning by a particular signifier (see S 11, 191/210). At one level, of course, this is just a variation of Lacan's earlier, Hegelian-Heideggerian meditation on the intimate connection between language and death. With respect to the account of the drives that we have been considering, however, this argument suggests that the driven subject—the subject locked in that relation to demand symbolized by the notation ($\lozenge$D)—is caught up in fading just as the fantasizing subject fades beneath the *objet a,* cause of the fantasy. Where the fantasizing subject fades into an identity with those mysterious, but real, *objets petit a,* the subject drifting in the drives apparently fades into an identity with the signifiers from the cultural field of the Other inscribed on his body by means of the fear of castration.

Curiously, in the 1973 interview *Télévision,* Lacan extends his account of the drives to cover the case of affect as well. Suggesting that "my idea that the unconscious is structured like a language allows one to verify affect more seriously" (T, 37/24), Lacan points out that philosophical accounts of the passions ever since Plato have distinguished between different passions by making reference to different parts of the body. These parts of the body are themselves distinguished from each other simply by means of distinctions borrowed from the symbolic register; it is language that differentiates body parts, just as it is language that differentiates erogenous zones and drives. Thus, if affects can be approached only by means of reference to parts of the body, then Lacan suggests that the body is "affected only by the structure" (*T*, 39/ 26): affect is a product of language. He concludes with a characteristic flourish: "Affect, therefore, befalls a body whose essence it is said is to dwell in language—I am borrowing plumage which sells better than my own—affect, I repeat befalls it on account of its not finding dwelling-room, at least not to its taste. This we call moroseness, or equally, moodiness. Is this a sin, a grain of madness, or a true touch of the real?" (*T*, 41/27–28). As the translators of *Télévision* point out, the borrowed plumage here is that of the later Heidegger,[30] but for our purposes the more intriguing dimension of the passage is Lacan's hint that affect is the product in the human body of some sort of conflict between the symbolic and the real. The body cannot quite dwell in language, and affect is the sign it takes on of its real resistance to such a dwelling. That this "touch of the real" may be confused with madness or sin suggests, once again, the distinctively Lacanian notion of the real as that which fails to conform to the signifying structures of language, which disrupts all coherence, and which refuses to be subsumed under any closed notion of possibility or reality.

The Gaze

We have seen that Lacan subverts the traditional philosophical notion of the subject in a number of ways, and in this chapter I have been particularly emphasizing the manner in which his difficult account of the real plays a special role in this intellectual subversion. One of the factors that makes Lacan's account of the real so difficult is that he so completely defies our expectations about any such account. In particular he destabilizes the customary distinction between the knowing subject and the known object to such an extent that the former begins to take on a tinge of the real, with all the unknowability that this entails for Lacan, while the latter becomes indistinguishable from the register of the symbolic. One way of highlighting this transformation is found late in the seminar of 1964, where Lacan uses his notion of the fading of the subject to mount a critique of "philosophical idealism." Lacan's target here is not simply the metaphysical claim that reality is in an important sense dependent upon the mind, but the much more widely accepted (indeed almost universally held) theory that the human subject is essentially involved in representing the world, that knowing is to be understood as a kind of mirroring or picturing of that which is outside the consciousness of the knower.[31] About this theory, Lacan offers the following observation:

And things might be thus, were there in the world subjects, each entrusted with the task of representing certain conceptions of the world. Indeed, this is the essential flaw in philosophical idealism which, in any case, cannot be sustained and has never been radically sustained. There is no subject without, somewhere, *aphanisis* [fading] of the subject, and it is in this alienation, in this fundamental division, that the dialectic of the subject is established. (S 11, 201/221)

Because the subject is constantly and inevitably involved in a number of different forms of fading—fading before the fear of castration (primal repression), fading before the signifiers of demand (in the drive), and fading before the *objets petit a* involved in fantasy—the subject lacks precisely the unity and coherence that the mirror analogy of the knowing subject demands. In fact, for Lacan the subject is not so much a representer as itself a representation, and it is this fact that most profoundly disrupts the idealism of the traditional theory of knowledge. In order to grasp Lacan's point here we must turn to the four sessions of *The Four Fundamental Concepts* that he devotes to the topic "Of the Gaze as *objet petit a*" (S 11, 63–109/65–119).

Lacan situates his discussion here very much in the field of more or less contemporary French philosophy. On the one hand, he opens his analysis by paying homage to his late friend, the phenomenologist Maurice Merleau-Ponty (S 11, 68–70/70–73).[32] In his posthumously published work, *The Visible and the Invisible* (1964),[33] Merleau-Ponty probes the mysterious conjunction of "the visible" and "the invisible," the fact that the things we see somehow manifest something that transcends both the features disclosed by vision and the consciousness of the one who sees. This transcendent "invisible" bears a certain relation to Lacan's mysterious notion of the real, both of these concepts integrally involving the operation of a gaze (*regard*) that paradoxically cannot be distinguished from the objects toward which the gaze turns. Thus Merleau-Ponty writes: "What there is then are not things first identical with themselves, which would then offer themselves to the seer, nor is there a seer who is first empty and who, afterward, would open himself to them—but something to which we could not be closer than by palpating it with our look, things we could not dream of seeing 'all naked' because the gaze itself envelops them, clothes them with its own flesh."[34] On the other hand, much of Lacan's actual argument is shaped by Sartre's influential claims in *Being and Nothingness* (1943) that "my fundamental connection with the Other-as-subject must be able to be referred back to my permanent possibility of *being seen* by the Other" and that "this relation which I call 'being-seen-by-another,' far from being merely one of the relations signified by the word *man,* represents an irreducible fact which can not be deduced either from the essence of the Other-as-object, or from my being-as-subject."[35] Thus, while he gives Merleau-Ponty credit for indicating the path he is to take, Lacan makes the Sartrean goal of that path quite clear: "What we have to circumscribe, by means of the path he [Merleau-Ponty] indicates for us, is the pre-existence of a gaze [*un regard*]—I see only from one point, but in my existence I am looked at from all sides" (S 11, 69/72).

Sartre's discussion in *Being and Nothingness* revolves around the curious example of Sartre's own peering through a keyhole "moved by jealousy, curiosity, or vice."[36] Among other things Sartre argues here that his presence at the keyhole—as an unreflective consciousness embodied in space and time and as a concrete complex of possibilities—is actually dependent upon the existence of the Other. In particular, his presence is dependent upon the fact that "the Other *is watching me.*"[37] Nevertheless, Sartre emphasizes that the reality of "being-looked-at" need not presuppose the immediate existence of a particular object or other person manifesting the gaze. The Other's gaze is in its essence "invisible," although its presence is for Sartre absolutely certain: "In a word what is certain is that *I am* looked-at; what is only probable is that the look is bound to this or that intra-mundane presence."[38]

What we have in both Merleau-Ponty and Sartre is the paradoxical logic reflected in Lacan's notion of the *objet petit a*: the logic of something that lies behind our more or less conscious experience, the effect of which is manifested in that experience without this something's itself being readily accessible to consciousness. This, of course, is the basic logic of the unconscious for Lacan, and it is equally the defining logic of the register of the real.

The direction Lacan will pursue in the seminar on the gaze is already hinted at in the essay, "Kant avec Sade," written in September 1962. Here, writing of desire in a Kantian context, he formulates the necessary intersubjectivity of desire—an intersubjectivity generally epitomized in the phrase "desire is desire of the Other"—in terms of the gaze: "The look [*le regard*] is indeed there, object that presents to each desire its universal rule by materializing its cause in binding to it the

division 'between the center and the absence' of the subject" (*E*, 785).
The gaze of another person—and here the gaze of every other is essentially equivalent, this fact grounding Lacan's invocation of a quasi-
Kantian "universal rule"—this gaze reveals the cause of the subject's
desire. As we have seen, this cause is the *objet petit a*, and it in effect
identifies the subject as something constituted in suspension between
self and other. In other words it is the gaze of another person that
determines the subjectivity of—that "subjectifies"—the human being,
and the gaze accomplishes this precisely by causing a particular sort of
desire.

By 1964 Lacan has shifted his attention primarily to the notion of
the drive, and the gaze emerges in *The Four Fundamental Concepts* in the
context of the scopic drive, that drive correlated with the eye as erogenous zone. The gaze is here defined as the *objet petit a* "in the field of the
visible" that as such supports the scopic fantasy (S 11, 97/105 and 78–
79/83). As we have seen in our review of Lacan's theories of fantasy and
of the drives, the gaze is correlated with a particular part of the subject's body—the eyes—in roughly the same sort of way that, for example, the breast is associated with the mouth. From the admittedly non-
Lacanian perspective of child development, we might say that what is
involved here is the *jouissance* initially inseparable from the loving gaze
of the parents: a *jouissance* rooted in the fact that the gaze incarnates the
parents' recognition of the infant as subject. (Recall that even as early as
"Function and Field" Lacan insists that "the first object of desire is to be
recognized by the other" [*E*, 268/58].) With the infant's maturation
the objects of vision proliferate endlessly, while recognition in the gaze
tends to be replaced by forms of recognition bound up with language
and discourse. The parental gaze thus becomes lost to the subject, and a
split is opened up between the eye and its object of satisfaction, the
gaze (S 11, 70/73). Noting that even in Sartre's analysis the gaze is "not
a seen gaze, but a gaze imagined by me in the field of the Other" (S 11,
79/84), Lacan sketches a similar account, maintaining that "the gaze is
outside, I am looked at, that is to say, I am a picture" within the
structure of the scopic fantasy (S 11, 98/106).

The scopic fantasy, then, identifies the subject as essentially "a
given-to-be-seen," which exists only in relation to an imagined gaze (S
11, 78–80/83–85). Even as the subject identifies with this given-to-
be-seen, this picture, however, he effectively alienates himself from
himself by identifying with the *objet a* gaze, by allowing himself to be
"stuffed" with this necessarily lost and impossible object. We have here

an almost archetypal case of the *moi* as frustration, a situation the
foundation for which is laid at the mirror stage of the infant, where he
recognizes himself only in an alienating image of the self as other (see
E, 97–99/4–6). Lacan highlights the alienating nature of the subject's
being given-to-be-seen by describing it sometimes as a "screen" and
sometimes as *la tache*: both the "spot" implicated in the phenomena of
animal mimicry, pheonomena themselves dependent upon the functioning of a preexistent gaze, and the "stain" of moral and existential
inadequacy (S 11, 71/74).

The alienating character of the scopic fantasy and the frustration of
the *moi* constituted in it as *tache* are by no means hidden from the
subject. Lacan writes:

> From the outset, we see, in the dialectic of the eye and the gaze, that there is
> no coincidence, but, on the contrary, a lure. When, in love, I solicit a look,
> what is profoundly unsatisfying and always missing is that—*You never look at
> me from the place where I see you.*
> Conversely, *what I look at is never what I wish to see.* (S 11, 94–95/102–3)

This awareness on the part of the subject that there is an ongoing
conflict between the gaze as *objet a* and the actual gaze of the other
person, this awareness that the *moi* as *tache* is never the body that is seen
nor the *je* of discourse, actually provides the subject with a means of
escape from the trap of the gaze as *objet petit a.* Rather than suffer
passively the effects of the gaze supporting the fantasy, one may exploit
the screen or stain or mask that is produced by the existence of this
gaze. "Only the subject—the human subject, the subject of the desire
that is the essence of man—is not, unlike the animal, entirely caught
up in this imaginary capture. He maps himself in it. How? Insofar as
he isolates the function of the screen and plays with it. Man, in effect,
knows how to play with the mask as that beyond which there is the
gaze. The screen is here the locus of mediation" (S 11, 99/107). In this
way the scopic fantasy, defined by its connection to the gaze as *objet petit
a,* can potentially lead to something other than the subject's alienation
in his being given-to-be-seen. It may in fact lead to the subject's using
this being given-to-be-seen as a means to facilitate a dealienating dialogue with the Other.

This ability of the human being to make use of the fact that, in the
scopic drive, he "makes himself seen" (*se faire voir*) (see S 11, 177–78/
195) is what grounds Lacan's attempt to clarify the problematic notion

of sublimation so integral to aesthetic theories shaped by psychoanalysis. Having argued that the subject is a "picture" (*tableau*) within the intersubjective structure of the scopic fantasy, Lacan devotes the final session of the seminar on the gaze to a sketchy theory of the painting (*tableau*) as a picture. One key to grasping Lacan's approach here is that the painting (or other work of visual art) manifests in the intersubjective dynamic of its structure the invisible, impossible, forever lost *objet a* gaze.[39]

Much of Lacan's seminar on the gaze is devoted to the way in which the development of "geometral optics" in sixteenth- and seventeenth-century painting has the effect of reducing the presupposed viewer of such paintings to a punctiform being, that spatial point in relation to which the perspective of the painting unfolds. This sort of optical theory and the painting derived from it thereby fail to exhaust "what the field of vision as such offers us as the original subjectifying relation" (S 11, 81/87). In failing to do justice to the subjective richness of the viewer these paintings unwittingly manifest "something symbolic of the function of the lack, of the appearance of the phallic ghost" (S 11, 82/88), a lack brilliantly illustrated in the anamorphic skull that floats in the foreground of Hans Holbein's painting *The Ambassadors* (1533).[40] While Lacan's remarks on this subject are of great interest (and have stimulated the important recent work of such art historians as Norman Bryson),[41] what is more important at the theoretical level is Lacan's insistence that painting as such involves a "subjectifying" function. In other words, paintings have the power to make or shape or transform human subjects, and from this it follows that painting is not essentially a matter of representation (S 11, 100/108). The history of painting is thus the sequence of "the variations of the subjectifying structure that have occurred in history" (S 11, 100/109).

Lacan is more than usually evasive in his account of how a painting subjectifies its viewer, but the heart of the process is that a painting can cause a viewer to give up his search for the gaze as *objet petit a*. In giving up the gaze, the viewer gives up as well—and more importantly—that part of his *moi* that has been stuffed or lined by this gaze. He renounces his being given-to-be-seen as constitutive of his identity, and this is a critical step on the way toward the viewing subject's dealienation from the *moi*.

The process of giving up the gaze begins with the viewer's search for the gaze in the painting. Naturally, something of an other's gaze is regularly found in any painting (inasmuch as there always is an other

responsible for the painting) (S 11, 93/101). However, Lacan argues for
the apparent paradox that "in any picture, it is precisely in seeking the
gaze in each of its points that you will see it disappear" (S 11, 83/89).
Careful inspection of any painting will reveal an inescapable conflict
between its manifestation of the invisible *objet a* gaze and the painting's
essentially physical, real presence. This conflict is rooted in the ineluctable nature of the painterly signifier, which, as something visible, is
always already subject to the "reality"-producing effects of the symbolic, even though by hinting at the invisible it ruptures this "reality"
with an evocation of the real. In a painting utilizing geometral conventions of representation, to use Lacan's example, there is always a "central field" whose absence can be observed (S 11, 99–100/108), and it is
with respect to this place that the viewer of the painting is expected to
position himself. In following through with this the viewer accepts the
subjectifying effect of the *objet a* gaze and allows this gaze to serve as the
cause of his (desiring/fantasizing) experience of the painting.[42] In contrast, it is possible for the viewer to recognize this absence but actively
resist positioning himself in its place. When this occurs the painting
allows the viewer to grasp and thus to avoid the subjectifying structure
inherent in the gaze.

This resistance to the gaze can be seen as a product of the intervention of the real in the painting, and it should by no means be taken as a
mark of the painter's failure. Rather it is precisely this effect of the real
which has the ability to shake the viewer out of his search for satisfaction through fantasy and to lead him toward giving up the *objet a* gaze
on which such fantasy depends. This point is put by Lacan in the
following obscure passage:

The painter gives something to the person who must stand in front of his
painting which, in part, at least, of the painting, might be summed up thus—
You want to look? Well, see this![43] He gives something for the eye to feed on, but
he invites the person to whom this picture is presented to lay down his gaze
there as one lays down one's weapons. This is the pacifying, Apollonian effect
of painting. Something is given not so much to the gaze as to the eye,
something that involves the abandonment, the *laying down,* of the gaze. (S 11,
93/101)

In laying down his gaze "as one lays down one's weapons," the viewer is
quite simply abandoning a crucial component of his imaginary *moi* and
is thus well on his way toward dealienation and authentic acceptance of

his status as a human subject. It is surely no coincidence that Lacan here alludes to his early paper on the mirror stage, where he describes the *moi*'s origins in the gaze of the specular image as "the assumption of the armor of an alienating identity" (*E*, 97/4).

In coming upon the absence at the center of the painting, this absence waiting to be filled by the viewer, the viewer comes upon himself as well, and this in a double sense: as the speaking body fading beneath the signifying chain of the symbolic register and as the *moi* which takes the place of the speaking body in fantasy (see S 11, 90/97 and 89/96).[44] The viewer's contact with absence in the painting thus has the power to compromise his faith in the imaginary *moi* and to strengthen the claims of the real presence of his speaking body. This is why Lacan says in the passage quoted above (S 11, 93/101) that the painting gives something to the eye and not to the gaze, the eye remaining an organ, a real part of the subject's real, speaking body.

We have here, then, Lacan's explanation of the social value of painting. We value painting because of its power to help us realize—make real—the truth, to help us come to the realization that the *moi* is nothing more than a frustrating illusion. With the renunciation of the *moi* and of the subject's dependence upon the gaze as *objet petit a,* there may not come happiness, but there will come—indeed there already has come—a real relation to other subjects (for example, the painter and other viewers) as real. This powerful combination of the simultaneous satisfaction and renunciation of fantasy is what Freud terms "sublimation" (see S 11, 102/111), and Lacan's account of painting does much to explain why things that produce such a paradoxical and almost incoherent effect are accorded such a high status among human artifacts.

Ethics and the Real

The preceding account of sublimation as illustrated by the example of visual art is at odds with some remarks Lacan makes about sublimation in the 1959-60 seminar, *L'éthique de la psychanalyse* (S 7). What is at stake, as we shall see, is nothing less than the value of sublimation and, to be as precise as possible, the value of sublimation from the perspective of an ethics informed by psychoanalysis. This issue of course raises much more general questions about the nature of ethics and of the theory of value, and here I mean to focus on the relatively narrow topic of the role of the real in Lacan's approach to ethics.

What comes to the fore in Lacan's thought around 1960 is a tension centering around the ethical status of desire. We have already seen that in 1964 Lacan praises painting for its "Apollonian" effect, arguing that the arts can help us give up our illusions and assume the truth of the human condition. In giving up the fantasies grounded in the gaze as *objet a* we are also giving up the desire which is supported by these fantasies: recognition of the real absence—the castration—inseparable from our being apparently entails a fading of desire itself. In contrast, Lacan in 1960 insists that "the only thing of which one can be guilty, at least in the analytic perspective, is to have given up on one's desire" (S 7, 368). If sublimation leads to a fading of desire, isn't this something of which we ought to be guilty?

More generally, there appears to be a shift from positive to negative in Lacan's own perspective on the value of desire. In the late 1950s desire certainly stands as a positive notion: the goal of psychoanalytic treatment is the analysand's assumption of his desire, and Hamlet stands as a tragic hero precisely because he shows us the ultimate importance and difficulty of assuming our desire. In contrast, by the 1960s and 1970s desire seems to take on something of a negative connotation in Lacan's work, as that which stands as a defense against or an obstacle to *jouissance*: in "The Subversion of the Subject" for example (*E,* 825/322), Lacan seems to promote the value of *jouissance* over that of the "perverted," fetishistic desire shaped by castration, and his account of women's sexuality raises profound questions about the ultimate ethical status of desire.

Our question here, then, is, Where does the ethics of psychoanalysis really lie? With Hamlet, on the one hand, and the ideal of the human subject's assuming his desire? Or, on the other hand, with Antigone, who is willing to go beyond the satisfaction of desire in her pursuit of *jouissance* itself? While I do not believe that the tensions inherent here are ever fully resolved by Lacan, I do think that a review of his account of how the real relates to both sublimation and ethics will help highlight the significance of these tensions.

Freud introduces the concept of sublimation in connection with his problematic analysis of instincts or drives (*Triebe),* and Lacan sees this as largely responsible for the fact that sublimation has proved to be such a difficult notion for psychoanalytic theory to clarify (S 7, 131). Recalling Freud's fourfold analysis of the drive in terms of pressure, aim, object, and source, we may see more clearly the difficulty attending the concept of sublimation by noting that Freud himself insists that sublimation must not be confused with the idealization of the object. In the essay "On Narcissism: An Introduction" (1914)—a text of great importance for Lacan, as we have seen—Freud makes it clear that sublimation concerns the aim of a drive. Sublimation consists in the drive's "directing itself towards an aim other than, and remote from, that of sexual satisfaction; in this process the accent falls upon deflection from sexuality." It does not involve any necessary change in the drive's object; such a change is, in contrast, the province of idealization. [45]

After reviewing Freud's texts on this distinction and noting that there is something "paradoxical" about the notion of drive satisfaction, Lacan offers his own account of sublimation. This account is put in terms of a distinction between *l'objet* (object) and *Chose* (Thing), a distinction that—as we shall see—he claims to find implicit in Freud's texts in a distinction between *die Sache* and *das Ding*. "Sublimation," Lacan says, "which brings to the *Trieb* a different satisfaction of its aim—this always defined as its natural aim—is precisely what reveals the proper nature of the *Trieb* insofar as it is not purely instinct but has a relation with *das Ding* as such, with the Thing insofar as it is distinct from the object" (S 7, 133). Sublimation then involves not a change in the drive's object but the introduction of a new relation between the drive and something in addition to the object, something separate from the object but somehow related to it. This new relation nevertheless does have some effect on the character of the object, since Lacan gives as "the most general formula" of sublimation that it "lifts up an object . . . to the dignity of the Thing" (S 7, 133). [46]

The fourth and fifth sessions of the seminar of 1959–60 are devoted to *das Ding*. These sessions provide a marvelous example of the radically revisionist reading of Freud in which Lacan often engages. Their basic purpose is to find a sharp distinction in Freud's theory between two different concepts of the thing, marked by the German terms *die Sache* and *das Ding*, despite the fact that Freud apparently never explicitly exploits this verbal distinction. [47] The Freudian context of Lacan's argument here is the distinction between thing-presentations (*Sachvorstellung*) [48] and word-presentations (*Wortvorstellung*). Freud uses this distinction both in the metapsychological essay "The Unconscious" (1915) and in *The Ego and the Id* (1923) to contrast the unconscious system, which involves only thing-presentations, with the preconscious system and even with consciousness, both of these involving a linkage of the thing-presentations with word-presentations. [49]

It is immediately apparent that such a reading of Freud is at odds with Lacan's linguistic rethinking of the unconscious, and it thus comes as little surprise to see Lacan arguing throughout these two sessions that there is something unavoidably linguistic about the very notion of *die Sache* involved in the thing-presentations that presumably constitute the unconscious. "*Sache* and *Wort* are thus tightly linked; they make a couple," Lacan insists, while "*das Ding* is situated elsewhere" (S 7, 58). *Das Ding* is a "stranger" (S 7, 65) to the human world of polar oppositions and qualitative differences, such oppositions and differences reflecting the signifying *coupure* that marks the reality surrounding the subject as a human and not an animal world (see S 7, 57 and 78). *Das Ding* stands beyond all human objects as *le hors-signifié*, the "outside-the-signified" in relation to which "the subject keeps his distance and is constituted in a mode of relation, of primary affect, prior to any repression" (S 7, 67–68).

Borrowing a distinction between two different kinds of judgment found in Freud's essay "Negation" (1925), Lacan argues that *die Sache* ultimately refers to particular qualities or clusters of qualities the possession of which by some thing in the human world can be affirmed or denied. In contrast *das Ding* ultimately refers to the very existence of a thing that can be affirmed or denied independently of the attribution to the thing of various qualities (see S 7, 65).[50] Inasmuch as Freud's distinction between these two sorts of judgment occurs in an analysis of the primordial distinction between what is "inside" and what is "outside" the subject, Lacan's notion of *das Ding* emerges as "the absolute Other of the subject," modeled on the Mother (S 7, 82), as the object forever lost around which the subject and his desire revolve (S 7, 65). Summing up his account, Lacan characterizes *das Ding* as paradoxically both exterior to the subject and yet at the subject's very heart, as something that "a representation merely represents" (S 7, 87).

Put into terms with which we are familiar we may say that *die Sache* or *l'objet* here designates an object in the human world; as such, the "object" is thoroughly determined by signifying chains in the symbolic register as well as given shape by fundamental constraints of the imaginary. *Das Ding* or *la Chose* here designates a real existent that transcends the "reality" produced through the intersection of the symbolic and the imaginary; as such, the "Thing" overlaps the realm of the *objets petit a*, and we may assimilate the Thing/object relation to the relation between the real *objet a*, forever lost to the subject, and the symbolic and imaginary objects that take its place in the subject's conscious life.

Thus when Lacan defines sublimation as involving the lifting up of an object "to the dignity of the Thing" (S 7, 133), what is involved is the subject's attempt to reclaim the lost *objet a* and in this way to map himself into the impossible and unmappable real from which the primal repression of language has separated him. While there is still a gap between the account of sublimation here and that found in Lacan's later seminar on the gaze, we now see that in both accounts the subject's attempt to refind himself in the real plays a significant role. It is precisely this that brings out the fundamentally ethical dimension of sublimation, because, as Lacan notes at the end of the second session devoted to *das Ding,* it is this notion of the Thing as fundamentally lost, as forbidden by the primordial threat of castration, that provides the very foundation of the "moral law" in modern ethical theory (S 7, 85).

This startling claim is, in a sense, the central theme of *L'éthique de la psychanalyse.* In the opening session of the seminar (S 7, 20–24) Lacan situates his discussion by describing the transformation in ethical theory found in the history of philosophy from Aristotle to Freud. This transformation concerns the role of happiness or pleasure in the ethical understanding of human life. For Aristotle (as for Greek thought in general) happiness is without question not only the desired goal of human life but something that the entire constitution and structure of the universe tend to further.[51] In stark contrast, Freud's *Civilization and its Discontents* paints the picture of a world in which, for the pursuit of human happiness, "absolutely nothing has been prepared, neither in the macrocosm nor in the microcosm" (S 7, 22).[52]

According to Lacan, the ethical consequences of this rather pessimistic appraisal of the world are most clearly elaborated in Immanuel Kant's *Critique of Practical Reason,* first published in 1788.[53] Put as simply as possible, what Kant argues here is that ethical judgment ultimately refers to the presence or absence of a "good will." Because he holds that there is a strict causal determinism within the natural universe, Kant cannot maintain that there is any guaranteed connection between the good will and human happiness; thus whatever it is that makes a will good, it is in no way related to its ability to produce happiness. Because the very idea of moral goodness implies that morality be a matter of something universally and necessarily true (that is, a priori), Kant argues that what makes a person's will a good will is that the person's reason for acting can be universalized so as to apply to any and every human agent. Any maxim for acting that cannot be so universalized is thus immoral. The result of all this is that, for Kant, the moral law is essentially empty of content: it is the very form of universality that is at issue in ethics, and any particular content specified in a maxim will only serve to deprive that maxim of the universality that would make it morally acceptable. It is the "categorical imperative"—"So act that the maxim of your will could always hold at the same time as a principle establishing universal law."[54]—that determines the goodness of the will, and any specific pleasure, desire, or interest that an individual might have must be isolated and purged from a will that is to be fully moral.[55]

In his essay "Kant avec Sade," itself very much a product of the 1959–60 seminar, Lacan accurately enough characterizes Kant's position as follows: "So that [the Good] is imposed as superior by reason of its universal value. Thus the weight of this does not appear except by excluding drive or feeling, everything that the subject can suffer by reason of its interest in an object, i.e., what Kant, for his part, designates as 'pathological' " (E, 766). The moral law according to Kant, then, rests on the exclusion, the prohibition, from the will of any particular object of human interest (any "object" in Lacan's sense). In Lacanian terms, however, this prohibited, lost object is of course *das Ding*, the "Thing," even the *objet petit a*, around which the desiring life of the human subject inevitably turns. In this way it is the impossible real, the fundamentally lost *Chose, das Ding*, that provides the foundation for the moral law in Kant (see S 7, 93–95).

To bring out the full significance of this analysis of the moral law as understood in modern ethical theory, Lacan goes on to argue that the truth of Kant's *Critique* is fully realized only in the Marquis de Sade's *Philosophy in the Bedroom*, published some seven years after Kant's text (see E, 765–66 and S 7, 94–97).[56] He is particularly interested in the pamphlet-length treatise, "Yet Another Effort, Frenchmen, If You Would Become Republicans," which is found about two-thirds of the way through Sade's dialogue.[57] Lacan is impressed by the way in which this pamphlet conforms to Kant's moral strictures: "It is precisely the Kantian criteria that are put forward to justify the positions of what might be called a kind of anti-morality" (S 7, 95). He points out that Sade's argument in effect revolves around a "maxim of *jouissance*," which is proposed in the universal form dictated by Kant's analysis of the moral law:

"I have the right to enjoy your body, someone may say to me, and this right I shall exercise without any limit stopping me in the caprice of [whatever] exactions I have the fancy to gratify."

Such is the rule to which one pretends to submit the will of all, however little society, by means of constraints, may implement it. (*E,* 768–69)

In "Kant avec Sade" Lacan argues at some length that this Sadean maxim of *jouissance* is in fact morally acceptable on Kant's own criteria: the maxim can be universalized and is empty of any particular content related to an individual's interest or desire (*E,* 769–71). Moreover, Sade's own argument throughout the pamphlet is couched in terms of "the doctrine of the rights of man," a doctrine itself very much in the spirit of Kant's elaboration of the moral law. Just as Kant argues that human freedom is the key to the moral law—a freedom realized in the purging of all particular interests and desires from the good will—Sade also argues that human freedom is made concrete only through his maxim of *jouissance* (see *E,* 771). (We have already seen in the previous chapter that Lacan argues as well that there is a clear and important parallel between Sade's views and the aesthetic theory of Kant, which also emphasizes the notion of "disinterestedness.")

The connection between the Kantian-Sadean moral law and the Freudian-Lacanian *das Ding* comes in the katharsis of interests, the purging of desires that is involved in the moral law's universalization. The law, by demanding that the will be empty of particular content, in effect situates the human subject in relation to a world devoid of particular qualities or attributes. Things of this world are stripped of all their characteristics, their good and their evil, and find a place within ethical theory only as bare existences, as the "we know not what" that Lacan designates as *das Ding.* In other words, the moral subject relates not to a world of objects but to the real Thing for which all these objects are symbolic or imaginary substitutes or both. As such, the moral subject finds himself in the same position that we have already seen Lacan put Antigone, namely, in the zone "between-two-deaths" (*entre-deux-morts*). The subject of modern ethics acts (or, rather, "wills") in the region between the "death" of all particular qualities of human interest and that Sadean "second death," wherein even the bare existence of the remaining unqualified things, of *das Ding*—symbolized in Sade's narratives by the apparently deathless victims of torture—is finally utterly negated (see *E,* 775–76).[58]

Lacan anticipates the results of his reading of Kant with Sade in a characteristically pithy sentence: "My thesis is that the moral law is articulated toward the target [*la visée*] of the real as such, of the real insofar as it can be the guarantee of the Thing" (S 7, 92). Along the same lines, he later suggests that all forms of religion and of mysticism also aim at *das Ding,* although the religious subject hopes to refind a relation to the Thing "somewhere beyond the law" (S 7, 101–2). (Antigone stands, perhaps, somewhere between the two.) Ethics then emerges as a relation to *das Ding* that takes the real as a kind of limit (whereas mysticism attempts to surpass any limit separating us from the real). The ethical subject carries out his actions in an asymptotic relation to the always elusive real,[59] forever attempting and yet failing to achieve the purity of the Kantian good will. (Even Kant is dubious of the human possibility of ethics.)

In the final sessions of the 1959–60 seminar Lacan finally addresses directly the implications for psychoanalysis of his reflections on ethics. "There is no reason," he insists, "that we should make ourselves the guarantors of the bourgeois dream." The "success" of an analysis should not be based on the resulting "comfort" of the analysand; psychoanalysis does not serve and should not serve as a socially approved system for the delivery of "goods" (*biens*)—"private goods, family goods, goods of the household, other goods that also solicit us, goods of a trade, of a profession, of the city" (S 7, 350). Psychoanalysis does not concern "the happiness of future generations." Rather, it focuses on "the problem of the real and present [*actuel*] relation of each man, in this short space of time between his birth and his death, with his own desire" (S 7, 351). Because "the function of desire ought to remain in a fundamental relation with death," coming to grips with one's desire—assuming one's death as one's own—is by no means an easy or happy task. Echoing the pessimism of the later Freud, Lacan describes the termination of the training analysis, which he sees as the only authentic (*véritable*) kind of psychoanalysis, as an anguished, anxiety-ridden confrontation with "the reality of the human condition." "At the end of the training analysis," he says, "the subject ought to attain and to recognize the field and the level of the experience of absolute distress [*désarroi*], at the level at which anxiety is already a protection, not *Abwarten* [waiting], but *Erwartung* [expectation]. Anxiety is already deployed while allowing a danger to outline itself, whereas there is no danger at the level of the final experience of *Hilflosigkeit* [helplessness]" (S 7, 351).[60] At the termination of analysis the analysand should be able "to deal with the boundary [*toucher au terme*] of what he is and of what he is not" (S 7, 351). While this goal of analysis is clearly consistent with Lacan's earlier account of the role of death in the subject's assumption of desire, there is here as well an insistence that analysis should yield a subject whose relations to the real are unambiguous, undistorted by imaginary fantasies, and free of symbolic contamination. The human subject, fully realized—made real—through the process of psychoanalysis, is a subject who authentically knows what is real and what is not, even though what is real—*das Ding*—is fundamentally unknowable.[61]

In the 1970s Lacan tends to redescribe the ethics of psychoanalysis as "the ethic of the Well-Spoken [*le Bien-dire*]," arguing in effect that all human action is essentially discursive because "only discourses ex-ist" (*T*, 65/45; compare 36–37/23–24 and S 20, 92). If it is only through discourse—through symbolically determined articulation—that the human subject stands out (and thus "ex-ists") in his essential humanity, then it is only in discourse that he can finally come to terms with what is real and what is not. In this sense ethical action is "speaking well," and, while the linguistic formulation does diminish their apparent Heideggerian quality, Lacan's later ethical claims are quite consistent with those of the seminar of 1959–60.[62]

In the final session of the seminar, after proposing that the ethics of psychoanalysis shows that "the only thing of which one can be guilty . . . is to have given up on one's desire" (S 7, 368), Lacan goes on to point out and to emphasize that the assumption of desire, as well as its satisfaction, comes only at a price. The price of which he speaks is *jouissance* itself, the "pound of flesh" sacrificed in the interest of saving what pleasure or happiness can be found in this life (S 7, 370–71). This returns us to the question with which we began the present section: Where does the ethics of psychoanalysis really lie? Lacan's eagerness to situate Freud's contributions to ethics within the context of Kant and Sade and his definition of ethics in terms of aiming toward *das Ding* and the real both suggest that his ultimate position puts the highest value on the side of desire as limited by the law rather than on the side of *jouissance*. The real appears to stand as the limit, what Sophocles called *Atē*, beyond which the ethical subject ought not to aim.

And yet at the end of "Kant avec Sade" Lacan disparages *Philosophy in the Bedroom* for failing to get beyond the point "where desire and the law are bound together [*se noue*]" (*E*, 789). Sade ultimately takes us no further than Kant or even Plato: what he gives us is "submission to the Law," but "as a treatise truly on desire, there is little here then—in fact, nothing" (*E*, 790). There is at least a hint in this text from 1962 that desire may take a form other than that constrained by the moral law and its treatment of *das Ding,* the real, as an unattainable limit. This new, shadowy configuration of desire and the reconceptualizing of the relation between *jouissance* and the real that it suggests are very much at the heart of the reflections on women's sexuality that so dominate Lacan's work of the 1970s. It is to these reflections that I now must turn.

Chapter Seven
Sexuality and Science

Lacan's seminar of 1972–73, published in 1975 under the title *Encore* (S 20),[1] marks his most spectacular and controversial effort to develop a discourse in which to theorize the real. What is perhaps most astonishing about *Encore* is its virtually simultaneous treatment of two apparently quite different theoretical domains: on the one hand, the question of sexuality in general and of women's sexuality in particular, and, on the other hand, the philosophical question of the scientific status of psychoanalysis. Lacan here makes every effort to show that Freud's classic question, "What does woman want?",[2] is inseparable from the equally classic question, Is psychoanalysis a science? Although the precise course of Lacan's argument is often shrouded in obscurity, what is clear is that these two questions find their interconnection in the by now familiar notion of the real as impossible.

Thus, speaking of sexual *jouissance* in the opening session of the seminar, Lacan notes that it is "specified by an impasse" distinguishing it from the broader notion of the *jouissance* of the body. Psychoanalysis shows this impasse to be the fact that "it is impossible to pose the sexual relation" in language (S 20, 14). In the eighth session the term *impasse* comes up again with special reference to the register of the real. "The real can only be inscribed," Lacan argues, "by an impasse of formalization" (S 20, 85). It is in the failures of a mathematically formalized theory—its paradoxes, its inconsistencies, its areas of incompleteness—that we can grasp "the limits, the points of impasse, of dead end [*sans-issue*], which show the real yielding [*accédant*] to the symbolic" (S 20, 86). With respect to both sexuality and formalized theory, then, we see that symbolic systems meet their match in a real that resists symbolization.

Elaborating his claims for a formalized writing (*écriture*), Lacan remarks: "This has the value of centering the symbolic . . . in order to retain a suitable truth [*une vérité congrue*], not the truth that claims to be all, but that of the half-saying [*le mi-dire*]" (S 20, 86). Truth, a notion the vicissitudes of which we have traced throughout this study, is now securely located in relation to speech and language: punning on *dementia* and *mensonge* ("falsehood"), as well as on *dimension*,[3] he describes truth as "la *dit-mension*, la mension du dit" (S 20, 97). With truth thus defined in terms of "saying" (*dire*) and "said" (*dit*) it comes as no surprise to find Lacan characterize the impossibility of the real as a matter of "*l'inter-dit.*" The real is that which is "prohibited" (*interdit*), but also that which "is said between the words, between the lines" (S 20, 108). We saw at the beginning of the previous chapter that Lacan regularly describes the real as "that which prevents one from saying the *whole* truth about it" (see *T,* 53/35 and 9/7), and it is this fundamental rift between the real and the symbolic systems of language, speech, and writing that provides the focus of much of Lacan's reflection during the final decade of his teaching.

It is also his insistence on *mi-dire*, on "half-saying," that leads Lacan to the very margins of intelligibility in his latest texts. In his pursuit of a discourse ruptured by paradox and inconsistency Lacan succeeded in producing during the 1970s a body of work unique (even within the context of French *préciosité*) both for its obscurity (its "preposterous difficulty," in the words of Juliet Mitchell)[4] and for its theoretically evocative power. While the very effort to translate Lacan's *mi-dit* into a coherent theoretical sketch is both doomed to failure from the start and, from the Lacanian perspective, something less than appropriate, I will attempt in this chapter to provide a relatively smooth path into the thickets and deserts of *Encore,* focusing first on issues of sexuality and then on the claim of psychoanalysis to be a science.

Women and Sexuality

The seminar of 1972–73 is regularly punctuated by a refrain that provides a simple but oblique summary of Lacan's topic. Lacan announces: "*The jouissance of the Other, of the Other [Autre] with a capital A, of the body of the Other that symbolizes it, is not the sign of love*" (S 20, 11, italics in the original). This refrain reflects the distinction between *jouissance* and love around which much of Lacan's discussion turns. We have already seen that the theme of *jouissance* in Lacan brings with it the notion of primary repression, whereby the human subject is constituted as a split by the fact of speech and language. What we will see in *Encore* is that the already familiar split between the subject and *jouissance* is itself rearticulated in the distinction between the sexes, where men find themselves on the side of linguistic subjectivity and love, and women find themselves on the side of an unspeakable *jouissance*. In turn, the distinction between the sexes itself gives way to a distinction between different kinds of *jouissance*, with the gulf between these forms of *jouissance* in effect reinforcing Lacan's shocking conclusion that "there is no sexual relation [*il n'y a pas de rapport sexuel*]" (see, for example, S 20, 35).

To begin to see what Lacan is attempting here it is essential to contrast his discussion with the familiar psychoanalytic controversies surrounding feminine sexuality that stem from Freud's work in the 1920s. It is worth emphasizing from the start that the specific focus on women's sexuality is itself something of a distortion of Freud's own theories of sexuality. Juliet Mitchell has noted that there is a transformation in the psychoanalytic literature during the 1920s and 1930s from an interest in "what distinguishes the sexes" to a concern, both feminist and antifeminist, with "what has each sex got of value that belongs to it alone."[5] This shift is evident even in the titles of Freud's relevant texts, which move from "Some Psychical Consequences of the Anatomical Distinction Between the Sexes" (1925),[6] to "Female Sexuality" (1931),[7] and finally to "Femininity" (1933).[8] While this shift of interest has had a major impact on the course of psychoanalytic research, it is crucial to bear in mind that a retrospective look at the works of Freud from the perspective of this shift is bound to distort his views.

This is certainly not the place to consider at length the tangled web of controversy associated with Freud's changing views on women and sexuality.[9] What we must stress, however, is that popular presentations of Freud's position rarely characterize his views correctly. In particular, while he certainly does not underestimate the importance of biological considerations on the development of human sexuality, Freud is by no means guilty of a crude biologism which would reduce all the complexities of sexual behavior and personality to facts of sexual anatomy. Rather, Freud's is a theory about how human psychosexual development is shaped by the biological fact of sexual difference: more specifically, it is a theory about how the "castration complex" organized around this biological fact decisively shapes the sexual identity of the developing human being. Freud repeatedly insists that it is not the biological presence or absence of the penis as such but the castration complex—the threat of castration and how that threat is experienced by the child in the context of his or her family situation—that is critical to the formation of sexual identity. At the heart of Freud's final account of sexuality, for example, is the claim that castration plays a fundamen-

tally different role in the two sexes: in boys the fear of castration
motivates the *resolution* of the Oedipus complex, while in girls the
perceived "fact" of castration makes possible and orients the *formation* of
the Oedipus complex by means of penis envy.[10] This alleged difference
between the sexes with respect to castration, then, is held to be responsible for personality characteristics stereotypically associated with each
sex.[11]

In line with his already clearly expressed hostility to developmental
theories in psychoanalysis, Lacan eliminates from Freud's account of
sexuality virtually every trace of chronological development.[12] In elimi-
nating considerations of development, he effectively eliminates the
realm of the biological as well, so that what remains decisive for Lacan
is simply the notion of castration. Of course the Lacanian notion of
castration itself is virtually divorced (as we have seen) from any biological framework by his insistence that the phallus is a signifier (and not
the penis). Where the Freudian drama of castration involves the child's
coming to grips over time with the implications of his or her biological
gender, the Lacanian drama is made up of a lifelong sequence of variations revolving around the basic language-created split, which structures the human being as a subject. The only developmental fact of
significance for Lacan is the fact that language is acquired, the fact that
children do grow up in a world richly structured by various symbolic
(and castrating) systems.

Thus in the course of the opening session of *Encore* Lacan remarks:
"The being of the body, certainly, is sexed, but this is secondary, as we
say. And as experience shows, it is not upon these traces that the
jouissance of the body—insofar as the body symbolizes the Other—
depends" (S 20, 11–12). Biological difference, then, is secondary to
bodily *jouissance* in the domain of experience explored by psychoanalysis. Moreover, this bodily *jouissance* is itself "asexual," because sexual
jouissance proper inescapably relates to the symbolic opposition of male
and female, which grounds the "reality" of biological difference (see S
20, 12–13). The *jouissance* of the body is real, then, in contrast to
biological difference, which derives from the order of the symbolic.
Women, for example, are sexed beings, not by virtue of some set of
properties inherent in their bodies and absent from the bodies of men,
"but by what results from a logical exigency in speech," speech being
understood as instantiating a logical coherence that exists quite apart
from any particular body (S 20, 15). For Lacan, to understand human
sexuality is to understand the logical exigencies brought to bear on

human bodies by the fact of speech and language. Of course, this is just Lacan's way of coming back to an agreement with Freud and of maintaining that sexual identity is ultimately shaped by castration.[13]

The logical exigency in question here follows from Lacan's notion of the phallus as a signifier, the primordial repression of which fixes the meaning of the signifying chains of every subject's discourse. It will be remembered that in his important lecture of 1958, "The Signification of the Phallus," Lacan describes the function of the phallus in Freudian theory as a signifier "intended to designate as a whole the effects of the signified, in that the signifier conditions them by its presence as a signifier" (*E*, 690/285). As such, the phallus must not be confused with any physical organ, any object, or any fantasy, even though certain organs, objects, or fantasies inevitably bear a metonymic relation to the phallus. By the time of *Encore* this account of the phallus has shifted toward stressing the failure of the phallic function to establish a fully adequate meaning. Lacan notes: "Of all signifiers this is the signifier for which there is no signified, and which, in relation to meaning [*sens*], symbolizes its failing. This is the *half-sense {mi-sens}*, the *inde-sense* par excellence, or if you like, the *reti-sense*" (S 20, 74/151). In fact Lacan here argues that psychoanalysis has shown that "meaning is mere semblance [*ce sens est du semblant*]," that the sexual and phallic meaning that analysis typically uncovers really marks the limits of analytic discourse and "indicates the direction in which it fails" (S 20, 74/150).[14]

The failure here appears to be the result of the fact that, while meaningful speech is possible only on the presupposition that there is a stable referential center for language—the phallus serving as this ultimate *point de capiton* in Lacan's earlier discourse—this presupposition of stability is in fact in error. The order of the symbolic rests on "the apparent necessity of the phallic function," on the assumption that only through the phallus can speech fulfill its role in human life. However, in a remark opening the door to a thoroughgoing feminism, Lacan insists that this phallic function is actually only contingent (see S 20, 87). There are, then, at least in principle, a variety of other ways to anchor language's *signification* and to yield speech's *sens*. Thus the meaning found in human life is only a semblance because it is ultimately grounded in the fraudulent insistence that the phallus is the only signifier capable of designating "as a whole the effect of there being a signified." Lacan's claim here is at least one of the sources for the development of an *"écriture féminine"* in French feminist circles (represented most forcefully by Hélène Cixous and Luce Irigaray), a practice of writing meant to stand as an alternative to the "phallocentric" discourse of ordinary speech and writing.[15]

That sexual difference is a result of speech and language is crystalized in Lacan's assertion that "there is not the least prediscursive reality" and thus that "men, women, and children are only signifiers" (S 20, 34). The difference in sexual identity between a man and a woman is not a prediscursive given of biology; it is rather a product of the symbolic system constituted by basic oppositions at the level of signifiers. (Elsewhere in *Encore* Lacan argues more generally that being [*l'être*] and what is said [*le dit*] are integrally related [see S 20, 93–94], thus repeating in a slightly different key his familiar claim that reality is a matter of the symbolic register.) There are men and women, then, only because of the preexisting oppositions between clusters of signifiers in the system of language. As early as the second year of his seminar Lacan had stressed the "androcentric" character of the symbolic, resting his case on Claude Lévi-Strauss's work on the structures of kinship (see S 2, 303–4/ 261–62). Given the fact that the symbolic system is organized (albeit only contingently) around the phallic signifier, it follows that "the Other, in my language, can thus be only the Other sex" (S 20, 40), the Other sex here clearly being that of the woman.

To illustrate the logical exigency of speech Lacan has recourse to the notations of symbolic logic (see the table at S 20, 73/149), which he interprets in a somewhat nonstandard way. The side of the man can be expressed in logical notation as $\forall x \Phi x$, "where all x is a function of Φx" (S 20, 67/143). In contrast, the side of the woman is expressed as $\overline{\forall x} \Phi x$, read as "not all x is a function of Φx" (S 20, 68/144). The function in question here, symbolized by the letter Φ, is clearly that of the phallus: from the perspective of the symbolic system, a man is one who is completely (*tout*) in the phallic function, while a woman is one who is "not-all" (*pas-tout*) in the phallic function. As Lacan makes clear (S 20, 69/145) the difference between men and women is not that women entirely escape the phallic function, while men are caught up in it. His use of the universal quantifier, $\forall x$, is apparently meant to designate symbolic, imaginary, and real elements or characteristics rather than sexed individuals. Thus $\forall x \Phi x$ says, in effect, that on the side of man *all* aspects of any individual are functions of the phallus, while $\overline{\forall x} \Phi x$ says that on the side of woman *not-all* characteristics are functions of the phallus. It must also be emphasized that the phallic function is something that anyone, male or female, can voluntarily "take up." "Everyone knows," Lacan insists, "that there are phallic women and that the phallic function does not prevent men from being homosexual" (S 20, 67/143). Indeed, being at least partially in the phallic function proves to be essential (as we will see) to the attempt at enjoying the sexual relation. Similarly, he insists, "when you are male, you don't have to put yourself on the side of $\forall x \Phi x$. You can also put yourself on the side of not-all. There are men who are just as good as women. It does happen" (S 20, 70/147). There could be no clearer statement than this of Lacan's strict opposition to any position that would ground sexual identity in biology.

"**Woman does not exist**" For Lacan there are a number of implications of the basic logical exigency enshrined in the bipolarity ("all" or "not-all") of the phallic function. The first of these implications is that woman as an abstraction—as *la femme*—does not exist. "There is no such thing as *The* woman," he argues, "where the definite article stands for the universal. There is no such thing as *The* woman since of her essence—having already risked the term, why think twice about it?—of her essence, she is not all" (S 20, 68/144). In contrast to *The* man, whose every characteristic is framed and given a cultural meaning by the phallus and who is thus easily definable, *The* woman simply cannot be found in discourse, since *not-all* her characteristics can be given meaning by the phallus. Lacan marks this essential lack of essence in women by urging that the definite article *la* or *the* be "crossed through" (*barrer*) in writing, thereby associating women with the "bar" (*barre*) separating the signifier from the signified—S/s—and the slash representing the human subject as fundamentally split by the fact of language—$. To these associations Lacan adds the signifier of the barred Other—S(Ⱥ)—clearly relating women to the Lacanian theme of castration (see S 20, 75/151), here symbolized by the fact that even the Other is castrated, that there is no Other of the Other to ground in an ultimate way the meaning (*sens*) of the symbolic order.

At one level there is something almost liberating about the claim that woman does not exist. It is man's concept of woman, a concept fully intertwined with man's phallic notion of sexuality, that fails to be actually instantiated. Despite her (partial) escape from man's limited and limiting notion of sex, however, each woman finds herself systematically excluded from reality as constructed in terms of the androcentric symbolic order. Lacan makes precisely this point in a passage that also reveals his own ambivalence about the organized women's movement of the 1970s: "There is woman only as excluded by the nature of things which is the nature of words, and it has to be said that if there is one thing they themselves are complaining about enough at the moment, it is well and truly that—only they don't know what they are saying, which is all the difference between them and me" (S 20, 68/144). As we will see, this idea that women are essentially excluded from the symbolically (and even from the imaginarily) constituted universe—an exclusion marked in part by their lack of a certain kind of *savoir*—provides a crucial undercurrent to Lacan's argument in *Encore*.

"There is no sexual relation" From the claim that woman does not exist, that woman is not-all in the phallic function, Lacan derives a second, equally alarming, consequence: "There is no sexual relation [*il n'y a pas de rapport sexuel*]." In the first session of *Encore*, where this claim is introduced, it is immediately explained in a single crucial sentence: "*Jouissance*, insofar as it is sexual, is phallic, that is, it is not related to the Other as such" (S 20, 14). Phallic *jouissance* makes it impossible for man "to enjoy [*jouir*] the body of woman." All he can enjoy is "the *jouissance* of the organ," of the phallus within the function of which he is totally defined (S 20, 13). In other words, within the sphere of male sexuality—which is the sphere of "sexuality" proper—the man relates only to himself, indeed only to a part of his own body, in the sexual act. Phallic sexuality is merely a form of masturbation, what Lacan calls later in *Encore* "the *jouissance* of the idiot" (S 20, 75/152).

When Lacan directly addresses the paradox that there is no sexual relation, he generally casts this as its impossibility of being said or written (see, for example, S 20, 35–36).[16] Since woman does not exist, the "not-all" of woman that can find a place in speech or writing are the roles women tend to play in man's symbolically structured reality—most notably, that of being a mother (S 20, 34 and 90–91)—or the fantasies of women that men use to support their phallic desires. The fundamental argument here seems to be that, in being able to speak of women within the phallic function only in terms of their symbolic identities or their fantasy roles, men are never able to use language to forge a link to the Other. Despite the fact that language fundamentally exists in and as the Other, language cannot be used to provide access to this Other. Instead, what language provides is actually a new, distinctly human and distinctly male, form of *jouissance*, a *jouissance* that "comes" with speaking (see, for example S 20, 61, 77, and 104).

"*All the needs of the speaking being are contaminated*," Lacan emphasizes at the beginning of the fifth session of the 1972–73 seminar, "*by the fact of being implicated in an other satisfaction {une autre satisfaction} . . . in relation to which they can be found lacking {faire défaut}*" (S 20, 49). This other satisfaction is quite precisely "other" than the *jouissance* of the body, and it serves as the substitute, both symbolic and imaginary, for the real *jouissance* of the body sacrificed when the human animal became a "speaking being," subject of and to language. "A subject as such does not have much to do with *jouissance*," Lacan remarks (S 20, 48). Supported by language, this other satisfaction brings a kind of *jouissance* to the subject's relation with reality (things made by words), but it accomplishes this only at the price of the repression of bodily *jouissance,* a repression that amounts to making such *jouissance* unspeakable (see S 20, 52–53 and 57). Satisfied with the *jouissance* that comes with speaking—with "*le blablabla*" (S 20, 53)—those beings "all" bound up in the phallic function accept the impossibility of *jouissance* proper. Indeed, this impossibility serves to define the phallic function itself (see S 20, 55). The success of language, then, consists in the failure of the sexual relation (S 20, 53).

Now, to the extent that a woman can be spoken of within the phallic function, she finds herself either subjected to the signifier of a symbolic role or implicated in the structure of man's fantasy. Fantasy, as we already have seen, is essentially a relation ($ \$ \Diamond a$) between the barred subject of language and the *objet petit a,* a relation that provides a *fantasmatic* identity for the subject. Given this analysis of fantasy and its relation to desire—desire now being understood to be phallic desire—a woman's role in man's fantasy life is simply that of being the *objet a* that makes up for the man's castration by language, his lack of the omnipotent phallus. Thus, man's sexual desire is ultimately narcissistic (see S 20, 12), and the object(s) of his desire are precisely those imaginarily detached body parts, those *objets a*—breasts, buttocks, mouths—that trigger his desire and his masturbatory *jouissance.* In short, it is because the man, as defined by the phallic function, relates to an *objet a* rather than to a human Other that "there is no sexual relation" (see S 20, 58).

Moreover, it follows, as Lacan announces in the seminar of 1974–75, that "a woman is a symptom" (S 22).[17] In particular, because she is "taken on" by the man merely as an *objet petit a,* as a cause of his phallic desire, a woman's status within phallic *jouissance* is that of a symptom of "the polymorphous perversion of the male." (Lacan defines the "act of love" in these terms at S 20, 68/143.) What we see here, then, is a return to Lacan's earlier claim that desire, and particularly male desire, is inherently perverted and fetishistic. Within the closed, masturbatory circuit of phallic *jouissance,* a woman plays the role of fetish object, substituting for the phallus and thereby hiding the man's own castration.[18] Again we see that it is this perverted character of male sexuality that leads to the failure of the sexual relation. That to which a man relates finally in sex is simply an *objet a*: thus the sexual act presents the Other "under an *a*-sexual form" (S 20, 115), thereby undercutting any authentically sexual relation.

Noting in his 1973 television interview that a woman "yields" (*se prête*) to man's perversion, Lacan adds that this involves her in the notion of "masquerade" (*T,* 64/44–45). Many women do, after all, to some extent play along with men's fantasies of them, and in this way they themselves directly enter, although not completely (*pas-tout*), the phallic function. In fact, "masquerade" apparently characterizes both the feminine and the masculine roles with regard to the sexual relation (see S 11, 176/193), since both women and men find themselves in the position of semblance in the course of their inevitably failed sexual encounters. Given Lacan's account of the structure of fantasy, it is clear that a woman as *objet a* is, in effect, seeming (to the man) to be the phallus that he lacks. Similarly, as Lacan had suggested toward the end of "The Signification of the Phallus," a man finds himself seeming (to the woman) to have the phallus that she lacks (see *E,* 693–95/288–91). Thus, while the fact of castration is structurally involved on both sides of the phallic attempt at sexual intercourse, it is "veiled" or "masked" in two different ways. For the man it is hidden by the woman's pretending to *be* the phallus; for the woman it is hidden by the man's pretending to *have* the phallus. It is this mutual masquerade that makes it possible for human beings to continue in their pursuit of the sexual relation, despite the fact that the success of sex is doomed from the start by the "other satisfaction" of phallic *jouissance.*

"There is something of One"   Thus far we have seen that Lacan's account of the phallic function as that which structures human sexuality in accordance with an "other satisfaction" different from bodily *jouissance* has two consequences: neither woman nor the sexual relation exist. Crucial to the argument of *Encore* is that each of these failures of existence finds an admittedly inadequate substitute. In place of the impossible sexual relation, we find love (S 20, 44). In place of the nonexistent woman, the Other sex, we find the soul (S 20, 78–79/ 154–56).

Turning first to love, we see once again that Lacan builds his argument primarily around the use of ordinary language. "*We are only one {Nous ne sommes qu'un}*. Each of us knows perfectly well that it has never happened that two have made only one, but still *we are only one*. It is from this that the idea of love comes. This is truly the most vulgar [*la plus grossière*] way of giving a signified to the sexual relation, to this term that clearly eludes us" (S 20, 46). This illusory notion of an impossible unity around which our discourse about love turns is reflected in the colloquial phrase *Y a d' l'Un* (There is something of One) (S 20, 12). Lacan claims that countless philosophical theories about love in all its manifestations can be framed in precisely these terms, and his argument in the seminar of 1972–73 often returns to this theme.

The "vulgarity" that Lacan sees in the notion of love lies primarily in the fact that love is inherently narcissistic. The One that is sought in love is really one's own unity (S 20, 46), forever lost as a result of primal repression, of the castration effected by speech and language. What the lover seeks in his beloved is nothing else than his own integral identity, and—just as in the fable told by Aristophanes in Plato's *Symposium*[19]—this means that the driving force of love relates not to an Other but to another part of oneself. Indeed, that toward which love directs the lover is precisely the *objet a* that substitutes for the lover's forever lost phallus (S 20, 12), and in this way the whole concept of love merely masks and repeats the fetishism characteristic of phallic *jouissance*. While the ideology of love promises a real relation between the lovers, a unity in which two become one, what love delivers is just a variant of the sexual relation's impossibility. Thus it comes as no surprise that Lacan insists "when one loves, it is not a matter of sex" (S 20, 27), and this is one reason why "the *jouissance* of the Other is not a sign of love" (S 20, 11).

There is, however, much more to be said about love. The belief that "there is something of One" carries with it a tendency to believe in the existence of "One alone" (S 20, 63–64/139). This suggests the "romantic" notion that there is but one true love. This notion is fostered to some degree by the very logic of a woman's place in the phallic function as "not-all," since this "not-all" apparently demands some sort of One to serve as the "all" by which the woman is defined (S 20, 93). The connection between love and "One alone" also establishes a framework within which God (as the "One alone") can enter into a love relationship with creation, as in the Gospel of John (S 20, 64/140).

No doubt the most dramatic example of the way in which love fosters the idea that there is "One alone" is found in the tradition of courtly love, which reached its peak between the eleventh and thirteenth centuries. About courtly love, Lacan remarks: "It is an altogether refined way of making up for the absence of sexual relation by pretending that it is we who put an obstacle to it. It is truly the most staggering thing that has ever been tried. But how can we expose its fraud? . . . For the man, whose lady was entirely, in the most servile sense of the term, his female subject, courtly love is the only way of coming off [*se tirer*] elegantly from the absence of sexual relation" (S 20, 65/141). Lacan here refers to his earlier account of courtly love in *L'éthique de la psychanalyse* (S 7, 174– 180), where he emphasizes that the inaccessibility of the lady within the troubadour tradition in effect transforms her from a woman of flesh and blood into a manifestation of *das Ding*. This treatment of the lady is "refined" precisely because it involves the purification of all the woman's attributes, her transubstantiation into an immaterial being (S 7, 180). Thanks to the power of love, the woman becomes a "real" Thing rather than an object of human "reality."

However, this process of transubstantiation is a "fraud" according to Lacan, and perhaps the best way to see why is to turn to his important remarks about the philosophical concept of the soul. At the heart of this account is Lacan's claim that the soul emerges as a theme in Western thought precisely as a substitute for the woman who does not exist. Lacan's discussion of this in the seventh session of the 1972–73 seminar is elliptical in the extreme, but everything turns around his use of *lalangue* to produce a new verb, *âmer*, fusing the notions of "soul" (*âme*) and of "loving" (*aimer*) (S 20, 78/155). Alluding to the Athenian context in which the philosophical theory of the soul originated—a social milieu in which, for a time, male homosexuality was something of a norm[20] and which is wonderfully portrayed in Plato's *Symposium*— Lacan remarks: "In effect, as long as soul souls for soul [*l'âme âme l'âme*], there is no sex in the affair. Sex does not count. The soul is conjured out of what is *hommosexual,* as is perfectly legible from history" (S 20, 78/ 155). Lacan goes on to maintain that the ethic of love bound up with the notion of soul is itself "outsidesex" (*hors-sexe*) (S 20, 78/155), suggesting that the conceptual move from human beings to souls involves again something like the move from objects in human reality to the real *das Ding* outside of all symbolic or imaginary constraints. The soul seems to be by definition something that eludes any simple characterization in terms of symbolic or imaginary categories. In this way the soul

occupies the same position within philosophical or theological specula-
tion that the lady occupies within the poetic tradition of courtly love.
This fact, then, explains the rather startling claim: "For the soul to
come into being, she, the woman, is differentiated from it, and this has
always been the case. Called woman [*dit-femme*] and defamed [*diffâme*].
The most famous things that have been handed down in history about
women have been strictly speaking the most defamatory that could be
said of them" (S 20, 79/156). In effect, the fact that woman is only
partially excluded from the phallic function—the fact that she is "not-
all" (and *not* "all-not")—means that interest in her seems to the man to
be a poor substitute for his pursuit of *das Ding*. Women still have
symbolic and imaginary roles in man's world, while the soul appears to
escape such constraints completely.[21]

However, the pursuit of the real in the form of *das Ding*—whether it
be through the elevation of the lady to an impossible object or through
the creation of a soul as an impossible object—is doomed to fail in light
of the fact that the real is at best a limit toward which we can progress
asymptotically. In the same way that the Kantian-Sadean ethic of the
pure will stumbles back into a reaffirmation of the law of castration,
neither courtly love nor soul-love succeeds in making up for the impossibility of the sexual relation. "What it is all about," Lacan notes, reflecting on Kant and Sade, "is the fact that love is impossible, and that the
sexual relation founders in non-sense, not that this should in any way
diminish the interest we feel for the Other" (S 20, 80–81/158). At the
very end of *Encore,* pointing out again that the extreme form of love,
"true love," is essentially an approach toward being in the form of *das
Ding* stripped of all predicates, Lacan adds that "true love opens out
onto hatred" (S 20, 133). Love of *das Ding*, the pursuit of the real, ends
in the utter devaluation of the human world.

"A *jouissance* beyond the phallus" Given all these difficult
and troubling implications of the "logical exigency" involved in the
phallic function, it comes as a distinct relief to learn in the course of
Encore that the "other satisfaction" of phallic *jouissance* is not the only
form of *jouissance* actually found in the human world. In fact, one of the
most influential assertions of Lacan's seminar is that there is something
in some women's experience of *jouissance* that goes beyond the limited
and self-defeating logic of the phallic function.

Because the phallic function narrowly restricts what can be said or written about sexuality, Lacan approaches the issue of women's *jouissance* obliquely. He seems most impressed by the fact that at least some women have an experience of *jouissance* about which they find they have nothing to say (see S 20, 56 and 82/159). Since knowledge (*savoir*) in Lacan's ordinary usage demands the possibility of articulation in language, it follows that women have an experience of *jouissance* about which they apparently know nothing. "There is a *jouissance* proper to her, to this 'her' which does not exist and which signifies nothing. There is a *jouissance* proper to her and of which she herself may know nothing, except that she experiences it—that much she does know. She knows it of course when it happens. It does not happen to all of them" (S 20, 69/145).

While there have been attempts to theorize women's *jouissance,* most notably by distinguishing between clitoral orgasm (as phallic) and vaginal orgasm (as nonphallic) (see S 20, 69–70/146), Lacan insists that such accounts fail because they do not recognize women's status as essentially excluded from the "androcentric" order of the symbolic. Because woman does not exist, the *jouissance* of a woman can only be described as "*supplementary"* to phallic *jouissance* (S 20, 68/144), and as such it falls outside of any attempt to theorize it in terms of the phallic function. A supplement is not a complement, however, and this means that a woman's *jouissance* is "beyond the phallus" (S 20, 69/145). In describing it by means of a parody of Nietzsche (*Beyond Good and Evil*) and Freud (*Beyond the Pleasure Principle*), Lacan is suggesting that women's *jouissance* escapes the bipolar oppositions—for example, good and evil, pleasure and reality—characteristic of the symbolic system of language. In this sense it seems fair to say that a woman's *jouissance* is an experience of privileged access to the real order of *das Ding*. It is precisely because it is an experience of this sort that women cannot say or know anything about it.

Lacan nevertheless persists in trying to say something about this unspeakable *jouissance*. At the beginning of *Encore,* before introducing any of the themes distinctive of his argument, he argues that within the framework of the law *jouissance* can be defined negatively as "that which is used for nothing" (S 20, 10): one can only "enjoy" the use of something that is not used as a tool for the eventual enjoyment of something else. From the perspective of phallic *jouissance,* this appears a reasonable description of a woman's *jouissance,* since a supplement is in no way necessary to the functioning of that which it supplements. Reflections such as these lead Lacan to describe a woman's *jouissance* as *plus-de-jouir,* which has been translated wonderfully by "over-coming" and which involves the double meaning of "end-of-coming" and "excess-of-coming" (see *T,* 53–54/36–37). From the man's point of view, a woman's *jouissance* is both excessive and threatening—useless to him and impossible for him finally to dominate.

Lacan also makes use of the notion that woman is "not-all" to characterize the *jouissance* in question here. "When I say that woman is not-all and that it is because of this that I cannot say *the* woman, this is precisely because I am raising the issue of a *jouissance* which is of the order of the infinite from the perspective of everything involved in the function Φx" (S 20, 94). In being "not-all" a woman escapes (at least partially) the totalizing effect of the phallic function and of language. She thus partakes in something that is not only beyond the phallus but beyond "the all" as the finite totality of everything that is determined by the phallic function. It is the infinity introduced into the phallic order by women that motivates the title of Lacan's seminar: with respect to any finite totality, a woman's supplementary response is always "Encore!"

If we allow Lacan this logical move, his final account of women's *jouissance* will not take us by surprise. In the sixth session of *Encore,* "Dieu et la jouissance de la femme" ("God and the *Jouissance* of The Woman"), he argues that it is in the great texts of mysticism that we find the best descriptions of a *jouissance* that goes beyond the phallus. After alluding to the texts of Hadewijch d'Anvers and Saint John of the Cross, Lacan suggests that Bernini's great statue of Saint Theresa (which graces the cover of *Encore)* perfectly epitomizes the issue in question: "You only have to go and look at Bernini's statue in Rome to understand immediately that she's coming, there is no doubt about it. And what is her *jouissance,* her *coming* from? It is clear that the essential testimony of the mystics is that they are experiencing it but know nothing about it" (S 20, 70–71/147). What we find in mysticism is a powerful—indeed, shattering—experience that breaks all the bounds of linguistic possibility. It is common to find the use of paradox, contradiction, and even *mi-dire* in the mystic's passionate attempt to convey something of this experience. Something similar, of course, is found in Lacan's own discourse, and when he adds that "the *Écrits* of Jacques Lacan" should be added to any list of "mystical ejaculations" (S 20, 71/147) it becomes clear that we are meant to take Lacan's lifework itself as constituting at least in part an attempt to go beyond theory so as to describe an ultimate, nonphallic *jouissance*.[22]

What Lacan is clearly suggesting is that certain kinds of human experience—among which women's *jouissance* and mystical experience stand out most clearly—give us access to "the *jouissance* of the body" which we have taken to be forever lost as a result of castration. In somehow going beyond the limitations of the symbolic and imaginary structures of language, such experiences apparently give us access as well to the order of the real, to *das Ding*.

This position raises inevitable questions: Does this *jouissance* beyond the phallus yield an authentic relation to the Other? Can a woman's *jouissance* successfully overcome the impossibility of the sexual relation as framed by the phallic function? It would seem that such an experience provides convincing evidence (to the one having the experience) that some authentic relation to the Other has been achieved. Thus the great classics of mysticism tend to speak of some kind of unity between the mystic and God, all the while stressing the inadequacy of any language to describe such an experience.

Lacan clears the way for an acceptance of the mystic's account by arguing that Freud and others were wrong to try "to reduce the mystical to questions of fucking" (S 20, 71/147). Religious experience should not be considered an illusory substitute for the frustration entailed by the impossibility of the sexual relation. In this sense, again, "the *jouissance* of the Other is not a sign of love" (S 20, 11). "If you look carefully," Lacan insists, "that is not what it is all about. Might not this *jouissance* which one experiences and knows nothing of, be that which puts us on the path of ex-istence? And why not interpret one face of the Other, the God face, as supported by feminine *jouissance?*" (S 20, 71/147).[23]

It appears, then, that women's *jouissance* may provide something that the sexual relation as determined by the phallic function cannot deliver: namely, a genuine relation to the Other. Moreover, it appears that this bodily *jouissance* may give us access to the real in a way that allows us to recognize the remarkable fact that as human beings we are fully part of the real even as we stand outside of it ("ex-ist") by inhabiting the orders of the symbolic and the imaginary. The irony, of course, is that such an experience cannot really be put into words—or at best it can only be *mi-dire*—despite the fact that it provides the ground out of which all the flowers of our rhetoric grow.

Psychoanalysis and Formalization

The second major theme broached in *Encore* is the controversial question of whether or not psychoanalysis is a science. Lacan's basic strategy both here and throughout his teaching is to approach this question by means of a careful reconceptualization of the nature of science. This approach is more or less dictated by his early adoption of structuralist principles of explanation, principles that cast into doubt Freud's framework for dealing with the question.

From his very early *Project for a Scientific Psychology* (1895)[24] to the end of his life,[25] Freud had been preoccupied with the task of demonstrating that the new discipline of psychoanalysis was a full-fledged natural science. As a product of his time, Freud understood scientificity largely in terms of the positivist epistemology of tracing all elements of scientific theory back to essentially repeatable empirical evidence[26] and in terms of the deterministic metaphysics of late nineteenth-century physics.[27] Thus Freud's chief interest was to show that there was sufficient empirical evidence for the basic claims of psychoanalytic theory, evidence that would at least eventually support strictly deterministic causal explanations of human behavior in terms of psychoanalytic laws.[28]

With Lacan's reorientation of psychoanalytic theorizing in the direction of structuralist principles, both Freud's positivistic empiricism and his determinism had to be reexamined. Although these are issues explored by Lacan throughout his teaching, there is a surprising consistency in his positions between 1953 and 1973. A brief sketch of the position developed in the course of Lacan's argument in "The Function and Field of Speech and Language in Psychoanalysis" will thus provide a useful point of departure for our consideration of his later claims in *Encore*.

It will be remembered that one of the themes of "Function and Field" (1953) is that the contemporary human subject finds himself alienated from modern scientific theory. There is more than a little irony in the fact that psychoanalytic theory itself has been one of the great sources of the objectifying jargon that has led to such alienation from self. Lacan chooses to confront this danger by turning his attention to the scientific standing of psychoanalysis. As we would certainly expect, Lacan comes to the conclusion that scientificity is fundamentally to be understood in terms that make the principles of structuralism paradigmatic of all science. He even goes to the extreme of arguing that twentieth-century physics and natural science in general are inherently, although perhaps unknowingly, structuralist (*E*, 286–87/74–75). Lacan's argument for structuralism as a paradigm derives from his claim that the question of the scientific status of psychoanalysis is basically a question concerning the principles of its "grounding." Freud's constant attempts to make psychoanalysis intellectually respectable all rest on his assumption that such respectability depends upon the empirical confirmation, validation, and thus grounding of psychoanalytic claims. Lacan, in contrast, defines the issue of grounding as "a problem of formalization" (*E*, 284/ 72), thus making it possible to see in the mathematically formulated phonological theory of Jakobson and Halle[29] and in the combinatorial diagrams of Lévi-Strauss splendid examples of the grounding of scientific theories (*E*, 284–85/73).

This in turn leads to the provocative claim that it is precisely the mathematization—that is, the formalization—of claims about the natural world that is of the essence of natural science, rather than the positivist idea that these sciences owe their status to empirical confirmation. Lacan writes:

It is clear that our physics is simply a mental fabrication whose instrument is the mathematical symbol.

For experimental science is not so much defined by the quantity to which it is in fact applied, as by the measurement it introduces into the real. (*E*, 286/74)

To put this point in another way, we might say that, where positivism defines a science in terms of the preexisting objects studied by that science, Lacan offers a definition of a science in terms of the kinds of signifiers, of formal vocabularies, that it adds to the objects it studies and that, in turn, transform those objects into the objects of science. Lacan illustrates this point in "Function and Field" by showing how experimental precision was impossible until the invention of Huyghens's clock in the seventeenth century, an invention that itself changed the nature of the objects studied by physics (*E*, 286–87/74–75).

Even the most casual reader of Lacan's writings after "Function and Field" will have been struck by his common and apparently confident use of quasi-algebraic formulations and elaborate diagrams or graphs.[30] A typical example of Lacanian algebra can be found in "The Agency of the Letter" (1957), where he "symbolizes" the structure of metonymy as follows:

$$f(S \ldots S')S \cong S(-)s$$

This formalization highlights the fact that the word-to-word connection characterizing metonymy—(S . . . S')—preserves the distinction between signifier and signified—S(−)s. The structure of metaphor is then symbolized:

$$f\left(\frac{S'}{S}\right) S \cong S(+)s$$

Here the substitution of one signifier for another—S' for S—highlights the fact that metaphor allows a "crossing of the bar" between signifier and signified—S(+)s—a crossing essential for "the emergence of signification" (*E*, 515−16/164). Lacan clearly means these attempted mathematizations of psychoanalytic theory to be taken seriously. Yet during the 1950s he is also willing to concede the intellectual dangers posed by such models. In "On a Question Preliminary to Any Possible Treatment of Psychosis" (1958), for example, after having spent a great deal of space elaborating a very complex graph describing the structure of the psychotic subject, Lacan insists: "However, it would be better to confine this schema to the waste-bin, if, like so many others, it was to lead anyone to forget in an intuitive image the analysis on which it is based" (*E*, 574/ 214). By the 1960s and 1970s the dangers posed by mathematical modeling—what Lacan comes to call his *mathèmes*—seem to worry him less. Indeed, as I noted earlier, Lacan eventually turns his attention to formalized models of paradoxes and other forms of logical and mathematical impasse, apparently convinced that the "intuitive images" involved here perfectly reflect the "analyses" on which they are based.

By the time of *Encore*, with its emphasis on the real as an order to be taken as seriously as the symbolic and the imaginary, Lacan reengages the question of science by asking about the relation between scientific knowledge (*savoir*) and the real. Traditional epistemology, and the positivistic notion of science that depends upon it, which Lacan traces back to Aristotle, rests on the assumption that the object of knowledge is in some way similar to the thought or knowledge a human being has of the object. On the basis of this assumption, which Lacan reduces to the claim that "being thinks" (S 20, 96), the epistemologist can claim that knowledge in some way represents its object. The fundamental epistemological question, then, becomes one of determining the accuracy or adequacy of such a representation. Within the tradition of the natural sciences, this question has tended to be answered by reference to sense perception. Thus, one scientific representation of reality is more accurate than another to the extent that it is better grounded in sense perception, and sense perception is taken to be the ultimate evidence capable of falsifying particular scientific representations of reality.

There are at least three problems with this positivistic epistemology from Lacan's perspective. In the first place, the apparently simple move from perception to science "avoids the abyss of castration" (S 11, 73/77). To move from simple perception to the generalizations characteristic of science requires the mediation of the symbolic structures of language. In ignoring the role of language here, the positivist in effect fails to give an account of just what is involved in the notion of *representation*.

In the second place, Lacan argues that the discoveries of contemporary science—the privileged example here is that of DNA—show that reality itself is thoroughly articulated by chains of signifiers (see S 20, 21–22). Because it is discourse that structures both reality and our knowledge of reality, the positivist is wrong to think that knowledge somehow involves a relation of representation. Moreover, the representational analysis of knowledge presupposes that we have some "metalanguage" in which we can describe both knowledge and reality and then go on to calibrate the degree of similarity between the two. But, Lacan insists, *"there is no metalanguage,"* and this means there is no "language of being" (S 20, 107) in reference to which our knowledge can be measured. Being is just "a fact of what is said [*un fait de dit*]" (S 20, 107), and what follows for Lacan is a sort of linguistic idealism in which all scientific knowledge is essentially speaking about speaking (compare *T,* 60/41).

Finally, the positivist idea that sense perception provides a decisive test of a scientific claim, that sense perception has the power to "falsify" the claims of a science, rests on the assumption that the goal of science is to produce an understanding of reality as a whole, in which all the results of all the sciences can be put together into an absolutely consistent and noncontradictory whole. But, Lacan argues, "this world conceived as the all . . . remains a conception . . . a view, a gaze, an imaginary capture" (S 20, 43). In short, the positivist rests his case on an impossible fantasy of completeness, thus leaving science in a position not unlike that of religion or mythology.

Even if we grant the force of Lacan's arguments against epistemology as traditionally conceived, there still remains within Lacan's own theory the question of the relation between the symbolically (and imaginarily) determined system of knowledge and the impossible and unspeakable real. The key to his approach to this question—and this serves as an important connection back to his theory of women and sexuality—lies in the rejection of "the idea of the *all {tout}*," an idea "to which the least encounter of the real makes an objection."[31] What Lacan's new emphasis on the real (as opposed to reality) demands is that the scientific project be reconsidered in the light of the "not-all." His challenge in *Encore* and other works of the 1970s is in effect to redefine the very character of the modern scientific revolution.

Lacan's standard way to do this is to invoke the specter of Copernicus, following Freud, who claims that "the universal narcissism of men" is threatened by psychoanalysis in a way that parallels that of Copernicus.[32] (Curiously enough, self-comparison to Copernicus goes back at least to Kant.)[33] Where Freud focuses (as does Kant) on the way the revolution in modern astronomy shifted the human world out of the center of the universe, Lacan insists that the revolution called "Copernican" is really that of Kepler. When Kepler established the elliptical orbits of the planets, he was not simply "changing the center." Rather, the elliptical orbiting of the planets "already puts in question the function of the center" (S 20, 42–43). In questioning the idea of the center, the modern scientific revolution is in effect questioning the idea of the sphere and the scientific ideal of absolute totality—the *all*—that the sphere represents (see also *E*, 796–99/295–97).[34]

Given this revisionist interpretation of the Copernican revolution, it is easy to see how Lacan might go on to show the way in which psychoanalysis is a science in precisely this tradition. The Freudian discovery of the unconscious is exactly the sort of radical decentering that upsets the imaginary goal of knowing "all" about the human subject or even about oneself. Throughout this study we have seen a variety of ways in which Lacan uses his theoretical framework to undercut and to overthrow conventional wisdom about human subjectivity and about the very nature of reality.

Yet, when he directly addresses the relation between psychoanalysis and science, Lacan proceeds in a different way altogether. As early as

The Four Fundamental Concepts of Psychoanalysis (1964) he insists on a distinction between "science" and "*La* science" (S 11, 209–10/231). "Science" is the abstraction that "has been the object of the meditation of philosophers," but "*La* science" is something quite different: "The science in which we are caught up, which forms the context of the action of all of us in the time in which we are living, and which the psychoanalyst himself cannot escape, because it forms part of his conditions too, is '*La* science.' " And, Lacan adds, "It is in relation to this second science, '*La* science,' that we must situate psychoanalysis" (S 11, 210/231).[35] In his television interview of 1973 Lacan makes it clear that "*La* science" for us today is "*La* physique," and he particularly emphasizes "the use of number and demonstration" as distinguishing this "*La* science" which the psychoanalyst working today cannot escape (*T,* 62/43). In *Encore* as well he suggests that the decentering effected by Kepler (and deriving originally from Galileo) involves the essential reduction of reality to the "little letters" that make up the mathematical formulas of physics (S 20, 43).

What then is the position of psychoanalysis with respect to "*La* science," understood as mathematically formalized physics? In *Encore* Lacan refers to "the pretensions of analytic discourse to being something of a science," to its being a "would-be science" (*serait science*) (S 20, 76/152). This suggests, as does Lacan's own teaching during the 1960s and 1970s, that psychoanalysis will succeed in becoming a science only when it has adequately formalized its fundamental results. Lacan's relentless pursuit of formalization can be seen, then, as a sustained attempt to do for Freud what Kepler and Newton did for Copernicus. However, one week before Lacan asserts that "mathematical formalization is our goal, our ideal" (S 20, 108), he also insists that "the analytic trick [*truc*] will not be mathematical. It is exactly for this reason that the discourse of analysis is distinguished from scientific discourse" (S 20, 105).

Thus it is not simply because psychoanalysis has not yet been fully formalized that it is only a "would-be science." There is apparently something inherent in analytic practice, in the tricks of the psychoanalytic trade, that resists mathematical formalization. It is at this point that Lacan's notion of the real reappears, defined earlier in *Encore* in terms of "an impasse of formalization" (S 20, 85). What the scientific push toward formalization allows is the recognition of formalization's limits: the real is then constituted by what remains outside of these limits as that which is impossible to formalize.[36] As we have already seen, Lacan's favorite examples of this are logical and mathematical paradoxes: formalization serves here to foreground and to delimit that which cannot be formalized. He also suggests that certain kinds of vector analysis—along the lines of the mathematical theory of plate tectonics, which models geological faults—show that a coherent formalization can nevertheless explain discontinuities within the field formalized (see S 20, 44).

When Lacan insists that mathematical formalization is the "ideal" of his own theoretical work, he immediately adds: "Why?—because only formalization is *mathème*, that is, capable of being transmitted integrally" (S 20, 108; see also 100 and 129). What Lacan has in mind here is the curious fact that mathematical formulas can be (and to a remarkable extent actually are) taught and learned without any reference to their meaning (*sens*). In fact, certain philosophers of mathematics— Lacan refers to Bertrand Russell, although David Hilbert would have been a better example[37]—have argued that mathematical expressions are best understood as having no meaning, and Lacan uses this paradoxical claim to suggest that what formalization reveals is a *signifiance* of language that runs contrary to *sens* (S 20, 85–86). It is in recognizing the *contre-sens* of *signifiance* that we grasp the real as an impasse of formalization.[38]

In the opening session of the seminar of 1964, a session marked by the drama of Lacan's recent "excommunication" from the IPA, Lacan raises the science question quite directly (S 11, 11–15/6–11). Here he compares chemistry to alchemy, arguing that in the latter "the purity of soul of the operator was, as such, and in a specific way, an essential element in the matter." If this is enough to rule out alchemy as a proper science, the standing of psychoanalysis as well is called into question, since the training analysis prerequisite to the practice of analysis clearly addresses itself to the question, "*What is the analyst's desire?*" (S 11, 14/ 9). This leads Lacan to reflect on the role of formalization in science, and he concludes here that "true science" (as opposed to "false science") requires something more than "*formula making*" (S 11, 14–15/10). This something more is precisely what training analysis yields. It is clear that Lacan has in mind here something like that "encounter with the real" that formalized science by its very definition always attempts to avoid. Such an encounter would also involve recognition of "the abyss of castration" (S 11, 73/77) typically avoided by natural science.

From all this it should at least be clear that Lacan's pursuit of mathematical formalization is by no means unambiguous or unambivalent. What we see here is another sign of the tension involved in his notion of the real as an order opposed to the reality constituted by the symbolic and the imaginary. Lacan wants to avoid a thoroughgoing linguistic idealism, which would seem to be the logical consequence of structuralism. However, he also wants to avoid any naive notion of a prelinguistic or prediscursive cognitive access to the real. Put another way, Lacan wants to defend the intelligibility of a kind of cognitive experience of the real that avoids the extreme intellectual heights of *savoir*—complete mediation by the symbolic structure of language— but also avoids falling into the extreme intellectual depths of *connaissance*—absolutely immediate contact without any mediation by language.

We have already seen that Lacan makes special use of the familiar distinction in French between *savoir*—roughly, knowledge as involving mediation, especially by means of language, as well as a direct relation to action (as in *savoir faire*)—and *connaissance*—roughly, knowledge as involving direct acquaintance or awareness. In the context of *Encore* Lacan offers serious criticisms of both notions of knowledge. That the real completely eludes *connaissance* is the burden of Lacan's frequent remarks concerning the fantasy of unity. Suggesting in 1970 that "the all is the index of *connaissance*,"[39] Lacan goes further in *Encore* to argue that there is no such thing as an "aware subject" (*sujet connaissant*), because such a subject would presuppose a world completely and totally knowable (S 20, 114–15). Any such ideal of totality is merely imaginary from Lacan's perspective, and one of the aims of psychoanalysis is clearly to encourage us to give up such cognitive fantasies, thereby freeing us from the imaginary chains of the *moi*. On the other hand, as we have seen throughout the latter part of this study, *savoir,* because it is essentially mediated by language, is always relative to a discourse, and one implication of this is that what *savoir* deals with is ultimately a "reality" (S 20, 33). Of course, the fact that the unconscious is "the discourse of the Other" means that the reality constituted by a discourse need not be an object of conscious awareness, of *connaissance*. Nevertheless, *savoir* as such would appear to miss the real, although the ruptures and paradoxes inherent in it provide our best guide to the real.

In an effort to clarify just what sort of knowledge is at stake in psychoanalysis, Lacan suggests the following in the seminar of 1964: "In the unconscious there is a corpus of knowledge [*un savoir*], which must in no way be conceived as knowledge to be completed, to be closed" (S 11, 122/134). The openness of psychoanalytic *savoir* here contrasts sharply with Lacan's later analysis of scientific knowledge—particularly that involved in physics—as being made possible by "mathematical closure" (*T,* 35/22). What we see, then, is an attempt to reconceptualize *savoir* to allow certain kinds of ruptures in the texture of scientific discourse nevertheless to find a place within the discourse of psychoanalysis. Such a *savoir* would be in a sense "impossible,"[40] but precisely for this reason it would also manage to touch upon the real.

By the end of his life Lacan becomes quite explicit about the implications of this open-ended notion of *savoir.* Thus in the seminar of 1977–78 he announces dramatically that psychoanalysis "is not a science" (S 25),[41] because it is not open to the kind of falsifiability that philosophers following Karl Popper have used to define the notion of science.[42] Psychoanalysis is then "irrefutable," because it takes fully into account the endless "chattering" (*bavardage*) that is our only source of evidence for the functioning of the unconscious. (The title of the sole session published from this seminar is "Une pratique de bavardage," situating psychoanalysis precisely as "a practice of chattering.") In contrast, the scientist who demands falsifiability is caught up in what "the imaginary exfoliates [*s'exfolie*]"—what Lacan calls *sexe-folie* or "sex-madness"—and the result of this is that "science itself is only a fantasy" (S 25).[43]

Examples of formalizations that are extraordinarily open-ended in their interpretative possibilities are scattered throughout Lacan's work. The complex "graph of desire" that serves as the armature for "The Subversion of the Subject" (see Figure 1) is a remarkably polyvalent effort at graphic formalization. In introducing it Lacan himself calls attention to the fact that it serves a number of different purposes in his teaching (*E,* 804/302–3). Much the same thing could be said about the algebraic definitions of metaphor and metonymy in "The Agency of the Letter." In each of these cases we have a more or less "intuitive representation"[44] of a theoretical position, which suggests numerous theoretical possibilities beyond those explicitly discussed by Lacan. The openness here seems to stem immediately from Lacan's own teaching practice: like many teachers he is fond of diagrams and schematic representations, which serve to give a kind of coherence to largely extemporaneous lectures. In a similar fashion Lacan's own diagrams and equations have provided the basis for further Lacanian research; thus, case studies often make essential reference to the "graph of desire" or other Lacanian formalizations.[45]

In the 1970s Lacan's seminars are largely devoted to the topology of

Figure 2. A Borromean Knot

Borromean knots, this domain of mathematics providing Lacan with countless diagrams in terms of which the relations between the real, the symbolic, the imaginary, and (ultimately) the "symptom" are illustrated. The tenth session of *Encore* is a good example of Lacan's procedure here. Lacan first defines Borromean knots as interlocking rings of string such that when any one of the rings is cut the entire interlocking system falls apart (see S 20, 112; Figure 2 is a simple example).[46] He then proceeds to construct several such knots, eventually producing a ring of such rings. Commenting on his pursuit of relatively pure topology here, Lacan insists that the Borromean knot can be used "to represent this rather diffuse metaphor expressing that which distinguishes the usage of language—precisely, the chain" (S 20, 115). Knot theory then gives us a formalization of what the term "signifying chain" only loosely represents, and it does this in a mathematically precise, if something less than totally lucid, way. In a supplement to this session of *Encore* Lacan adds that what the Borromean knot particularly emphasizes is "the fall from privilege" of any one of the rings that constitute the knot (S 20, 122). In the seminar of 1974–75—entitled *R.S.I.*, for real, symbolic, and imaginary—this moral is reemphasized, with Lacan using various shadings of different Borromean knots to elaborate the complete interconnection of his three fundamental orders and their parallels—at one level—in *jouissance* of the Other, *sens,* and phallic *jouissance,* and—at another level—in anxiety, the symptom, and inhibition. He also emphasizes, however, that the Borromean knot itself is the real and not a part of reality. Indeed, by the end of the seminar Lacan argues that the real is best described as "being knotted" (*se nouer*) (S 22).[47] This suggests—as does Lacan's title—that by 1975 the real has emerged as the most important of Lacan's orders, as something of a "first among equals," even though it is literally impossible to know or to speak about it as such.

This is certainly not the place to pursue Lacan's topology any further, particularly since most of the seminars in which it is developed remain either very difficult to find or unpublished.[48] The challenge facing a commentator on this late work of Lacan is to determine just how to construe the extraordinary blending of formal mathematical proof (or at least construction), psychoanalytic theory, and even poetry that makes of these final seminars something unique in the history not only of psychoanalytic theory but of theoretical writing in general.[49]

I would like to end this chapter with a brief review of one last example of formalization, that involved in Lacan's account of "the four discourses," which plays a fairly extensive role in *Encore.* Introduced in the as-yet-unpublished seminar of 1969–70, *L'envers de la psychanalyse* (which I would render as "The seamy side of psychoanalysis"),[50] the theory of the discourses is meant to provide a formalized account of intersubjectivity, of "the social bond" forged by our use of language (see S 20, 21, 51 and 76/152–53). It does this by defining four different intersubjective structures, each of which involves a different configuration of the same four terms (see Figure 3, reproduced from S 20, 21).

The four terms involved are: S_1, the "master signifier" or the signifier as such; S_2, *savoir,* understood as knowledge articulated by a signifying chain; *a,* the *objet a* understood here as *le plus-de-jouir,* which marks both the cause of desire and the end of phallic *jouissance*; and S, the subject as divided by language. These four terms are then arranged in the four discourse structures in such a way that a simple quarter turn of the terms is all that distinguishes one discourse from the next.

The discourse structures themselves represent two subjects, each split by a bar separating the conscious subject from his unconscious. The subject on the left is the "agent" or speaker, while that on the right is "the other" or listener. What is repressed in the speaker is "the truth," while what is repressed in the listener is "the production," the unconscious effect of the speaker's discourse. There are in turn subordinate relations of "impossibility" and "impotence"—left essentially

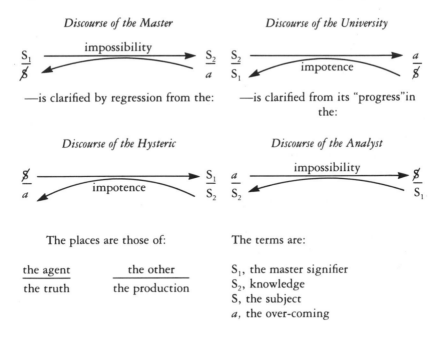

Figure 3. "The Four Discourses"

undefined in the texts we have—which further characterize the subjects' consciousnesses and their unconsciouses respectively.

It should be clear that the range of possible interpretations of these discourses is open-ended, and this is not the place to pursue such interpretations at length. While all sorts of intriguing intersubjective scenarios suggest themselves here, what remains decisive for Lacan is that the formalization advanced in his seminars allows us to predict the outcomes of certain kinds of discourses spoken in particular discursive situations. In making such predictions possible, the formalization also suggests ways in which a particular discourse can be undermined and transformed by an alteration in its discursive situation. Thus, the *discourse of the hysteric,* in which the barred subject expects to speak to an other simply representing his master signifier or identity, is met in the course of a psychoanalysis with the *discourse of the analyst,* in which the analyst as embodying the *objet a* speaks (through her punctuation of the analysand's discourse) to precisely the barred subject. Where the hysteric expects to produce *savoir* in the other, the analyst expects to produce the master signifier in the hysteric, thereby opening the possibility of the hysteric's finally assuming his desire. Obviously the details of such an account remain to be worked out, but what Lacan seems to have been working toward was a formalization of precisely the intersubjective conflicts out of which human history grows. In arguing that such conflicts have their roots and solutions in discursive structures, Lacan is clearly reaffirming a rather strong form of structuralist explanation. At the same time, in insisting that the power of the formalization actually consists in the way that intersubjectivity can interfere with and rupture its own discursive structure, Lacan is once again returning to his notion of the real as an impasse in any formalization.

What we see in the four discourses, then, as well as in Lacan's topology and algebra, is essentially the same valorization of the "not-all" found in his discussion of women's sexuality and in his critique of modern science. The irony of Lacan's latest teaching is that it is only through the thoroughgoing pursuit of the "all" that the value of the "not-all" finally crops up. Only by means of an extraordinary explosion of theoretical activity can the limits of theory be revealed and grasped. By the end of his life Lacan seems to situate the very power and success of psychoanalytic theory in its ultimately necessary failure. This is the true significance of the human subject's encounter with the real: failure is success, and success is failure.

Notes and References

Preface

1. "L'instance de la lettre dans l'inconscient ou la raison depuis Freud" ("The Agency of the Letter in the Unconscious or Reason Since Freud") (1957) (*E*, 493/146).

Chapter One

1. Biographical sources for Lacan remain widely scattered. The only lengthy biography to date is that which occupies the better part of the second volume of Elisabeth Roudinesco, *La bataille de cent ans: Histoire de la psychanalyse en France*, 2 vols. (Paris: Seuil, 1982, 1986). A very helpful, shorter biography can be found in Marcelle Marini, *Jacques Lacan* (Paris: Pierre Belfond, 1986), 101–43. In English, the only significant source is Michael Clark, *Jacques Lacan: An Annotated Bibliography*, 2 vols. (New York: Garland Publishing, Inc., 1988), 1:xviii–xxxiii. Sherry Turkle, *Psychoanalytic Politics: Freud's French Revolution* (New York: Basic Books, 1978) is helpful in situating psychoanalysis in postwar French culture and includes much useful information on the various institutional conflicts that marked Lacan's professional career. Stuart Schneiderman, *Jacques Lacan: The Death of an Intellectual Hero* (Cambridge: Harvard University Press, 1983) provides an unusual glimpse of what it was like to engage in training analysis with Lacan, while Catherine Clément, *The Lives and Legends of Jacques Lacan*, trans. Arthur Goldhammer (New York: Columbia University Press, 1983) proves a source for amusing anecdotes. A more serious and moving memoir is Eileen Simpson, "A Courier for Jacques Lacan," *The Yale Review* 76 (1987): 440–47. My primary source for this biographical chapter is Roudinesco.

2. Roudinesco, *La bataille*, 2:119.

3. In fact, Lacan remarks in 1955 that he heard "from Jung's own mouth" the famous anecdote that Freud, upon arriving in New York in 1909, turned to Jung and said, "They don't realize we're bringing them the plague." See *E*, 403/116.

4. Now available in *De la psychose paranoïaque dans ses rapports avec la personnalité, suivi de premiers écrits sur la paranoïa* (Paris: Éditions du Seuil, 1975).

5. This patient, whom Lacan names Aimée, surprisingly reemerges later in Lacan's life: her son, Didier Anzieu, became a psychoanalyst in the 1950s after having trained with Lacan; she herself, through a very odd turn of

events, ended up as Alfred Lacan's cook after the death of Lacan's mother in 1948. See Roudinesco, *La bataille*, 2:135–36.

6. See "Motifs du crime paranoïaque: le crime des soeurs Papin," in *De la psychose paranoïaque*, 389–98.

7. See "Écrits 'inspirés': Schizographie" and "Le problème du style et la conception psychiatrique des formes paranoïaques de l'expérience," in *De la psychose paranoïaque*, 365–82 and 383–88.

8. Kojève's lectures were eventually published in Alexandre Kojève, *Introduction à la lecture de Hegel: Leçons sur la "Phénoménologie de l'esprit" professés de 1933 à 1939 à l'école des hautes études*, assembled by Raymond Queneau (Paris: Gallimard, 1947). There is an abridged English version: Alexandre Kojève, *Introduction to the Reading of Hegel: Lectures on the "Phenomenology of Spirit"*, assembled by Raymond Queneau, ed. Allan Bloom, trans. James H. Nichols, Jr. (Ithaca: Cornell University Press, 1969). Kojève's influence on Jean-Paul Sartre and on French thought of the 1940s and 1950s cannot be overemphasized. On Kojève's influence, see Vincent Descombes, *Modern French Philosophy*, trans. L. Scott-Fox and J. M. Harding (Cambridge: Cambridge University Press, 1980), 27–48.

9. See *Les complexes familiaux dans la formation de l'individu: Essai d'analyse d'une fonction en psychologie* (Paris: Navarin, 1984).

10. See Stephen Barber, "A Foundry of the Figure: Antonin Artaud," *Artforum* 26, no. 1 (September 1987): 88–95, 89.

11. Roudinesco, *La bataille*, 2:161.

12. See "Le temps logique et l'assertion de certitude anticipée: Un nouveau sophisme" (*E*, 197–213), and "Le nombre treize et la form logique de la suspicion," *Ornicar?* 36 (1986): 7–20.

13. Most of the documents relating to the conflict within the SPP and to its eventual schism can be found in Jacques-Alain Miller, ed., *La scission de 1953: La communauté psychanalytique en France I*, published as a supplement to *Ornicar?* 7 (1976).

14. See Martin Heidegger, "Logos," trans. Jacques Lacan, *La psychanalyse* 1 (1956): 59–79.

15. Documents relating to the SFP's attempt to join the IPA are collected in Jacques-Alain Miller, ed., *L'excommunication: La communauté psychanalytique en France II*, published as a supplement to *Ornicar?* 8 (1977). Most of the important documents from this collection, as well as several important later texts, have been translated into English: see "Dossier on the Institutional Debate," trans. Jeffrey Mehlman, *October* 40 (1987): 51–133.

16. The complete opening session of this seminar is currently available only in English; see "Introduction to the Names-of-the-Father Seminar," trans. Jeffrey Mehlman, *October* 40 (1987): 81–95.

17. See the opening session, "Excommunication," of the 1964 seminar (S 11, 7–17/1–13).

18. "Fondation de l'EFP," in Miller, ed., *L'excommunication*, 149–52; trans. Jeffrey Mehlman as "Founding Act," *October* 40 (1987): 96–105.

19. For Lacan's contribution to the symposium, which he delivered at least partially in English, see "Of Structure as an Inmixing of an Otherness Prerequisite to Any Subject Whatever," in Richard Macksey and Eugenio Donato, eds., *The Structuralist Controversy: The Languages of Criticism and the Sciences of Man* (Baltimore: Johns Hopkins University Press, 1970), 186–200.

20. *Écrits* (Paris: Éditions du Seuil, 1966).

21. *Écrits I* and *Écrits II* (Paris: Éditions du Seuil Collection Points, 1970, 1971).

22. See Louis Althusser, "Freud and Lacan," in *Lenin and Philosophy and Other Essays*, trans. Ben Brewster (New York: Monthly Review Press, 1971), 189–219.

23. The procedure of the pass was introduced in "Proposition du 9 octobre 1967 sur le psychanalyste de l'École," *Scilicet* 1 (1968): 14–30. For a useful discussion of the issues at stake, see Turkle, *Psychoanalytic Politics*, 119–38. For a sympathetic but critical assessment of the pass and of the EFP in general, see Moustapha Safouan, *Jacques Lacan et la question de la formation des analystes* (Paris: Éditions du Seuil, 1983).

24. Most numbers of the journal did, however, list the contributing authors; see *Scilicet* 1–6/7 (1968–1976).

25. The difficulties facing Miller in his task are nicely described in Roudinesco, *La bataille*, 2:568–73. For Miller's own, revealing account of the editorial principles involved in his editing of the seminars, see Jacques-Alain Miller, *Entretien sur le séminaire avec François Ansermet* (Paris: Navarin, 1985).

26. *Les quatre concepts fondamentaux de la psychanalyse*, text established by Jacques-Alain Miller (Paris: Éditions du Seuil, 1973).

27. The text of this interview was published as *Télévision* (Paris: Éditions du Seuil, 1974). An English translation is now available: "Television," trans. Denis Hollier, Rosalind Krauss, and Annette Michelson, *October* 40 (1987): 5–50.

28. For texts of these lectures, see "Conférences et entretiens dans des universités nord-américaines," *Scilicet* 6/7 (1976): 5–63. Turkle, *Psychoanalytic Politics*, 234–47, offers an amusing account of the American reception accorded Lacan's topological discourse.

29. *Ornicar?* remains to this day the official journal of the Champ freudien.

30. *The Four Fundamental Concepts of Psychoanalysis*, ed. Jacques-Alain Miller, trans. Alan Sheridan (New York: W.W. Norton, 1977), and *Écrits: A Selection*, trans. Alan Sheridan (New York: W.W. Norton, 1977).

31. "Lettre de Dissolution," *Ornicar?* 20/21 (1980): 9–10, 10; trans. Jeffrey Mehlman as "Letter of Dissolution," *October* 40 (1987): 128–30, 129.

32. See the texts by Lacan collected in *Ornicar?* 20/21 (1980): 9–20, and in *Ornicar?* 22/23 (1981): 7–14.

33. For a useful chronology of the dissolution of the EFP, as well as some important interviews and texts, see *Almanach de la dissolution* (Paris: Navarin, 1986).
34. "Le séminaire de Caracas," in *Almanach de la dissolution*, 81–87.
35. Ibid., 82.
36. Roudinesco, *La bataille*, 2:679.

Chapter Two

1. Considerations of space prevent a serious treatment of the thesis here. For a useful introduction to the work and an excellent review of Aimée's case history, see Bice Benvenuto and Roger Kennedy, *The Works of Jacques Lacan: An Introduction* (New York: St. Martin's Press, 1986), 31–46.
2. *De la psychose paranoïaque*, 351–62. Indeed, one of these references is to a paper actually translated by Lacan. See Sigmund Freud, "Sur quelques mécanismes névrotiques dans la jalousie, la paranoïa et l'homosexualité," trans. Jacques Lacan, *Revue française de psychanalyse* 3 (1932): 391–401.
3. This description is that of Benvenuto and Kennedy, *The Works of Jacques Lacan*, 32.
4. See Henri Wallon, ed., *Encyclopédie française*, vol. 8, *La vie mentale* (Paris: Larousse, Société de gestion de l'*Encyclopédie française*, 1938).
5. For Freud's most extensive discussion of the "primal horde," see Sigmund Freud, *Totem and Taboo* (1913), *SE*, 13:xiii–162, 140–61.
6. The central source for this is Sigmund Freud, *Three Essays on the Theory of Sexuality* (1905), *SE*, 7:130–243.
7. It is crucial to keep clear the distinction between Lacan's account of the *moi* and the theory of the ego developed in non-Lacanian psychoanalysis. In quotations from Lacan I indicate his usage, since he generally uses the term *ego* only when he is discussing and criticizing the views of others.
8. Jacqueline Rose notes that Lacan's account of the mirror stage "is not restricted to the field of the visible alone," but it is clear that this account does take visual experience as paradigmatic of all conscious experience even for the infant. See Jacqueline Rose's introduction in Jacques Lacan and the école freudienne, *Feminine Sexuality*, ed. Juliet Mitchell and Jacqueline Rose, trans. Jacqueline Rose (New York: W.W. Norton, 1982), 30.
9. In his later work, Lacan will relate this gap to the phenomenon of splitting *(Spaltung)* described in Sigmund Freud, "Splitting of the Ego in the Process of Defence" (1938), *SE*, 23:275–78.
10. In his important text on psychosis, "D'une question préliminaire à tout traitement possible de la psychose" ("On a Question Preliminary to Any Possible Treatment of Psychosis") (1957–58) (*E*, 531–83/179–225), Lacan goes so far as to suggest that our capacity for imagining ourselves as mortal is rooted in this *béance* (*E*, 552/196).
11. I retain the French expression, in order to emphasize Lacan's insis-

tence on the distinction between the *moi* and the *je*, the *ego* and the *I*, a distinction crucial to Lacanian theory.

12. In "Variantes de la cure-type" (Variants in the form of the treatment) (1955) (*E*, 323–62), Lacan suggests that this first confrontation with alienation is the basis for the fundamental philosophical distinction between essence and existence (*E*, 345).

13. Sigmund Freud, *The Question of Lay Analysis: Conversations with an Impartial Person* (1926), *SE*, 20:183–258, 225–28.

14. The classic source here is René Descartes, *Meditations on First Philosophy* (1641), in particular the "Second Meditation." See *The Philosophical Writings of Descartes*, 2 vols., trans. John Cottingham, Robert Stoothoff, and Dugald Murdoch (Cambridge: Cambridge University Press, 1984), 2:16–23.

15. For a useful introduction to the work of Husserl, see Erazim Kohák, *Idea and Experience: Edmund Husserl's Project of Phenomenology in "Ideas I"* (Chicago: University of Chicago Press, 1978).

16. Jean-Paul Sartre, *Being and Nothingness: An Essay on Phenomenological Ontology*, trans. with an introduction by Hazel E. Barnes (New York: Philosophical Library, [1956]).

17. There is in the metaphor of "precipitation" a reference to Heidegger's notion of "thrownness," elaborated in Martin Heidegger, *Being and Time* (1927), trans. John Macquarrie and Edward Robinson (New York: Harper & Row, 1962), section 38, 219–24.

18. See the helpful discussion of "quadrature" in John P. Muller and William J. Richardson, *Lacan and Language: A Reader's Guide to "Écrits"* (New York: International Universities Press, 1982), 39.

19. A fundamental implication of this is drawn in "Some Reflections on the Ego," *International Journal of Psycho-Analysis*, 34 (1953): 11–17, where Lacan notes: "We are nevertheless convinced that our researches justify the epigram of the philosopher who said that speech was given to man to hide his thoughts; our view is that the essential function of the ego is very nearly that systematic refusal to acknowledge reality (*méconnaissance systématique de la réalité*) which French analysts refer to in talking about the psychoses" (12). In this same essay—Lacan's sole publication in the official journal of the International Psychoanalytic Association and a remarkable synthesis of the two earlier papers discussed here—he links the ego (that is, the *moi*) explicitly with Freud's notion of *Verneinung* (denegation or denial), noting that "what we have been able to observe is the privileged way in which a person expresses himself as the ego; it is precisely this—*Verneinung*, or denial" (11).

20. See, for example, Sigmund Freud, *The Ego and the Id* (1923), *SE*, 19:12–66, 23–27; it should be emphasized, however, that Freud is quite insistent about the fact that parts of the ego remain unconscious as well.

21. Anna Freud, *The Ego and the Mechanisms of Defence*, trans. Cecil Baines (New York: International Universities Press, 1946).

22. Sigmund Freud, "Negation," *SE*, 19:235–39, 235. Freud's term here is *Verneinung*, which Lacan generally renders as *dénégation*, emphasizing the duplicity involved in saying "No" (the double negation tantamount to affirmation).

23. Here again, "Some Reflections on the Ego," 11–12, offers a compact restatement of this position.

24. Sigmund Freud, "On Narcissism: An Introduction," *SE*, 14:73–102.

25. Ibid., 100.

26. For example, "a vital dehiscence that is constitutive of man, and which makes unthinkable the idea of an environment that is preformed for him" (*E*, 116/21).

27. Closely related to this is René Girard's notion of "mimetic desire," used as a central concept in his analysis of myth and religion. See, in particular, René Girard, *Violence and the Sacred*, trans. Patrick Gregory (Baltimore: Johns Hopkins University Press, 1977), and René Girard, *Des choses cachées depuis la fondation du monde: Recherches avec Jean-Michel Oughourlian et Guy Lefort* (Paris: Bernard Grasset, 1978), especially 307–22.

28. The interrelation of the *moi* and others is summed up in the claim that "the narcissistic relation to a fellow being is the fundamental experience in the development of the imaginary sphere in human beings." See "The Neurotic's Individual Myth" (1953), trans. Martha Noel Evans, *The Psychoanalytic Quarterly* 48 (1979): 405–25, 423; the original version of this essay is "Le mythe individuel du névrosé," *Ornicar?* 17/18 (1979): 289–307. A similar position is sketched in "Variantes de la cure-type," *E*, 342–43.

29. See the letter of 13 May 1871 to Georges Izambard: "C'est faux de dire: Je pense. On devrait dire: On me pense. Pardon du jeu de mots [penser/panser ("to think/to groom")]. / Je est un autre." ("It is false to say: I think. One ought to say: People think me. Pardon the pun. / I is an other.") This letter is included in Arthur Rimbaud, *Complete Works, Selected Letters*, trans. Wallace Fowlie (Chicago: University of Chicago Press, 1966), 302–5. It would be fair to claim that much of Lacan's work is an elaboration of this passage from Rimbaud.

30. See also "Some Reflections on the Ego," 12.

31. Throughout Lacan's discussion in "Aggressivity in Psychoanalysis," the key term is *connaissance*. In later texts, he will use *savoir* much more. It would not be unreasonable to see the distinction between paranoiac knowledge and Lacanian theory as marked by the *connaissance/savoir* distinction. In a discussion of "Subversion of the Subject," Jane Gallop argues that *connaissance* "is associated with psychology and its perception of the person as a unified whole with natural developmental cognitive states. *Savoir* is associated with Hegel, desire, and language. *Connaissance* is an unmediated experience; *savoir* is intricated with discourse." See Jane Gallop, *Reading Lacan* (Ithaca: Cornell

University Press, 1985), 174–75. In general, Gallop tends to translate *connaissance* as *recognition* and *savoir* as *knowledge.*

Chapter Three

1. In addition to the translation by Alan Sheridan included in *Écrits: A Selection* (1977), one must acknowledge the pioneering effort of translator Anthony Wilden in *Speech and Language in Psychoanalysis* (Baltimore: Johns Hopkins University Press, 1968), originally published as *The Language of the Self: The Function of Language in Psychoanalysis.* For ease of reference I have quoted from Sheridan's version, but Wilden's translation has much to recommend it, among other virtues some sixty-five pages of translator's notes to Lacan's text.

2. A helpful introduction to the history of ego psychology is "The Development of Ego Psychology" (1951), in *Selected Papers of Ernst Kris* (New Haven: Yale University Press, 1975), 375–89.

3. Characteristic themes of ego psychology are highlighted in Heinz Hartmann, "Psychoanalysis and the Concept of Health" (1939), "Psychoanalysis and Developmental Psychology" (1950), and "Psychoanalysis as a Scientific Theory" (1959), in *Essays on Ego Psychology: Selected Problems in Psychoanalytic Theory* (New York: International Universities Press, 1964), 3–18, 99–112, 318–50. See also the early formulation of Hartmann's theory in Heinz Hartmann, *Ego Psychology and the Problem of Adaptation* (1939) (New York: International Universities Press, 1958).

4. It is worth emphasizing that there is nothing whatsoever in Lacan's discussion to prohibit the possibility of variable-length sessions running longer than the canonical fifty minutes of the IPA.

5. A useful introduction to object relations theory is Jay R. Greenberg and Stephen A. Mitchell, *Object Relations in Psychoanalytic Theory* (Cambridge: Harvard University Press, 1983).

6. Among the many introductions to structuralism, one of the most useful is John Sturrock, ed., *Structuralism and Since: From Lévi-Strauss to Derrida* (Oxford: Oxford University Press, 1979). For a rather sophisticated philosophical treatment, see Philip Pettit, *The Concept of Structuralism: A Critical Analysis* (Berkeley: University of California Press, 1977).

7. Ferdinand de Saussure, *Course in General Linguistics,* ed. Charles Bally and Albert Sechehaye, in collaboration with Albert Riedlinger, trans. Wade Baskin (New York: McGraw-Hill, 1966). For a very useful introduction to the work of Saussure, see Jonathan Culler, *Ferdinand de Saussure* (New York: Penguin, 1977).

8. In the interest of absolute accuracy, it should be noted that Saussure distinguishes between *langage* and *langue,* using the former at times to refer to the fact of human speech in general (see, for example, *Course,* 9). Lacan does

not regularly observe this Saussurean distinction; *langage* and *langue* are often taken to be essentially synonymous.

9. Saussure, *Course,* 11–15.

10. Ibid., 67–70.

11. Ibid., 14.

12. Ibid., 98–100.

13. Ibid., 120.

14. Ibid., 117. It is this dimension of Saussure's theory that makes it possible for Lacan to unite structural linguistics and an existentialist reading of Hegel.

15. See Claude Lévi-Strauss, *The Scope of Anthropology,* trans. Sherry Ortner Paul and Robert A. Paul (London: Jonathan Cape, 1967), 16–19.

16. Saussure, *Course,* 16–17.

17. Claude Lévi-Strauss, *Structural Anthropology,* trans. Claire Jacobson and Brooke Grundfest Schoepf (New York: Basic Books, 1963), 31–54.

18. Ibid., 33.

19. Ibid., 44; compare the diagrammatic representation of the argument (45).

20. Claude Lévi-Strauss, *The Elementary Structures of Kinship,* rev. ed., trans. James Harle Bell, John Richard von Sturmer, and Rodney Needham (Boston: Beacon Press, 1969).

21. It should be noted, however, that "Function and Field" will argue for the very different claim that human discourse "is only apparently two-way, for any positing of its structure in merely dual terms is as inadequate to it in theory as it is ruinous for its technique" (*E,* 265/56).

22. On the "fundamental rule," see in particular Sigmund Freud, "Recommendations to Physicians Practising Psycho-Analysis," *SE,* 12:111–20, especially 112, 115, as well as "On Beginning the Treatment (Further Recommendations on the Technique of Psycho-Analysis I)," *SE,* 12:123–44, especially 134–35.

23. For Freud's most important theoretical accounts of repression, see the metapsychological essay of 1915, "Repression," *SE,* 14:146–58, and its complement, "The Unconscious," *SE,* 14:166–204.

24. Compare "Variantes de la cure-type" (*E,* 346). Along similar lines, Lacan insists, for example, that "regression is simply the actualization in the discourse of the phantasy relations reconstituted by an 'ego' at each stage in the decomposition of its structure. After all, this regression is not real" (*E,* 252/44).

25. We have already seen that Lacan himself undertook the translation of a landmark text by Heidegger on the pre-Socratic philosopher Heraclitus and published it in the first number of *La psychanalyse,* which also included "Function and Field." On Lacan's relation to Heidegger, see the important essay by the noted Heideggerian William J. Richardson, "Psychoanalysis and the

Being-question," in Joseph H. Smith and William Kerrigan, eds., *Interpreting Lacan* (New Haven: Yale University Press, 1983), 139–59, as well as Edward S. Casey and J. Melvin Woody, "Hegel, Heidegger, Lacan: The Dialectic of Desire," in the same volume, 75–112. Lacan himself addresses the presence of Heidegger in his work at the end of "The Agency of the Letter," dating from 1957; see *E*, 527–28/175. For an amusing account of the personal relation between Lacan and Heidegger, see Roudinesco, *La bataille*, 2:308–10.

26. For the most relevant discussion of related questions in Heidegger, see his analysis of "anticipatory resoluteness" in section 65, "Temporality as the Ontological Meaning of Care," in *Being and Time*, 370–80.

27. The issues raised by this question for psychoanalysis in general are sensitively explored in D. A. Spence, *Narrative Truth and Historical Truth* (New York: W.W. Norton, 1982).

28. In his later work, Lacan will make a difficult distinction between the real (*le réel*) and reality (*la réalité*), subsuming the latter under the rubric of the symbolic; however, this distinction has not yet been articulated here. In "Some Reflections on the Ego" (1953) Lacan suggests that language has "a sort of retrospective effect in determining what is ultimately decided to be real" (11).

29. For a very helpful account of Freud's use of the notion of deferred action, see J. Laplanche and J.-B. Pontalis, *The Language of Psycho-Analysis*, trans. Donald Nicholson-Smith (New York: W. W. Norton, 1973), 111–14.

30. Sartre's response to the challenge of determinism is to redefine causality in the human agent as a function of the agent's utterly free choice of an initial project. Only in the light of an agent's assumption of a project can certain psychological states or events be said to motivate or cause decisions or actions. See Sartre, *Being and Nothingness*, part 4, chapter 1, especially 445–51.

31. Crucial to this mechanism is the power of the demand for love addressed to the analyst. What motivates the analysand's assumption of his history is precisely the promise that this will yield recognition by the other (the analyst).

32. Lacan's presentation of this point is found in a stylistic tour de force (one of many in "Function and Field") metaphorically linking these features of the analysand's symbolic behavior with the documentary evidence used by historians; see *E*, 259/50.

33. See "La direction de la cure et les principes de son pouvoir" ("The Direction of the Treatment and the Principles of its Power") (*E*, 585–645/226–80), dating from 1958.

34. "The Agency of the Letter," *E*, 495/147.

35. Sigmund Freud, *The Interpretation of Dreams*, SE, 4–5:xxiii–625.

36. Lacan's reference here is to *SE*, 4:277–78.

37. On these mechanisms, see *SE*, 4:279–309. Basically, condensation involves the reduction of a multiplicity of ideas into a very few, multivalent

dream images and situations; displacement involves the transference of affect from a highly charged idea to an apparently unimportant idea. Both of these mechanisms serve to distort the latent dream thoughts, while preserving their essential content, in the manifest dream.

38. Sigmund Freud, *The Psychopathology of Everyday Life*, SE, 6.

39. Overdetermination is the fact, crucial to psychoanalytic theory but also to any dialectical theory (for example, Marxism), that certain events or situations can be given more than one causal explanation or specification of meaning. Thus, Laplanche and Pontalis define it as "the fact that formations of the unconscious (symptoms, dreams, etc.) can be attributed to a plurality of determining factors." See *The Language of Psycho-Analysis*, 292–93.

40. Sigmund Freud, *Jokes and Their Relation to the Unconscious*, SE, 8.

41. It is also the necessity of this "third" that leads Lacan at the end of section 1 to insist that "any positing of its [discourse's] structure in merely dual terms is as inadequate to it in theory as it is ruinous for its technique" (*E*, 265/56).

42. Compare Saussure, *Course*, 117, 120.

43. Lacan is here trading on the meaning of the Greek *sumbolon*, as Wilden notes in *Speech and Language*, 118–22.

44. Sigmund Freud, *Beyond the Pleasure Principle*, SE, 18:7–64; see 14–17.

45. Ibid., 15.

46. It is a striking example of Lacan's willful distortion of Freud that Freud himself has rather little to say about the linguistic dimension of his grandson's game. As we shall see, Lacan will go on to relate this linguistic accomplishment to *Beyond the Pleasure Principle*'s introduction of the concept of the death instinct, thus finding in Freud the inseparability of language and death.

47. Kojève, *Introduction to the Reading of Hegel*, 142–43.

48. The most important of these texts, all collected in *Écrits*, are "The Freudian Thing, or the Meaning of the Return to Freud in Psychoanalysis" (1955), "The Agency of the Letter" (1957), "The Direction of the Treatment" (1958), and "The Signification of the Phallus" (1958) (*E*, 685–95/281–91).

49. Saussure, *Course*, 65–67.

50. Lacan often uses an image to capture this feature of the signifying chain: "rings of a necklace that is a ring in another necklace made of rings" (*E*, 502/153).

51. On this, compare "The Agency of the Letter," *E*, 513–14/162–63.

52. Roman Jakobson and Morris Halle, *Fundamentals of Language* (The Hague: Mouton, 1956), part 2, "Two Aspects of Language and Two Types of Aphasic Disturbances," 55–82.

53. For Freud's account of the dream-work, see *The Interpretation of Dreams*, chapter 6, especially 277–338.

54. On the translation of *manque à être*, Stuart Schneiderman writes: "Lacan's concept of *manque-à-être* has been translated as 'want-to-be,' and to me, at least, this expression is unsatisfactory. One of the scenes of the word 'want' is 'lack,' but this is not rendered in the idea of 'want-to-be.' Thus I have adopted, with Lacan's approval, the expression 'want-of-being' where the genitive can be either subjective or objective." See Stuart Schneiderman, ed. and trans., *Returning to Freud: Clinical Psychoanalysis in the School of Lacan* (New Haven: Yale University Press, 1980), vii.

55. In "Variantes de la cure-type" Lacan paradoxically identifies desire as the desire that desire be recognized (*E*, 343).

56. In "The Signification of the Phallus" Lacan argues that this inability of language to articulate desire—which itself leads to desire's being "alienated in needs"—constitutes "primal repression" in the Freudian sense. See *E*, 690/285–86.

57. Compare *E*, 431/141 and 628/264. In "The Agency of the Letter" the Other is described as "the locus of signifying convention" (*E*, 525/173).

58. Lacan uses a Z-shaped figure—the so-called Schema L—to illustrate the imbrication of subject and Other, emphasizing the way this relation shapes and is shaped by the subject's relation to objects and to the *moi*. On Schema L, see *E*, 429–30/139–40, 548–49/193–94, and 630–31/265–66.

59. Compare *E*, 413/125. *Ça* is, it should be noted, Lacan's translation of Freud's *Es*, normally translated into English as *id*.

60. A now classic discussion and critique of Lacan and Lévi-Strauss is Gayle Rubin, "The Traffic in Women: Notes on the 'Political Economy' of Sex," in Rayna R. Reiter, ed., *Toward an Anthropology of Women* (New York: Monthly Review Press, 1975), 157–210.

61. Lévi-Strauss, *Elementary Structures of Kinship*, 10

62. Thus, Lévi-Strauss writes, the prohibition of incest "is the fundamental step because of which, by which, but above all in which, the transition from nature to culture is accomplished" (ibid., 24).

63. Ibid., 481.

64. Ibid., 495–96.

65. Lest this mathematical reading of Lévi-Strauss seem extreme, it should be noted that chapter 14 of *Elementary Structures of Kinship* is entitled "On the Algebraic Study of Certain Types of Marriage Laws (Murngin System)" and was written by the mathematician André Weil.

66. For Freud's exposition of the Oedipus complex, see Sigmund Freud, *Introductory Lectures on Psycho-Analysis* (1915–17), lecture 21, "The Development of the Libido and the Sexual Organizations," *SE*, 16:320–38; *The Ego and the Id* (1923), *SE*, 19:31–39; and "The Dissolution of the Oedipus Complex" (1924), *SE*, 19:173–79.

67. *Nom* and *non*, "name" and "no," are homophones in French.

68. "The Neurotic's Individual Myth," 422–23.

69. Ibid., 423.

70. For a useful, more clinically oriented summary of Lacan's position on the Oedipus complex, see Benvenuto and Kennedy, *The Works of Jacques Lacan,* chapter 7, 126–41.

71. We have begun to see how "Function and Field" also marks Lacan's attempt to leave the phenomenological dimension of this earlier account behind, offering in its place a more rigorously structural analysis.

72. Further Freudian discussions of these issues include Sigmund Freud, "Neurosis and Psychosis" (1924), *SE,* 19:149–53, and "The Loss of Reality in Neurosis and Psychosis" (1924), *SE,* 19:183–87.

73. I quote here the translation of Jacqueline Rose (having corrected an unfortunate substitution of 'signified' for 'signifier' at the beginning of the second sentence) in Lacan and école freudienne, *Feminine Sexuality,* 79–80.

74. The other side of this is the fact that the phallus, as that which is itself never successfully signified can play a role as the signifier of that part of our being that manages to escape the barriers raised by signifying convention. This observation lies at the heart of Lacan's approach to comedy (see S 7, 362).

75. In "The Direction of the Treatment" Lacan maintains that the refusal of castration on the part of a subject is "first of all a refusal of the castration of the Other (initially, the mother)" (*E,* 632/267).

76. See Sigmund Freud, "Psycho-Analytic Notes on an Autobiographical Account of a Case of Paranoia (*Dementia Paranoides)*" (1911), *SE,* 12:9–82. Schreber's *Memoirs* were published in English as *Memoirs of My Nervous Illness,* trans. I. Macalpine and R. A. Hunter (London: Dawson and Sons, 1955). Lacan devoted much of his seminar of 1955–56, *Les psychoses,* to the case of Dr. Schreber, and his views are largely summarized in "On a Question Preliminary."

77. See, for example, the radio play, *To Have Done with the Judgment of God* (1947), in Antonin Artaud, *Selected Writings,* ed. Susan Sontag, trans. Helen Weaver (New York: Farrar, Straus and Giroux, 1976), 553–71.

78. See, for example, the collection of reports published in conjunction with the Quatrième rencontre internationale du champ freudien, *Hystérie et obsession: Les structures cliniques de la névrose et la direction de la cure* (Paris: Fondation du champ freudien, 1985).

79. On repression, see Laplanche and Pontalis, *The Language of Psycho-Analysis,* 390–94.

80. On negation, see ibid., 261–63.

81. In his later work Lacan occasionally suggests that the alienation of the modern, scientific subject is actually much more closely related to psychosis and thus is a product of foreclosure (for which, see below). For a discussion of this, see Jonathan Scott Lee, "From Knowledge to the Real: Philosophy after Lacan," *PsychCritique: The International Journal of Critical Psychology and Psychoanalysis* 1 (1985): 235–54.

82. For example, by Laplanche and Pontalis in *The Language of Psycho-Analysis*, 166–69.

83. For an extensive discussion of Lacan's approach to psychosis, see Alphonse De Waelhens, *Schizophrenia: A Philosophical Reflection on Lacan's Structuralist Interpretation* (1972), trans. Wilfried Ver Eecke (Pittsburgh: Duquesne University Press, 1978).

Chapter Four

1. Sigmund Freud, "Notes upon a Case of Obsessional Neurosis" (1909), *SE*, 10:155–318. For a Lacanian reading of this case study, see Stuart Schneiderman, *Rat Man* (New York: New York University Press, 1986).

2. This is the issue motivating much of the earlier work of the French philosopher, Jacques Derrida. See, for example, his classic critique of Lévi-Strauss, "Structure, Sign, and Play in the Discourse of the Human Sciences," in *Writing and Difference*, trans. Alan Bass (Chicago: University of Chicago Press, 1978), 278–93.

3. The idea that universal and particular are united in the individual is quite common in Hegel; for a brief and very general discussion, see *Hegel's Logic: Being Part One of the "Encyclopaedia of the Philosophical Sciences" (1830)*, 3d ed., trans. William Wallace (Oxford: Clarendon Press, 1975), 226–30.

4. Lacan puts this point with unusual clarity in "The Signification of the Phallus," *E*, 692/287.

5. An important and controversial study in this direction is Fredric Jameson, *The Political Unconscious: Narrative as a Socially Symbolic Act* (Ithaca: Cornell University Press, 1981).

6. Compare "The Freudian Thing," *E*, 413–414/125. The performative dimension of language was most fully introduced into philosophical discourse by J. L. Austin in *How to Do Things with Words*, 2d ed., ed. J. O. Urmson and Marina Sbisà (Cambridge: Harvard University Press, 1975).

7. Lacan's special attention to the performative dimension of language is a focus of Shoshana Felman, *Jacques Lacan and the Adventure of Insight: Psychoanalysis in Contemporary Culture* (Cambridge: Harvard University Press, 1987).

8. A similar critique of models of language that emphasize communication and representation is found in the rethinking of traditional humanism characteristic of the later works of Heidegger. See, for example, "The Way to Language" (1959), in *On the Way to Language*, trans. Peter D. Hertz (New York: Harper & Row, 1971), 111–36, and "Letter on Humanism" (1947), in *Basic Writings*, ed. David Farrell Krell (New York: Harper & Row, 1977), 193–241.

9. In "On a Question Preliminary" Lacan emphasizes that "the question of existence" occurs "as an articulated question" in the analysand's speech and

that it "bathes the subject, supports him, invades him, tears him apart even" (*E, 549/194*).

10. It is this emphasis on truth that distinguishes Lacan from Derrida. For a pre-Derridian critique of Derrida, see "The Freudian Thing," *E,* 405–6/ 118. For Derrida's critique of Lacan (first published in 1975), see "Le facteur de la vérité," in *The Post Card: From Socrates to Freud and Beyond,* trans. Alan Bass (Chicago: University of Chicago Press, 1987), 411–96.

11. For Heidegger's own account, see *Being and Time,* section 44, 256–73, especially 262–63.

12. The prosopopoeia "The thing speaks of herself" can be found at *E,* 408–11/121–23, and should be compared with a passage in "The Neurotic's Individual Myth": analytic experience "always implies within itself the emergence of a truth that cannot be said, since what constitutes truth is speech, and then you would have in some way to say speech itself which is exactly what cannot be said in its function as speech" (406).

13. Heidegger, *Being and Time,* 376–77. *Dasein* is Heidegger's technical term for the being characteristic of the human being.

14. For the Rat Man's "fateful constellation," see "The Neurotic's Individual Myth," 410–11.

15. For the claim that the subject of the enunciation is not to be identified with the subject of the statement, see the difficult text of 1960, "Subversion du sujet et dialectique du désir dans l'inconscient freudien" ("The Subversion of the Subject and the Dialectic of Desire in the Freudian Unconscious") (*E,* 793–827/292–325), *E,* 800–801/298–99. In "The Agency of the Letter," *E* 516–18/165–66, Lacan makes the same point in terms of the "subject of the signified" and the "subject of a signifier."

16. See, for example, "Of Structure as an Inmixing," 186–200, especially 193–94.

17. The central sources for Freud's formulation of the later topography are *The Ego and the Id,* (1923), *SE,* 19:12–59, and *New Introductory Lectures on Psycho-Analysis* (1933), lecture 31, "The Dissection of the Psychical Personality," *SE,* 22:57–80.

18. References in "Function and Field" to this "wall of language" (*mur du langage),* in addition to that quoted below, include *E,* 282/71, 291–92/79, 308/94, 312/97, and 316/101.

19. In "The Freudian Thing" Lacan elaborates a critique of this emphasis on adaptation, arguing that such a theory treats the ego or *moi* as a thing in no way different from a desk; see *E,* 420–27/131–37.

20. Freud, *New Introductory Lectures, SE,* 22:80.

21. Freud's fundamental contributions to the theory of transference can be found in the papers on technique from the period just before World War I; see, in particular, Sigmund Freud, "The Dynamics of Transference" (1912), "Remembering, Repeating and Working-Through (Further Recommenda-

tions on the Technique of Psychoanalysis II)" (1914), and "Observations on Transference-Love (Further Recommendations on the Technique of Psychoanalysis III)," *SE*, 12:99–108, 147–56, and 159–71. For a very rich discussion of the complexities of the notion of transference in psychoanalytic theory, see Laplanche and Pontalis, *The Language of Psycho-Analysis*, 455–62.

22. One of Freud's very last and most important papers deals directly with this question; see Sigmund Freud, "Analysis Terminable and Interminable" (1937), *SE*, 23:216–53.

23. Freud, "Recommendations to Physicians," *SE*, 12:115.

24. For a remarkable description of the effect of Lacan's very short sessions, see the remarks of Gérard Pommier in Roudinesco, *La bataille*, 2:428–29.

25. Compare "The Agency of the Letter," where Lacan writes: "It is in the chain of the signifier that meaning [*sens*] 'insists' but . . . none of its elements 'consists' in the signification of which it is at the moment capable" (*E*, 502/153).

26. For further examples, see "The Agency of the Letter," *E*, 502/153, and the seminar of 6 June 1956 (S 3, 293–306).

27. Compare "On a Question Preliminary," *E*, 532–33/180.

28. "The Direction of the Treatment," *E*, 593–94/232–33.

29. Indicative of the continuing importance of these issues was the recent colloquium "On Time in Psychoanalysis," held at Columbia University in October 1987.

30. That there are deep similarities between Zen and psychoanalysis has often been noted. See, for example, the influential study by D. T. Suzuki, Erich Fromm, and Richard De Martino, *Zen Buddhism and Psychoanalysis*, (New York: Harper & Row, 1970).

31. In his later work Freud typically traces the negative therapeutic reaction back to an unconscious sense of guilt, arguing that there is a dimension of the analysand's personality that finds satisfaction in the continuation of neurosis. See, for example, *The Ego and the Id, SE*, 19:49–50, and *New Introductory Lectures, SE*, 22:109–10.

32. See, for example, the discussion in Frank J. Sulloway, *Freud, Biologist of the Mind: Beyond the Psychoanalytic Legend* (New York: Basic Books, 1979), 393–415. It was certainly the speculative biology of *Beyond the Pleasure Principle* that most inspired Freud's own circle; for a remarkable example of this, see Sándor Ferenczi, *Thalassa: A Theory of Genitality*, trans. Henry Alden Bunker (New York: W. W. Norton, 1968), in which dubious use of evolutionary theory provides the basis for an explanation of the high value placed upon genital sexuality by "healthy" adults.

33. Heidegger, *Being and Time*, 294–95.

34. "The Direction of the Treatment," *E*, 642/276–77.

35. See, in particular, "The Freudian Thing," *E*, 429–30/139–40; com-

pare "Variantes de la cure-type," *E,* 348, where the analyst is urged to take on the role of "the absolute master, death," as well as "The Direction of the Treatment," *E,* 589–90/229–30. The bridge analogy typically accompanies some discussion of Schema L.

36. Kojève, *Introduction to the Reading of Hegel,* 140. Kojève later considers the consequences for the human being of Hegel's identification of the Concept and Time, emphasizing the essential temporality of the human subject (147–48). There is every reason to believe that this Heideggerian approach to Hegel helped shape Lacan's own appropriation of both German philosophers.

37. G. W. F. Hegel, *Phenomenology of Spirit,* trans. A. V. Miller (Oxford: Clarendon Press, 1977), chapter 4, "The Truth of Self-Certainty," especially 111–19.

38. See, in particular, Sartre, *Being and Nothingness,* part 3, chapter 1, section 3, "Husserl, Hegel, Heidegger," 233–52.

39. This reversal of fortunes lies at the heart of Marx's early analysis of alienation; see Karl Marx, "The Economic and Political Manuscripts of 1844," in Robert C. Tucker, ed., *The Marx-Engels Reader,* 2d ed. (New York: W. W. Norton, 1978), 66–125, especially 70–81.

40. This summary of Hegel's argument avoids countless interpretative problems, not the least of which is the fact that the entire *Phenomenology of Spirit* is designed to operate simultaneously at the level of individuals and at the level of social totalities. Thus, the master-slave dialectic is both intrasubjective and intersubjective.

41. See, for example, the conclusion of "The Direction of the Treatment," *E,* 640–42/275–77.

42. "Some Reflections on the Ego," 15.

43. "The Freudian Thing," *E,* 427/137.

44. "Some Reflections on the Ego," 16.

45. Donald Moss identifies Lacan's reference to Freud here as the following remark from "Recommendations to Physicians," *SE,* 12:115: "A surgeon of earlier times took as his motto the words: 'Je le pansai, Dieu le guérit.' ['I dressed his wounds, God cured him.'] The analyst should be content with something similar."

46. Lacan, "Founding Act," 150/98.

47. For a lively critique of Lacanian psychoanalysis from precisely this angle, see Catherine Clément, *The Weary Sons of Freud* (1978), trans. Nicole Ball (London: Verso, 1987).

48. Even in the "Founding Act," Lacan characterizes the praxis of psychoanalytic theory as the "ethics of psychoanalysis" (151/98).

49. "The Neurotic's Individual Myth," 407–8.

50. This account of what it is to be a hero is elaborated in the final third of S 7 and summarized on 368–75.

51. "Some Reflections on the Ego," 17.

52. Muller and Richardson suggest a similar account when they remark: "Death is the limit, the boundary that de-fines man and the point from which he begins to be. To speak of 'desire for death' in this Heideggerean context can only mean, as Lacan says three paragraphs later, that it is 'in the full assumption of his being-for-death,' that is, in authentically accepting his ownmost possibilities, that he can affirm himself for others. Anything short of this, such as narcissistically identifying with the other or struggling to be the object of the other's desire is to be caught up in the imaginary structures of the ego." See Muller and Richardson, *Lacan and Language*, 120–21.

53. I adopt here Wilden's translation, Sheridan's attempt failing to make any grammatical sense; see Wilden, *Speech and Language in Psychoanalysis*, 85.

54. An excellent source is Swami Nikhilananda, trans., *The Upanishads*, 4 vols. (New York: Ramakrishna-Vivekananda Center, 1949–59), 3:321–22. Lacan had already alluded to the Upaniṣads as early as "The Mirror Stage" (*E*, 100/7), where he evokes the great dictum of the *Chāndogya Upaniṣad*, "Thou art that [*Tat-tvam-asi*]." See *The Upanishads*, 4:306–24.

55. T. S. Eliot, *The Waste Land* (1922) in *The Complete Poems and Plays: 1909–1950* (New York: Harcourt, Brace & World, 1952), 49–50. Eliot's poem "The Hollow Men" (1925), is quoted earlier in "Function and Field" (*E*, 282/71).

Chapter Five

1. Two representative and excellent collections of literary criticism from a Lacanian perspective are those edited by Robert Con Davis: *The Fictional Father: Lacanian Readings of the Text* (Amherst: University of Massachusetts Press, 1981), and *Lacan and Narration: The Psychoanalytic Difference in Narrative Theory* (Baltimore: Johns Hopkins University Press, 1983). Among recent books on Lacan published by professors of literature are Felman, *Jacques Lacan and the Adventure of Insight*; Gallop, *Reading Lacan;* Juliet Flower MacCannell, *Figuring Lacan: Criticism and the Cultural Unconscious* (Lincoln: University of Nebraska Press, 1986); and Ellie Ragland-Sullivan, *Jacques Lacan and the Philosophy of Psychoanalysis* (Urbana: University of Illinois Press, 1986).

2. "Some Reflections on the Ego" had, of course, appeared originally in English as early as 1953, but its publication in the *International Journal of Psychoanalysis* would have kept it out of the mainstream of North American literary culture.

3. Two later Lacanian readings of literature deserve special mention, although I will not explore them here. In 1965 Lacan published the extraordinary "Hommage fait à Marguerite Duras, du *Ravissement de Lol V. Stein*," *Cahiers Renauld-Barrault* 52 (1965):7–15. An English version is available: "Homage to Marguerite Duras, on *Le ravissement de Lol V. Stein*," trans. Peter Connor, in *Marguerite Duras* (San Francisco: City Lights Books, 1987), 122–

29. In 1975–76 Lacan devoted a substantial portion of his seminar *Le sinthome* to the work of James Joyce: transcriptions of the relevant seminar sessions, together with related texts, can be found in Jacques Aubert, ed., *Joyce avec Lacan*, (Paris: Navarin, 1987), 21–67.

4. Curiously, when Lacan made a selection from the *Écrits* for publication in English, not only did he not introduce the collection with the "Seminar," but he dropped it completely. I have used Jeffrey Mehlman's admirable translation of the "Seminar" here, referring to this version in the usual way after the French pagination. Regrettably, this translation does not include the long sequence of introductory texts with which the seminar in the *Écrits* concludes. For Mehlman's translation, see "Seminar on 'The Purloined Letter,'" trans. Jeffrey Mehlman, in John P. Muller and William J. Richardson, eds., *The Purloined Poe: Lacan, Derrida, and Psychoanalytic Reading* (Baltimore: Johns Hopkins University Press, 1988), 28–54 (translation originally published in *Yale French Studies* 48 [1972]: 38–72). Muller and Richardson's collection brings together a number of important studies of Lacan's "Seminar," most notably their own invaluable overview, map, and notes to Lacan's text.

5. For an admirable situating of the "Seminar" in the context of other literary critical and psychoanalytic approaches to Poe, see Felman, *Jacques Lacan and the Adventure of Insight*, 26–51. Muller and Richardson's *The Purloined Poe* includes a version of Felman's chapter, as well as selections from Marie Bonaparte's classic psychoanalytic reading of Poe; see 133–56 and 101–32.

6. It is perhaps worthy of note that the original presentation of "The Purloined Letter" in the seminar of 1955 is significantly less attentive to the details of Poe's text than is the formally published version found in the *Écrits*. This is a particularly dramatic example of the way Lacan's written texts transform the very workings of his oral presentations. Also worthy of note is the fact that the difficult introductory material included with the "Seminar" in the *Écrits* is somewhat closer in detail to the actual content of the seminar.

7. For Poe's text, see Muller and Richardson, *The Purloined Poe*, 6–23. For the first scene of the drama, see 8–9.

8. Ibid., 21–23.

9. In the introductory material added to the "Seminar" in 1966, Lacan emphasizes that intersubjectivity properly understood requires more than two positions: a dual relationship between subjects would simply repeat the imaginary relation between a subject and his mirror image. Thus, the three positions articulated here are the minimum for an intersubjective structure. See *E*, 57.

10. For Freud's presentation of the apparent conflict between repetition and the pleasure principle, see *Beyond the Pleasure Principle, SE*, 18:22–23.

11. Ibid., 36–39, 62.

12. Muller and Richardson, *The Purloined Poe*, 6–13.

13. Ibid., 14–23; for the reflections on methodology, see 14–20.

14. For a very useful review of the complex mathematical reasoning involved here, see ibid., 67–76. We see here a spectacular example of the move toward formalization that Lacan makes as he pursues the question of the scientific status of psychoanalysis.

15. Space prevents me from considering at any length the influential critique of the "Seminar" in particular and of Lacan's thought in general offered by Jacques Derrida in "Le facteur de la vérité." Derrida's basic objections to Lacan and to Lacan's reading of Poe are summarized in *Positions,* trans. Alan Bass (Chicago: University of Chicago Press, 1981), 107–13, where he argues that the "Seminar" offers a "profoundly traditional reading of Poe's text then, a reading that is ultimately hermeneutic (semantic) *and* formalist" (112). For a full translation of Derrida's text, which was first published in 1975, see Derrida, *The Post Card,* 413–96.

16. Although the complete text of this seminar has not yet been published, a substantial account of it can be found in the *compte rendu* of its first twelve sessions prepared by J.-B. Pontalis. See "Le désir et son interprétation," abstracted by J.-B. Pontalis, *Bulletin de Psychologie* 13 (1959–60): 263–72, 329–35.

17. The complete text of the sessions devoted to *Hamlet,* as edited by Jacques-Alain Miller, can be found in the following numbers of *Ornicar?*: sessions 1 and 2 in *Ornicar?* 24 (1981): 5–31; sessions 3 and 4 in *Ornicar?* 25 (1982): 13–36; and sessions 5, 6, and 7 in *Ornicar?* 26/27 (1983): 7–44. An English translation has appeared of the final three sessions in a slightly abridged version: see "Desire and the Interpretation of Desire in *Hamlet,*" translated by James Hulbert, *Yale French Studies* 55/56 (1977): 11–52. References to the seminar on *Hamlet* in this chapter will be by session number, followed by the page number of the French version and (where available) that of the English version; for example, (D, 5:16/20).

18. For Freud's most sustained remarks on *Hamlet,* see Freud, *The Interpretation of Dreams, SE,* 4:264–66; Lacan reviews these remarks during the first session of his seminar, 8–11. The classic treatment of *Hamlet* in the psychoanalytic literature is Ernest Jones, *Hamlet and Oedipus* (New York: W. W. Norton, 1949).

19. In this respect at least, Lacan's approach to literature parallels that of Aristotle in the *Poetics.* In his definition of tragedy (*Poetics,* chapter 6, 1449b 24–28), Aristotle emphasizes formal features of plot and language, but he also stresses the performative function of tragedy in transforming its audience, "through pity and fear effecting the proper purgation [*katharsis*] of these emotions." For a useful edition and translation of Aristotle's text, one originally published in 1894, see S. H. Butcher, *Aristotle's Theory of Poetry and Fine Art,* 4th ed. (New York: Dover, 1951).

20. Sigmund Freud, "The Dissolution of the Oedipus Complex," *SE,* 19:173–79.

21. Ibid., 176.

22. Sigmund Freud, "Mourning and Melancholia," *SE*, 14:243–58.

23. Ibid., 244–45, 249, 256.

24. Ibid., 255.

25. Ibid., 249.

26. Jones, *Hamlet and Oedipus*, 70.

27. Throughout the fourth session there are a number of clear allusions to Lacan's important article of the previous year, "The Signification of the Phallus," where he argues that it is because the phallus is repressed or "veiled" as a signifier that the unconscious is constituted as a language (*E*, 690/285, 693/288), thus suggesting that all human speech (and by extension action) is a more or less failed metonymic attempt to cover over the fundamental want-of-being characteristic of our castrated condition.

28. The algebraic symbols that crop up in this seminar refer to the completed "graph of desire" elaborated most fully in Lacan's important essay of 1960, "The Subversion of the Subject"; for the graph, see *E*, 817/315 and chapter 6, figure 1.

29. Thus, the claim here that "there is no Other of the Other" is equivalent to Lacan's later formulation that "there is no metalanguage." See "Subversion of the Subject" (*E*, 813/310–11).

30. Describing the symptoms of melancholia as "a profoundly painful dejection, cessation of interest in the outside world, loss of the capacity to love, inhibition of all activity, and a lowering of the self-regarding feelings," Freud himself calls attention to the way Hamlet fits this description; see Freud, "Mourning and Melancholia," *SE*, 14:244, 246.

31. The *petit a*, the "lower-case a," stands for *autre* (other), as opposed to the *Autre* (Other). As we have already seen, the relation between the human subject and ordinary objects and other people is itself mediated in a variety of ways by the subject's relation to the Other, as the place of speech, the domain of language.

32. Lacan notes that this process is "the inverse" of foreclosure (*D*, 6:30/38), the mechanism responsible for psychosis. For a study of the *Hamlet* seminar elaborating the relation between mourning and psychosis, see John P. Muller, "Psychosis and Mourning in Lacan's *Hamlet*," *New Literary History* 12 (1980): 147–65.

33. Sigmund Freud, "Fetishism" (1927), *SE*, 21:152–57.

34. This claim leads Lacan into an intriguing digression concerning the role of the signifier in Marx's analysis of the fetish character of the commodity in the first volume of *Capital*; see *D*, 5:12.

35. Lacan's claim here is ultimately derived from Freud's account of the way every form of love or desire is modeled on the infant's earliest relation to the mother's breast. "The finding of an object," Freud writes, "is in fact a refinding of it." See Freud, *Three Essays on the Theory of Sexuality, SE*, 7:222.

36. Because he is not a real person, Lacan remarks, it is possible for Hamlet to be both a hysteric and an obsessional at the same time (see *D*, 3:25).

37. How successfully any given performance of the play achieves this effect is very much a product of the actor's ability to use his body to mediate the imaginary and symbolic registers of the action. For a suggestive analysis of the power of theatrical performance in general, see *D*, 3:17–18.

38. The translation here is that of Benjamin Jowett as revised in Jonathan Barnes, ed., *The Complete Works of Aristotle*, 2 vols. (Princeton: Princeton University Press, 1984).

39. G. W. F. Hegel, *Aesthetics: Lectures on Fine Art*, 2 vols., trans. T. M. Knox (Oxford: Clarendon Press, 1975), 1:464. See also 2:1217–18.

40. For a provocative treatment of Hegel's reading and of the modern history of interpretation of Sophocles' play, see George Steiner, *Antigones* (Oxford: Oxford University Press, 1984). On Hegel, in particular, see 19–42; Steiner dismisses Lacan's reading without much analysis (no doubt in part because the seminar had not yet been published), remarking that "Sophocles' *Antigone* will not suffer from Lacan" (297).

41. The translation of *Antigone* used here is that of Elizabeth Wyckoff in David Grene and Richmond Lattimore, eds., *The Complete Greek Tragedies*, 4 vols. (Chicago: University of Chicago Press, 1959), 2:157–206.

42. See *Poetics* 13, 1453a 7–12. On *hamartia*, see Butcher, *Aristotle's Theory*, 317–25.

43. More literally—and this will clarify Lacan's later discussion—the law here might be translated as follows: "Nothing in the life of great mortals creeps beyond *Atē*."

44. The contrast between Creon's mistake and Antigone's *Atē* that Lacan sees in these lines is by no means a feature of traditional commentaries. Wyckoff, for example, translates the relevant text: "his crime, / the doom he brought on himself," a translation that is consistent with the commentary on these lines found in the standard student edition of the play. See Sophocles, *Antigone*, with a commentary, abridged from the large edition of Sir Richard C. Jebb by E. S. Shuckburgh (Cambridge: Cambridge University Press, 1902), 226.

45. For Lacan's later reflections on the relation between Kant and Sade, see "Kant avec Sade" (Kant with Sade), first published in 1963 and included in *Écrits (E*, 765–90). I am grateful to William J. Richardson for allowing me to quote from his unpublished translation of this important essay.

46. See Immanuel Kant, *The Critique of Judgement*, trans. James Creed Meredith (Oxford: Clarendon Press, 1952), part 1, 58.

47. Ibid., 43; see also, the definition of "the beautiful" on 50.

48. On overvaluation, see Freud, *Three Essays on the Theory of Sexuality*, *SE*, 7:150–55. On the relation of this to loving idealization, see Freud, *Group Psychology and the Analysis of the Ego* (1921), *SE*, 18:69–143, especially 111–16.

49. The conflict between love and the social community is a central theme of Freud's later writings. See, most notably, Sigmund Freud, *Civilization and its Discontents* (1930), *SE,* 21:64–145, especially 99–109.

Chapter Six

1. This seminar has not yet been published in an authorized version, and thus I have not been able to include a discussion of Lacan's commentary here. The sessions on Plato were at the center of a storm of controversy in 1985–86, as a result of a lawsuit instigated by Lacan's literary heir, Jacques-Alain Miller, against the editors of *stécriture,* a newsletter published in conjunction with the journal *Littoral. stécriture* had offered, over a number of issues, an unauthorized transcription of all eleven sessions devoted to Plato, a transcription at least partly intended to call into question Miller's editorial practice in his authorized editions of Lacan's seminars. The suit was settled in Miller's favor, and publication of *stécriture* has ceased. For Miller's own account of his editorial principles, see his *Entretien sur le séminaire.*

2. For a sketch of this still-unpublished seminar, see Marini, *Lacan,* 193–95.

3. On Lacan's puns, see Françoise Meltzer, "Eat Your *Dasein*: Lacan's Self-Consuming Puns," in Jonathan Culler, ed., *On Puns: The Foundation of Letters* (Oxford: Basil Blackwell, 1988), 156–63.

4. On *lalangue,* see S 20, 126–27.

5. "Vers un signifiant nouveau," *Ornicar?* 17/18 (1978): 7–23, 18.

6. See S 11, 22/18, where Lacan attempts to distance his work of 1964 from that of the 1950s by making special reference to his former, merely "propaedeutic" use of Heidegger.

7. See also Lacan's preface to the English-language edition of S 11, vii, where the unconscious as real is similarly contrasted with reality.

8. For Kant's notoriously difficult "refutation of idealism," see Immanuel Kant, *Critique of Pure Reason,* trans. Norman Kemp Smith (London: Macmillan, 1929), 244–47.

9. Compare similar remarks on rats and labyrinths in S 20, 127–29.

10. Although this seminar has not yet been published, see the abstracts of it by J.-B. Pontalis, published as "Les formations de l'inconscient," *Bulletin de psychologie* 11 (1957–58): 293–96; 12 (1958–59): 182–92, 250–56.

11. See "Le désir et son interprétation."

12. Lacan notes here that it is this translation of the Other's question that allows psychoanalysis to function.

13. The French term, perhaps most naturally translated as "enjoyment," is sufficiently wide to cover the legal notion of ownership, according to which one "enjoys" the use of property and even the exercise of rights, while its cognate verb, *jouir,* includes the sexual sense "to come."

14. In the seminar of 1964 this theme of castration is portrayed in the

myth of the "lamella" (*la lamelle*), the libido "*qua* pure life instinct, that is to say, immortal life" (S 11, 180/198), which is forever lost by the subject precisely because "he is only a sexed living being" (S 11, 186–87/205).

15. This contrast is elaborated in "Kant avec Sade," *E*, 773; compare also S 11, 32/31.

16. See Georges Bataille, *Erotism: Death and Sensuality*, trans. Mary Dalwood (San Francisco: City Lights Books, 1986), which first appeared in French in 1957. Bataille was of course the first husband of Lacan's second wife, Sylvia.

17. I use the masculine pronoun throughout the discussion of desire and fantasy in order to emphasize the fact that the desire in question here is essentially that of men. Lacan suggests that women's desire may escape the perversion inherent in fantasy. See chapter 7.

18. "La science et la vérité" (Science and truth), *E*, 855–77, 873.

19. Clément, *Lives and Legends*, 179.

20. Lacan also discusses this sign, which he sometimes calls the *losange*, at S 11, 190/209.

21. James Strachey's rationale for avoiding "drive" and using "instinct" in the translation of the *Standard Edition*—for which see *SE*, 1:xxiv–xxvi—has come under attack from quarters far removed from Lacan. See, for example, Bruno Bettelheim, *Freud and Man's Soul* (New York: Alfred A. Knopf, 1983), 103–12.

22. On this passage, see the useful discussion in Gallop, *Reading Lacan*, 174–75.

23. In the seminar of 1964 Lacan remarks that "In the unconscious there is a *savoir*, which must in no way be conceived as *savoir* to be completed, to be closed" (S 11, 122/134).

24. Sigmund Freud, "Instincts and Their Vicissitudes," *SE*, 14:117–40.

25. Ibid., 122–23.

26. See, for example, Sigmund Freud, "A Short Account of Psychoanalysis" (1924), *SE*, 19:190–209, especially 203.

27. Freud, "Instincts and Their Vicissitudes," 117.

28. Ibid., 122.

29. Later Lacan characterizes the *objet a* in its relation with the signifier, with special reference to the sexual drives: "This object supports that which, in the drive, is defined and specified by the fact that the coming into play of the signifier in the life of man enables him to bring out the meaning [*sens*] of sex" (S 11, 232/257).

30. See Heidegger, "Letter on Humanism," 193–242. The translators of *Télévision* make special reference to 204, where Heidegger finds language to be the key component of what he calls "the ek-sistence of man." This Heideggerian inflection of the notion of existence—marking the permeation of human existence by the division of the subject, his standing "outside" (*ek-*) of

himself—becomes a regular part of Lacan's vocabulary in the 1960s and
1970s. The classic text for Heidegger's reflections on the notion of dwelling is
"Building Dwelling Thinking" (1951), *Basic Writings,* 323–39.

31. For a compelling philosophical critique of this position, see the
influential study by Richard Rorty, *Philosophy and the Mirror of Nature* (Princeton: Princeton University Press, 1979).

32. Compare also Lacan's moving tribute to Merleau-Ponty's work,
"Maurice Merleau-Ponty," *Les temps modernes* 184/185 (1961): 245–54.

33. Maurice Merleau-Ponty, *The Visible and the Invisible,* ed. Claude
Lefort, trans. Alphonso Lingis (Evanston, Ill.: Northwestern University Press,
1968).

34. Ibid., 131.

35. Sartre, *Being and Nothingness,* 256–57.

36. Ibid., 259 ff.

37. Ibid., 263–64. For the claims that the Other's gaze spatializes and
temporalizes the subject, see 266–67.

38. Ibid., 276–77.

39. It is rather surprising that, despite the very wide use of Lacan in
contemporary art criticism—and the still wider mention of his name—most
such work has been limited to quite specific themes and issues in current art
and criticism, most notably to questions bound up with the politics of representation. For an important example of this trend, see Kate Linker, "Representation and Sexuality," reprinted in Brian Wallis, ed., *Art after Modernism:
Rethinking Representation* (New York: The New Museum of Contemporary Art,
1984), 391–415. In contrast, very little attention has been paid to his fairly
explicit remarks on the aesthetics of painting.

40. A reproduction of Holbein's painting appears on the cover of the
French version of S 11.

41. Norman Bryson, *Vision and Painting: The Logic of the Gaze* (New
Haven: Yale University Press, 1983).

42. Under the rubric of "suture," this basic notion of the viewing subject's being himself presupposed by the structure of the visual work of art has
emerged as perhaps the dominant concept of contemporary film theory. Influenced by Jacques-Alain Miller more directly than by Lacan, Stephen Heath
sketches the key concept as follows: "The major emphasis in all this is that the
articulation of the signifying chain of images, of the chain of images as
signifying, works not from image to image but from image to image through
the absence that the [viewing] subject constitutes." See Stephen Heath, "Notes
on Suture," *Screen* 18, no. 4 (Winter 1977/78): 48–76, 58. The fundamental
text by Miller, which originated as an intervention in Lacan's seminar of 1965,
can be found in the same number of *Screen*; see Jacques-Alain Miller, "Suture
(elements of the logic of the signifier)," trans. Jacqueline Rose, *Screen* 18, no.4
(Winter 1977/78): 24–34. Other important Lacanian contributions to film

theory include Christian Metz, *The Imaginary Signifier: Psychoanalysis and the Cinema,* trans. Celia Britton, Annwyl Williams, Ben Brewster, and Alfred Guzzetti (Bloomington: Indiana University Press, 1982) and Kaja Silverman, *The Acoustic Mirror: The Female Voice in Psychoanalysis and Cinema* (Bloomington: Indiana University Press, 1988).

43. I have modified Sheridan's rendering of this italicized remark.

44. Note Sheridan's rendering of "Mais moi, je suis dans le tableau" as "But I am not in the picture" (S 11, 89/96).

45. Freud, "On Narcissism," *SE,* 14:94–95.

46. In the preceding session of the seminar Lacan offers a similar account, remarking in somewhat disparaging terms that culture uses the sublimation involved in works of art "to colonize with imaginary formations the field of *das Ding*" (S 7, 118–19). A somewhat parallel distinction between object and thing also plays an important role in the later work of Heidegger; see, in particular, "The Thing" (1951), in *Poetry, Language, Thought,* trans. Albert Hofstadter (New York: Harper & Row, 1971), 165–86.

47. Indeed, since Lacan takes *das Ding* to designate the object forever lost and thus outside of language, he celebrates the fact that *das Ding* "is nowhere articulated by Freud" (see S 7, 72).

48. Unfortunately for Lacan's argument, Freud does seem to use *Dingvorstellung* as a synonym for *Sachvorstellung,* for example in "Mourning and Melancholia," *SE,* 14:256; on this see the editor's note, *SE,* 14:201.

49. See Freud, "The Unconscious," SE 14:201–3, and *The Ego and the Id, SE,* 19:20–23.

50. See Freud, "Negation," *SE,* 19:236–37.

51. This is the presupposition underlying particularly book 1 of the *Nicomachean Ethics,* where Aristotle argues that the good that is the goal of all human action is in fact happiness. For a useful and philosophically sophisticated translation of Aristotle's text, see Aristotle, *Nicomachean Ethics,* trans. Terence Irwin (Indianapolis: Hackett, 1985).

52. See especially the second chapter of Freud, *Civilization and its Discontents, SE,* 21:74–85.

53. See Immanuel Kant, *Critique of Practical Reason,* trans. Lewis White Beck (Indianapolis: Bobbs-Merrill, 1956).

54. Ibid., 30.

55. Ibid., 19–26.

56. For a useful modern translation, see the Marquis de Sade, *The Complete Justine, Philosophy in the Bedroom, and Other Writings,* trans. Richard Seaver and Austryn Wainhouse, (New York: Grove, 1965), 185–367. Man Ray's 1938 *Portrait du marquis de Sade* illustrates the cover of *L'éthique de la psychanalyse*

57. Ibid., 296–339.

58. Lacan notes as well that both Sade and Kant find "pain" (*la douleur*)

to be the key experience opening the human mind to *das Ding*; see S 7, 97, and Kant, *Critique of Practical Reason*, 75.

59. On the real as something approached only asymptotically, see Fredric Jameson, "Imaginary and Symbolic in Lacan: Marxism, Psychoanalytic Criticism, and the Problem of the Subject," *Yale French Studies* 55/56 (1977): 338– 95, 383. Compare Ragland-Sullivan, *Jacques Lacan*, 187–95.

60. For the context of Lacan's terminology here, see Sigmund Freud, *Inhibitions, Symptoms, and Anxiety* (1926), *SE*, 20:87–172, especially 164–68.

61. As in so many other respects, Lacan's theory here closely parallels that of Kant, in this case Kant's epistemology.

62. Even in *L'éthique de la psychanalyse* Lacan claims that the ten commandments of Judeo-Christian ethics simply "make explicit that without which no speech is possible" (S 7, 84). Here, however, he also tries to distinguish between speech (*parole*) and discourse (*discours*).

Chapter Seven

1. Although this seminar is not yet available in English, a somewhat abridged version of its two most important sessions has been included in Lacan and école freudienne, *Feminine Sexuality*, 137–61. References to this English version occur after the slash in parenthetical page references.

2. On this question see the editor's note to Sigmund Freud, "Some Psychical Consequences of the Anatomical Distinction between the Sexes" (1925), *SE*, 19:244 n.1.

3. There is also surely a reference here, through the English "mansion," to Heidegger's claim in "Letter on Humanism" that "language is at once the house of Being and the home of human beings" (239).

4. Juliet Mitchell, introduction to Lacan and école freudienne, *Feminine Sexuality*, 4.

5. Ibid., 20.

6. Freud, "Some Psychical Consequences," *SE*, 19:248–58.

7. Sigmund Freud, "Female Sexuality," *SE*, 21:225–43.

8. Sigmund Freud, *New Introductory Lectures*, lecture 33, *SE*, 22:112– 35.

9. For the best general review of the issues and literature on this difficult topic, see Juliet Mitchell, *Psychoanalysis and Feminism: Freud, Reich, Laing, and Women* (New York: Pantheon Books, 1974). Mitchell's admirably critical yet sympathetic treatment of Freud is nicely summarized in her introduction to Lacan and école freudienne, *Feminine Sexuality*, 1–26. My presentation of Freud on these issues owes much to Mitchell.

10. See Freud, "Some Psychical Consequences," 256–57.

11. See Freud, *New Introductory Lectures*, 130–35.

12. It is a particular weakness of many introductions to Lacan's theories about women that they are cast in precisely the developmental terms that he repeatedly rejects. See, for a dramatic example of this, Ragland-Sullivan, *Jacques Lacan*, 267–308.

13. We have already seen that for Lacan the very notion of the drive is thoroughly shaped by the system of the symbolic, the genital drive (for example) being "subjected to the circulation of the Oedipus complex, to the elementary and other structures of kinship" (S 11, 173/189).

14. This claim in turn simply reflects the ordinary range of meaning of the French term *sens*, which includes "direction," as well as "meaning" or "sense."

15. See, for example, Hélène Cixous and Catherine Clément, *The Newly Born Woman* (1975), trans. Betsy Wing (Minneapolis: University of Minnesota Press, 1986), and Luce Irigaray, *This Sex Which Is Not One* (1977), trans. Catherine Porter with Carolyn Burke (Ithaca: Cornell University Press, 1985). For a very helpful introduction to Cixous and Irigaray, emphasizing their relation to psychoanalysis and to Lacan, see Jane Gallop, *The Daughter's Seduction: Feminism and Psychoanalysis* (Ithaca: Cornell University Press, 1982).

16. More generally, in the course of *Encore* Lacan explores definitions of necessity, impossibility, and contingency in terms of various permutations of "ceasing to be written," permutations involving various positionings of the signifiers of negation(s). See S 20, 55 and 86–87.

17. Jacques Lacan, "Séminaire du 21 janvier 1975," *Ornicar?* 3 (1975): 104–110; see 108 and 110. This session has been translated in Lacan and école freudienne, *Feminine Sexuality*, 162–71; for the passages noted here, see 168 and 170.

18. As Lacan notes at S 20, 80/157, this account of phallic *jouissance* shows that its satisfaction is nothing more than a fantasy satisfaction.

19. In Aristophanes' fable, love results from Zeus's physical severing of primordially doubled human beings. It is thus quite literally a longing by the lover for his other half. Freud was quite fond of this portion of the *Symposium*, and his interest in it no doubt contributed to Lacan's choosing the *Symposium* for an elaborate commentary in the seminar of 1960–61. For a delightful translation of Plato's text, see *The Symposium of Plato*, trans. Suzy Q. Groden, ed. John A. Brentlinger (Amherst: University of Massachusetts Press, 1970); Aristophanes' speech is found at 189c–194e. Freud's references to the fable include *Three Essays on the Theory of Sexuality*, SE, 7:136, and *Beyond the Pleasure Principle*, SE, 18:57–58.

20. On this topic see Eva C. Keuls, *The Reign of the Phallus: Sexual Politics in Ancient Athens* (New York: Harper & Row, 1985).

21. Lacan's later remarks on Aristotle's theory of the soul as nothing more than a perspective on the body (see S 20, 99–100) suggest that any

conception of the soul is nevertheless dependent upon certain symbolic or imaginary categories. Thus reflection on the soul does not manage to yield a theory of *das Ding*. Indeed, in the strict sense any linguistically formulated theory would fail to be a theory of *das Ding*.

22. For an important and amusing discussion, "Jacques Lacan, Blessed Lady," see Clément, *Lives and Legends*, 61–67.

23. On a woman's close relation to God stemming from the radical Otherness of her *jouissance*, see also S 20, 65/140–41 and 77/153.

24. Sigmund Freud, *Project for a Scientific Psychology*, SE, 1:295–397.

25. See, for example, the final lecture, "The Question of a *Weltanschauung*," in Freud, *New Introductory Lectures*, SE, 22:158–82.

26. See, for example, the brief remarks in Freud, "On Narcissism," *SE*, 14:77, and "Instincts and Their Vicissitudes," *SE*, 14:117–18.

27. See chapter 12, "Determinism, Belief in Chance and Superstition—Some Points of View," in Freud, *The Psychopathology of Everyday Life*, SE, 6:239–79.

28. For an important contemporary appraisal of psychoanalysis along these lines, see Adolf Grünbaum, *The Foundations of Psychoanalysis: A Philosophical Critique* (Berkeley: University of California Press, 1984). Grünbaum predictably dismisses Lacan's work (65) without addressing Lacan's real interest in rethinking the nature of science.

29. See Jakobson and Halle, *Fundamentals of Language*, 3–51.

30. *Écrits* even includes an appendix in which Jacques-Alain Miller offers commentary on these graphs (*E*, 903–8/332–35).

31. "L'Éveil du printemps" (1974), *Ornicar?* 39 (1986): 5–7, 6.

32. See, for example, Sigmund Freud, "A Difficulty in the Path of Psycho-Analysis" (1917), *SE*, 17:137–44.

33. See Kant, *Critique of Pure Reason*, 22 and 25 n.

34. Further reflections on the Copernican revolution can be found in a valuable radio interview from 1970; see "Radiophonie," *Scilicet* 2/3 (1970): 55–99, especially 81–83.

35. Alan Sheridan regrettably renders "*La* science" as "Science *itself*," thereby turning Lacan's distinction upside down and suggesting that it is "*La* science" that has been the object of philosophical reflection.

36. Lacan insists that this is the same notion of the real to be found in Newton; see "Radiophonie," 83.

37. Hilbert's "formalism" claims that the notion of mathematical proof is best understood as a finite series of lawlike manipulations of symbols; the actual meaning of the symbols manipulated is irrelevant to the question of whether or not a series of formulas constitutes a proof. For a useful introduction to Hilbert and to related issues in the philosophy of mathematics, see Morris Kline, *Mathematical Thought from Ancient to Modern Times* (New York: Oxford University Press, 1972), 1203–8.

38. As Ellie Ragland-Sullivan has noted, similar reflections can be found as early as the seminar of 1955–56; Ragland-Sullivan, *Jacques Lacan*, 186, commenting on session fourteen of *Les psychoses*, "Le signifiant, comme tel, ne signifie rien" (The signifier, as such, signifies nothing) (S 3, 207–20).

39. "Radiophonie," 93.

40. See "Radiophonie," 77, on the idea that the unconscious itself is an impossible *savoir.*

41. "Une pratique de bavardage," *Ornicar?* 19 (1979): 5–9, 5.

42. Lacan's reference here is to the classic discussion of falsifiability in the sciences in Karl R. Popper, *The Logic of Scientific Discovery* (New York: Basic Books, 1959), 78–92.

43. "Une pratique de bavardage," 9.

44. This is the expression Lacan uses to describe his use of topological figures in "Function and Field" (*E, 320–21/105*).

45. For a number of such examples, see Fondation du champ freudien, *Hystérie et obsession,* and Néstor A. Braunstein, ed., *El Discurso del Psicoanálisis* (México: Siglo Vientiuno Editores, 1986).

46. The most important mathematical source for the topology involved here is J. W. Alexander, "Topological Invariants of Knots and Links," *Transactions of the American Mathematical Society* 30 (1928): 275–306.

47. "Séminaire du 8 avril 1975," *Ornicar?* 5 (1975/76): 49–50. Jane Gallop points out quite relevantly that the French term for "knot"—*noeud*—is also slang for "penis"; see Gallop, *Reading Lacan,* 156.

48. Lacan himself provides an important, but extremely difficult, introduction to his use of topology in "L'étourdit," *Scilicet* 4 (1973): 5–52, especially 26ff. For a practical, and even amusing, introduction to the basic topological notions employed by Lacan, see Jeanne Granon-Lafont, *La topologie ordinaire de Jacques Lacan* (Paris: Point Hors Ligne, 1985).

49. Sherry Turkle does a very good job of laying out the fundamental questions here; see Turkle, *Psychoanalytic Politics,* 234–39.

50. Available sources for the theory include the conclusion of "Radiophonie," 96–99, the second session of *Encore* (particularly S 20, 20–22), and scattered remarks in *Télévision* (particularly *T, 25–27/17–18* and 36/23). Helpful discussions of the four discourses include Lacan and école freudienne, *Feminine Sexuality,* 160–61 n. 6; Alain Juranville, *Lacan et la philosophie* (Paris: Presses Universitaires de France, 1984), 341–53; and Stephen Melville, "Psychoanalysis and the Place of *Jouissance*," *Critical Inquiry* 13 (1987): 349–70.

Selected Bibliography

PRIMARY WORKS

Books

De la psychose paranoïaque dans ses rapports avec la personnalité, suivi de premiers écrits sur la paranoïa (1932). Paris: Éditions du Seuil, 1975.

Les complexes familiaux dans la formation de l'individu: Essai d'analyse d'une fonction en psychologie (1938). Paris: Navarin, 1984.

Écrits. Paris: Éditions du Seuil, 1966. *Écrits: A Selection.* Translated by Alan Sheridan. New York: W.W. Norton, 1977.

Télévision. Paris: Éditions du Seuil, 1974. "Television." Translated by Denis Hollier, Rosalind Krauss, and Annette Michelson. *October* 40 (1987): 5–50.

Jacques Lacan and the école freudienne. *Feminine Sexuality.* Edited by Juliet Mitchell and Jacqueline Rose. Translated by Jacqueline Rose. New York: W. W. Norton, 1982.

Seminars

Abstracts and excerpts are readily available for many of the unpublished seminars, including some abstracts prepared or approved by Lacan himself. For bibliographic details, see Michael Clark, *Jacques Lacan: An Annotated Bibliography.*

S 1: *Les écrits techniques de Freud* (1953–54). Text established by Jacques-Alain Miller. Paris: Éditions du Seuil, 1975. *Freud's Papers on Technique: 1953–1954.* Translated by John Forrester. New York: W. W. Norton, 1988.

S 2: *Le moi dans la théorie de Freud et dans la technique de la psychanalyse* (1954–55). Text established by Jacques-Alain Miller. Paris: Editions du Seuil, 1978. *The Ego in Freud's Theory and in the Technique of Psychoanalysis: 1954–1955.* Translated by Sylvana Tomaselli, with notes by John Forrester. New York: W. W. Norton, 1988.

S 3: *Les psychoses* (1955–56). Text established by Jacques-Alain Miller. Paris: Éditions du Seuil, 1981.

S 4: *La relation d'objet et les structures freudiennes* (1956–57). Unpublished.

S 5: *Les formations de l'inconscient* (1957–58). Unpublished.

S 6: *Le désir et son interprétation* (1958–59). Text established by Jacques-Alain Miller (seven sessions). *Ornicar?* 24 (1981): 7–31; 25 (1982): 13–36; and 26/27 (1983): 7–44. The final three sessions are translated by James Hulbert as "Desire and the Interpretation of Desire in *Hamlet.*" *Yale French Studies* 55/56 (1977): 11–52.

S 7: *L'éthique de la psychanalyse* (1959–60). Text established by Jacques-Alain Miller. Paris: Éditions du Seuil, 1986.

S 8: *Le transfert dans sa disparité subjective* (1960–61). Unpublished.

S 9: *L'identification* (1961–62). Unpublished.

S 10: *L'angoisse* (1962–63). Unpublished.

S 11: *Les quatre concepts fondamentaux de la psychanalyse* (1964). Text established by Jacques-Alain Miller. Paris: Éditions du Seuil, 1973. *The Four Fundamental Concepts of Psychoanalysis.* Translated by Alan Sheridan. New York: W. W. Norton, 1977.

S 12: *Problèmes cruciaux pour la psychanalyse* (1964–65). Unpublished.

S 13: *L'objet de la psychanalyse* (1965–66). Opening session published as "La science et la vérité" in *Écrits*, 855–77.

S 14: *La logique du fantasme* (1966–67). Unpublished.

S 15: *L'acte psychanalytique* (1967–68). Unpublished.

S 16: *D'un autre à l'Autre* (1968–69). Unpublished.

S 17: *L'envers de la psychanalyse* (1969–70). Unpublished.

S 18: *D'un discours qui ne serait pas du semblant* (1970–71). Unpublished.

S 19: *. . . ou pire* (1971–72). Unpublished.

S 20: *Encore* (1972–73). Text established by Jacques-Alain Miller. Paris: Éditions du Seuil, 1975. Partially translated (two sessions) by Jacqueline Rose in *Feminine Sexuality*, 137–61.

S 21: *Les non-dupes errent* (1973–74). Unpublished.

S 22: *R. S. I.* (1974–75). Text established by Jacques-Alain Miller. *Ornicar?* 2 (1975): 87–105; 3 (1975): 95–110; 4 (1975): 91–106; and 5 (1975): 15–66. Partially translated (one session) by Jacqueline Rose in *Feminine Sexuality*, 162–71.

S 23: *Le sinthome* (1975–76). Text established by Jacques-Alain Miller. *Ornicar?* 6 (1976): 3–20; 7 (1976): 3–18; 8 (1976): 6–20; 9 (1977): 32–40; 10 (1977): 5–12; and 11 (1977): 2–9.

S 24: *L'insu que sait de l'une-bévue, s'aile à mourre* (1976–77). Text established by Jacques-Alain Miller. *Ornicar?* 12/13 (1977): 4–16; 14 (1978): 4–9; 15 (1978): 5–9; 16 (1978): 7–13; and 17/18 (1979): 7–23.

S 25: *Le moment de conclure* (1977–78). Text established by Jacques-Alain Miller (one session). *Ornicar?* 19 (1979): 5–9.

S 26: *La topologie et le temps* (1978–79). Unpublished.

S 27: *Dissolution!* (1980). *Ornicar?* 20/21 (1980): 9–20 and 22/23 (1981): 7–14. Partially translated by Jeffrey Mehlman as "Letter of Dissolution" and "The Other Is Missing." *October* 40 (1987): 128–33.

Articles

These are important articles not collected in *De la psychose paranoïaque* or *Écrits: A Selection*.

"Some Reflections on the Ego" (1951). Translated by Nancy Elisabeth Beaufils. *International Journal of Psycho-Analysis* 34 (1953): 11–17.

"Intervention sur le transfert" (1951). In *Écrits*, 215–26. "Intervention on Transference." Translated by Jacqueline Rose. In *Feminine Sexuality*, 61–73.

"Le mythe individuel du névrosé" (1953). Text established by Jacques-Alain Miller. *Ornicar?* 17/18 (1979): 289–307. "The Neurotic's Individual Myth." Translated by Martha Noel Evans. *The Psychoanalytic Quarterly* 48 (1979): 405–25.

"Discours de Jacques Lacan (26 septembre 1953)" (1953). *La psychanalyse* 1 (1956): 202–11, 242–55.

"Le séminaire sur 'La Lettre volée' " (1957). In *Écrits*, 11–61. "Seminar on 'The Purloined Letter.' " Translated by Jeffrey Mehlman. In *The Purloined Poe: Lacan, Derrida, and Psychoanalytic Reading*, edited by John P. Muller and William J. Richardson, 28–54.

"Maurice Merleau-Ponty" (1961). *Les temps modernes* 184/185 (1961): 245–54.

"Kant avec Sade" (1963). In *Écrits*, 765–90.

"Introduction to the Names-of-the-Father Seminar" (1963). Text established by Jacques-Alain Miller and translated by Jeffrey Mehlman. *October* 40 (1987): 81–95.

"Fondation de l'EFP par Jacques Lacan" (21 June 1964). In *L'excommunication: La communauté psychanalytique en France II*, edited by Jacques-Alain Miller, 149–52. Supplement to *Ornicar?* 8 (1977). "Founding Act." Translated by Jeffrey Mehlman. *October* 40 (1987): 96–105.

"Hommage fait à Marguerite Duras, du *Ravissement de Lol V. Stein*" (1965). *Cahiers Renauld-Barrault* 52 (1965): 7–15. "Homage to Marguerite Duras, on *Le ravissement de Lol V. Stein*." Translated by Peter Connor. In Marguerite Duras, *Marguerite Duras*, 122–29. San Francisco: City Lights Books, 1987.

"Of Structure as an Inmixing of an Otherness Prerequisite to Any Subject Whatever" (1966). In *The Structuralist Controversy: The Languages of Criticism and the Sciences of Man*. Edited by Richard Macksey and Eugenio Donato, 186–200. Baltimore: Johns Hopkins University Press, 1970.

"Proposition du 9 octobre 1967 sur le psychanalyste de l'École." *Scilicet* 1 (1968): 14–30.

"Radiophonie" (1970). *Scilicet* 2/3 (1970): 55–99.

"L'étourdit" (1972). *Scilicet* 4 (1973): 5–52.

"Joyce le symptôme I" (1975). In *Joyce avec Lacan*, edited by Jacques Aubert, 21–29. Paris: Navarin, 1987.

"Conférences et entretiens dans des universités nord-américaines" (1975). *Scilicet* 6/7 (1976): 5–63.
"Joyce le symptôme II" (1979). In *Joyce avec Lacan*, edited by Jacques Aubert, 31–36. Paris: Navarin, 1987.
"Le séminaire de Caracas" (1980). In *Almanach de la dissolution*, 81–87. Paris: Navarin, 1986.

SECONDARY WORKS

Bibliography

Clark, Michael. *Jacques Lacan: An Annotated Bibliography*. 2 vols. New York: Garland, 1988. Full descriptions of primary sources, but neither as helpful nor as complete for secondary sources.

Books

Benvenuto, Bice, and Roger Kennedy. *The Works of Jacques Lacan: An Introduction*. New York: St. Martin's Press, 1986. Introduces major texts with special emphasis on psychoanalytic context.
Bowie, Malcolm. *Freud, Proust, and Lacan: Theory as Fiction*. Cambridge: Cambridge University Press, 1987. Provocative literary approach to the concept of theory in Lacan, reprinting Bowie's classic introductory study of 1979.
Clément, Catherine. *The Lives and Legends of Jacques Lacan*. Translated by Arthur Goldhammer. New York: Columbia University Press, 1983. Captures the spirit of 1970s *lacanisme*, while introducing Lacanian themes in a feminist context.
————. *The Weary Sons of Freud*. Translated by Nicole Ball. London: Verso, 1987. A stinging critique of the tendency in Lacanian theory to discount the importance of therapeutic practice.
Davis, Robert Con, ed. *The Fictional Father: Lacanian Readings of the Text*. Amherst: University of Massachusetts Press, 1981. A valuable collection of Lacanian literary criticism, focused on literary treatments of paternity.
————, ed. *Lacan and Narration: The Psychoanalytic Difference in Narrative Theory*. Baltimore: Johns Hopkins University Press, 1983. Literary studies using the Lacanian theory of the subject to explore narrative strategies.
Deleuze, Gilles, and Félix Guattari. *Anti-Oedipus: Capitalism and Schizophrenia*. Translated by Robert Hurley, Mark Seem, and Helen R. Lane. New York: Viking, 1977. A classic, radical critique of Lacanian psychoanalysis from a post-1968, poststructuralist perspective.
Derrida, Jacques. *The Post Card: From Socrates to Freud and Beyond*. Translated

by Alan Bass. Chicago: University of Chicago Press, 1987. Includes Derrida's important critique of Lacan's notion of truth, "Le facteur de la vérité."

Felman, Shoshana. *Jacques Lacan and the Adventure of Insight: Psychoanalysis in Contemporary Culture*. Cambridge: Harvard University Press, 1987. A literary approach, with special emphasis on the performative aspect of language.

Gallop, Jane. *The Daughter's Seduction: Feminism and Psychoanalysis*. Ithaca: Cornell University Press, 1982. A valuable introduction to French feminism and its ambivalence toward Lacan.

————. *Reading Lacan*. Ithaca: Cornell University Press, 1985. An introductory study, focusing mostly on Gallop's polyvalent acts of reading.

Granon-Lafont, Jeanne. *La topologie ordinaire de Jacques Lacan*. Paris: Point Hors Ligne, 1985. A valuable introduction to the various topological figures used by Lacan in the course of his teaching, including amusing (and illuminating) instructions for their construction.

Julien, Philippe. *Le retour à Freud de Jacques Lacan: L'application au miroir*. Toulouse: érès, 1985. A good, relatively nontechnical introduction to and critique of Lacan's celebrated "return to Freud."

Juranville, Alain. *Lacan et la philosophie*. Paris: Presses Universitaires de France, 1984. A challenging exploration of the significance of Lacan for contemporary philosophy.

Lacoue-Labarthe, Philippe, and Jean-Luc Nancy. *Le titre de la lettre (Une lecture de Lacan)*. Paris: Éditions Galilée, 1973. An important critique of Lacan's high structuralism, singled out for special comment by Lacan himself in the seminar of 1972–73.

Lemaire, Anika. *Jacques Lacan*. Translated by David Macey. London: Routledge & Kegan Paul, 1977. The first doctoral thesis devoted to Lacan, not for the uninitiated.

MacCabe, Colin, ed. *The Talking Cure: Essays in Psychoanalysis and Language*. New York: St. Martin's Press, 1981. The best collection of interpretative and critical articles available in English on specific aspects of Lacan's linguistic rereading of Freud.

MacCannell, Juliet Flower. *Figuring Lacan: Criticism and the Cultural Unconscious*. Lincoln: University of Nebraska Press, 1986. A literary reading of Lacan that aims to clarify the relations between history, society, and literature.

Macey, David. *Lacan in Contexts*. London: Verso, 1988. A provocative critique of Lacan's theoretical importance and of his originality, including a particularly challenging interpretation of Lacan's theory of feminine sexuality in the light of his early and persistent enthusiasm for surrealism.

Marini, Marcelle. *Jacques Lacan*. Paris: Pierre Belfond, 1986. A general introduction, featuring a valuable short biography and a well-annotated bibliography of Lacan's works.

Miller, Jacques-Alain. *Entretien sur le séminaire avec François Ansermet.* Paris: Navarin, 1985. Describes and defends the editorial practice used in establishing the published texts of Lacan's oral seminars.

Muller, John P., and William J. Richardson. *Lacan and Language: A Reader's Guide to "Écrits".* New York: International Universities Press, Inc., 1982. An invaluable accompaniment to the English translation of the *Écrits*, featuring detailed textual and interpretative notes.

——, eds. *The Purloined Poe: Lacan, Derrida, and Psychoanalytic Reading.* Baltimore: Johns Hopkins University Press, 1988. Collects most of the important material in the literary debate between Lacan and Derrida and includes the editors' extremely helpful annotations to Lacan's seminar on Poe.

Ragland-Sullivan, Ellie. *Jacques Lacan and the Philosophy of Psychoanalysis.* Urbana: University of Illinois Press, 1986. Argues for Lacan's decisive philosophical importance and appeals to current work in empirical psychology to support fundamental Lacanian claims.

Roudinesco, Elisabeth. *La bataille de cent ans: Histoire de la psychanalyse en France.* 2 vols. Paris: Éditions du Seuil, 1982, 1986. The definitive book on its subject; the second volume is essentially a biography of Lacan.

Safouan, Moustapha. *Jacques Lacan et la question de la formation des analystes.* Paris: Éditions du Seuil, 1983. A sympathetic but critical assessment of Lacan's attempts to institutionalize psychoanalytic training.

Schneiderman, Stuart. *Jacques Lacan: The Death of an Intellectual Hero.* Cambridge: Harvard University Press, 1983. Impressionistic memoir of Schneiderman's training analysis with Lacan, probing the psychoanalytic significance of death.

——. *Rat Man.* New York: New York University Press, 1986. A Lacanian reading of Freud's case study, originating in a course given in Paris in 1977.

——, ed. and trans. *Returning to Freud: Clinical Psychoanalysis in the School of Lacan.* New Haven: Yale University Press, 1980. An important collection of Lacanian case studies by major figures in the French psychoanalytic world; includes Lacan's own case presentation of a psychotic patient.

Smith, Joseph H., and William Kerrigan, eds. *Interpreting Lacan.* New Haven: Yale University Press, 1983. An excellent collection of mostly philosophical and psychoanalytic articles, emphasizing the range of theory on which Lacan draws.

Turkle, Sherry. *Psychoanalytic Politics: Freud's French Revolution.* New York: Basic Books, 1978. A remarkable sociological analysis of the French psychoanalytic scene, including very helpful accounts of Lacan's conflicts with other psychoanalytic traditions.

De Waelhens, Alphonse. *Schizophrenia: A Philosophical Reflection on Lacan's Structuralist Interpretation.* Translated by Wilfried Ver Eecke. Pittsburgh: Duquesne University Press, 1978. A detailed, critical reading of "On a

Question Preliminary to Any Possible Treatment of Psychosis" from a phenomenological perspective.

Wilden, Anthony. *Jacques Lacan: Speech and Language in Psychoanalysis*. Baltimore: Johns Hopkins University Press, 1968. A pioneering translation, with copious notes and a sophisticated commentary, of "Function and Field," this book originally appeared under Wilden's name as *The Language of the Self: The Function of Language in Psychoanalysis*.

Articles

Heath, Stephen. "Notes on Suture." *Screen* 18, no.4 (1977/78):48–76. The classic source for the Lacanian intervention in English and American film theory, using the work of Miller as a starting point.

Lee, Jonathan Scott. "From Knowledge to the Real: Philosophy after Lacan." *PsychCritique: The International Journal of Critical Psychology and Psychoanalysis* 1 (1985): 235–54. Sketches the concept of a Lacanian philosophical practice, focusing on the question of foreclosure.

Meltzer, Françoise. "Eat Your *Dasein*: Lacan's Self-Consuming Puns." In *On Puns: The Foundation of Letters,* edited by Jonathan Culler, 156–63. Oxford: Basil Blackwell, 1988. A delightful introduction to the interpretative issues involved in Lacan's use of language.

Melville, Stephen. "Psychoanalysis and the Place of *Jouissance*." *Critical Inquiry* 13 (1987): 349–70. A provocative study of Lacan's late interest in formalization and the question of *jouissance*.

———. "Sexuality and Convention: On the Situation of Psychoanalysis." *SubStance* 50 (1986): 75–92. Explores the implications of the Lacan-Derrida debate for the question of the relation between philosophy and psychology.

Miller, Jacques-Alain. "D'un autre Lacan." *Ornicar?* 28 (1984): 49–57. Argues that too many commentators, obsessed with structuralism's emphasis on the symbolic, have missed Lacan's important work on the real. Translated in part by Ralph Chipman as "Another Lacan." *Lacan Study Notes* 3 (1984): 1–3.

———. "Encyclopédie." *Ornicar?* 24 (1981): 35–44. An encyclopedia article on Lacan that manages to elaborate a powerful interpretation of his work in a very short space.

———. "Suture (elements of the logic of the signifier)." Translated by Jacqueline Rose. *Screen* 18, no. 4 (1977/78): 24–34. Uses Frege's number theory to generalize the concept of the signifier, purifying it of any essential linguistic reference.

Muller, John P. "Psychosis and Mourning in Lacan's *Hamlet*." *New Literary History* 12 (1980): 147–65. Elaborates the argument of Lacan's *Hamlet* seminar by means of close study of Shakespeare's text.

Special Issues of Journals

L'ARC 58 (1974). "Jacques Lacan." A remarkable collection of articles, all (but an extract from Lacan's thesis) written by women and all engaging the dialogue between Lacanian psychoanalysis and feminism.

Lacan Study Notes 1–6/9 (1982–88). A newsletter published by Helena Schulz-Keil, having had its origins in the New York Lacan Study Group.

Magazine littéraire 121 (1977): 8–36. A "dossier" on Lacan, providing a valuable glimpse of the popular Parisian reception of Lacan in the late 1970s, as well as the text of Lacan's surrealist poem "Hiatus irrationalis" (1929).

Newsletter of the Freudian Field (1987–present). The North American journal of the Fondation du champ freudien.

October 40 (1987). Special issue editor, Joan Copjec. Includes a translation of *Télévision* and a selection of texts (many by Lacan) that deal with Lacan's troubled relations with various psychoanalytic institutions.

Ornicar? (1975–present). The official journal of the Fondation du champ freudien.

PsychCritique: The International Journal of Critical Psychology and Psychoanalysis 2, no. 1 (1987). A valuable collection of essays on and around Lacan, many by French analysts.

Scilicet 1–6/7 (1968–76). The official journal of the École freudienne de Paris.

Yale French Studies 48 (1972). "French Freud: Structural Studies in Psychoanalysis." Special editor, Jeffrey Mehlman. The first significant collection of essays in English on Lacan, the issue features the translation of Lacan's "Seminar on 'The Purloined Letter.' "

Yale French Studies 55/56 (1978). "Literature and Psychoanalysis: The Question of Reading: Otherwise." Special editor, Shoshana Felman. Features a partial translation of Lacan's seminar on *Hamlet,* as well as important articles by Felman, Fredric Jameson, John Brenkman, and Barbara Johnson, among others.

Index